UNIVERSITY LIBRARY
W. S. U. - STEVENS POINT

7.95
01

D1267210

THE POLITICS AND ECONOMICS
OF
STATE-LOCAL FINANCE

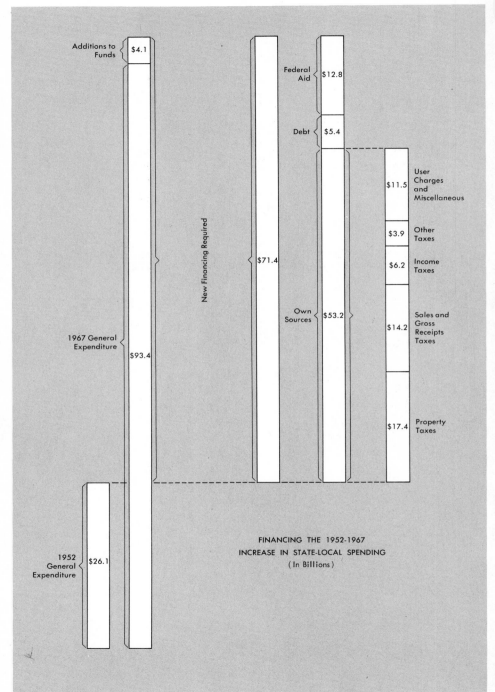

Additions to Funds $4.1

Federal Aid $12.8

Debt $5.4

New Financing Required

$71.4

Own Sources $53.2

User Charges and Miscellaneous $11.5

Other Taxes $3.9

Income Taxes $6.2

Sales and Gross Receipts Taxes $14.2

Property Taxes $17.4

1967 General Expenditure $93.4

1952 General Expenditure $26.1

FINANCING THE 1952-1967
INCREASE IN STATE-LOCAL SPENDING
(In Billions)

L. L. Ecker-Racz
Washington Center for Metropolitan Studies

THE POLITICS AND ECONOMICS
OF
STATE-LOCAL FINANCE

PRENTICE-HALL, INC., Englewood Cliffs, New Jersey

© 1970 by PRENTICE-HALL, INC., Englewood Cliffs, New Jersey

All rights reserved.
No part of this book may be reproduced in any form or by any means
without permission in writing from the publisher.

C—13-686055-9
P—13-686048-6

Library of Congress Catalog Card Number: 73-110490

Printed in the United States of America

Current printing (last digit)

10 9 8 7 6 5 4 3 2 1

PRENTICE-HALL INTERNATIONAL, INC., *London*
PRENTICE-HALL OF AUSTRALIA PTY. LTD., *Sydney*
PRENTICE-HALL OF CANADA, LTD., *Toronto*
PRENTICE-HALL OF INDIA PRIVATE LTD., *New Delhi*
PRENTICE-HALL OF JAPAN, INC., *Tokyo*

HJ
275
.E35

To *Robert W. Bruère*
because he wanted very much to read this book

184841

acknowledgments

My debt for help received is extensive.

Milton Christie, Royce Hanson, Jacob Jaffe, I. M. Labowitz, Allen Manvel, James A. Maxwell, Joseph A. Pechman, Cornelia B. Rose, Jr., and Kathryn Stone read the manuscript and were generous with constructive suggestions. Susannah Eby Calkins researched, drafted, and verified; Frank Tippett provided facts and figures; and Elvera C. Raspanti and Elmer Molis produced draft after draft of manuscript copy.

The Lincoln Foundation funded my appointment as Visiting Scholar at the University of Hartford and this in turn financed the research, statistical, stenographic, and other expenses incurred in writing a book without benefit of fringe benefits one takes for granted in professional employment. The Washington Center for Metropolitan Studies where I am now a Senior Fellow, generously provided staff assistance indispensable to readying the manuscript for publication.

why
still another
book?

This book has been in my mind's eye for a dozen years and longer. It was going to be a dispassionate examination of some current and emerging issues in state-local finance that would help people to an informed position on public questions that are critical to their families' and businesses' futures. I planned to put together a carefully balanced, impersonal exposition of both sides of some important government finance issues. That, however, is more easily said than done, especially in the present urban environment, where the eyes and ears constantly remind man of his failure to use his governmental instruments to help his deprived neighbors. The reader will quickly perceive my bias in favor of government's responding to people's needs.

People differ, of course, in what they want their government to do and how they want it done. All too often, their differences stem as much from conflicting and incomplete information as from differing values. The less people know about what government is trying to do and why, the more prone they are to become dissatisfied, and—what is perhaps worse, to become indifferent.

A book like this can help Americans to a better understanding of, and, hopefully, a greater support for, their government. Many Americans have an almost militant aversion to taxes, and tend to be negative about government, what it accomplishes, and how it gets things done. They see government as an unwelcome intruder into the orderly processes of private enterprise and an ineffective user of the tax dollars extracted from them—dollars they would prefer to spend in their own ways.

Despite the inefficiencies of active government, life in today's world would be very difficult without it. Consider what havoc just a few hours' stoppage of police protection, garbage collection, or even public transportation creates in today's city. Our tax dollars buy services essential to our prosperity and our welfare, such as education, health, hospital, and welfare services, police protection, traffic control, trash collection, recreation facilities, and libraries.

It is the purpose of this book to arouse public concern for the fiscal problems that confront state and local governments, and to explore possible solutions to these problems. If it contributes to an understanding of what state and local government finances are all about, the case for still another book will have been made.

contents

ix

part II

GATHERING OUR TAX DOLLARS

part V

COMING TO TERMS

> *Needs Grow Faster than Revenues. The People Could Af-
> ford More—If They Would. The System Needs Updating.
> The Fiscal Balance Can Be Altered.   Increased Federal
> Support of Schools Is a Possibility.   The Congress Has
> Other Options.   Federal Involvement in Local Schools Is
> Resisted.   Federal Financing of Welfare Is More Likely.
> Revenue Sharing Is Another Possibility.   There Is No Sub-
> stitute for State and Local Effort. The Federal Govern-
> ment Could Help to Contain Tax Competition.   More Fed-
> eral Money Is Not Enough.   Federal Strings Could Be
> Helpful.*

part I

THE SHACKLES THAT BIND US

chapter 1

governments
in need

State and local governments are suffering fiscal pains that grow more acute as the years roll by. Their financial condition is particularly ominous in the older industrial areas where millions of Americans most dependent on government services are congregating. Even the newer middle-income suburbs are finding it difficult to finance the quality education and social programs they would like, rely increasingly on questionable taxing methods, and live in hopes of increases in state and federal aid. The future, moreover, promises only further confrontation between strident demands for costlier social programs and diminishing local revenue resources.

WE HAVE THE RESOURCES

It is not that America lacks the means. The wealthiest and most prosperous nation the world has ever known is capable of buying and paying for the government services essential to its well-being, continued prosperity, and domestic peace. Its tax burden, in relation to its income, is moderate compared with that borne by several of the industrialized nations of the Western world. No one can doubt this nation's capability to finance a level of govern-

3

mental service adequate to satisfy the requirements of families aspiring to security and dignity and to the amenities we want the world to associate with the American image. Few question the logic of providing business with the services it must have for efficiency and sustained growth and prosperity.

If any doubt existed that we can afford to support adequate government services, the performance of the economy in recent years has dispelled it. For example, the increase in this nation's production of goods and services in 1968 over 1967, the one year's increase alone, would finance the aggregate budgets of all American public school systems for nearly two years. A third of the increase in national production during any of the past several years, if used that way, would have gone a long way toward lifting all of America's 30 million economically underprivileged above a poverty standard of living.

THEY ARE IN THE WRONG PLACES

Part of the answer to the seeming paradox of governmental poverty amid economic plenty is that the resources are in the wrong places. In pursuit of a unique brand of political decentralization, America has splintered herself into tens of thousands of politically independent governmental fragments, and within these fragments needs do not match resources. On the contrary, the states and communities with the greatest needs tend to be those with the least resources; and under our governmental system, each community depends largely on its own resources for meeting its needs. Moreover, fear of losing taxpayers to their neighbors is restraining rich and poor alike from effective use of their revenue resources.

THE GOVERNMENTAL APPARATUS IS OUTDATED

Our ingenious governmental apparatus, with its widely dispersed political powers, was designed by brilliant 18th century minds for a self-sufficient agricultural economy that by today's standards needed very few government services. Its architects anticipated little need for such essentials of urban living as fire and police protection, traffic control, sanitation, trash collection, sewage disposal, air and water pollution control, health and welfare services, recreation, or mass transportation. In the 18th century, these basic necessities of urban survival either were not needed or residents furnished them for themselves. They pumped their own water, buried their own refuse, relied on their own guns for security, stored their own rainwater for fire protection, and families and neighbors provided for the poor.

In that environment it was logical and practical to decentralize domestic government responsibility and political decision-making to local jurisdiction. Such a system kept government close to the people, gave them maximum scope in shaping the content and level of services they procured through government, and produced intercommunity differences in the scope and quality of governmental services. Each community was free to buy as much government as its inhabitants wanted without affecting the inhabitants of other communities. Differences among the communities reflected the differences in their people's preferences and willingness to pay for public projects. In that setting it made good sense to hold those responsible for spending funds responsible also for raising them, and to minimize intergovernmental financial aids. This made for careful handling of the people's money.

Very little of that old rural environment remains. Most Americans now live and work in urban areas and move among them with increasing frequency. Decentralization of all domestic government functions is no longer compatible with the public interest. Omissions and commissions of local governments anywhere are likely to affect people everywhere. Despite its increasing unsuitability, however, the philosophical basis of the original government conception continues to have a strong hold over the people. Such little interest as they take in community problems is concentrated on their own towns. Crises down the road are beyond their direct concern— even when the flames of burning cities are brought into their family rooms in living color. Those concerned with community affairs remain nostalgic for the small community where neighbors and public officials greet each other by their first name. They like to participate in choosing their many public officials. At the last count, Americans were selecting more than half a million officials in popular elections to guide and operate over 80,000 separate governments.

WE HAVE TOO MANY GOVERNMENTS

The nation carries its preference for small, decentralized, and fractionated governmental responsibility to extremes. The 1967 census tallied 22,000 separate school districts, 35,000 municipalities and townships, 21,000 special districts, and some 3,000 counties. At that time, seven states each had more than 3,500 local governments and together supported over 31,000 governments. In some places, residents were served by as many as a dozen different local jurisdictions.

The maze of governments that overlap one another geographically in the functions they perform and the taxes they levy on people, is especially incongruous in the densely populated urban areas where people and commerce ignore municipal boundaries and the complex business of govern-

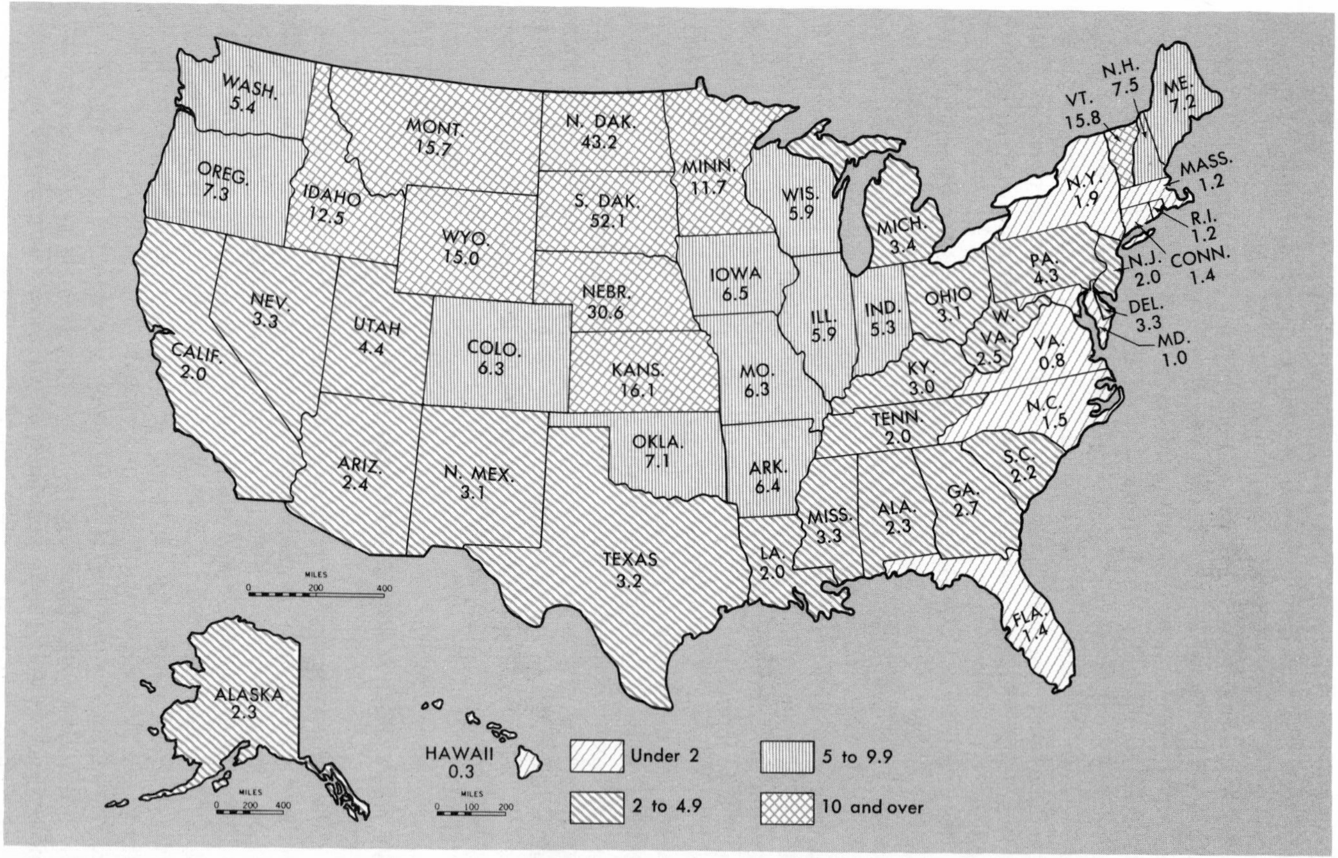

figure 1 Number of Governmental Units Per 10,000 Population : 1967

Legend:

Under 2

2 to 4.9

5 to 9.9

10 and over

State values:

WASH. 5.4
OREG. 7.3
CALIF. 2.0
NEV. 3.3
IDAHO 12.5
MONT. 15.7
WYO. 15.0
UTAH 4.4
ARIZ. 2.4
N. MEX. 3.1
COLO. 6.3
N. DAK. 43.2
S. DAK. 52.1
NEBR. 30.6
KANS. 16.1
OKLA. 7.1
TEXAS 3.2
MINN. 11.7
IOWA 6.5
MO. 6.3
ARK. 6.4
LA. 2.0
WIS. 5.9
ILL. 5.9
IND. 5.3
MICH. 3.4
OHIO 3.1
KY. 3.0
TENN. 2.0
MISS. 3.3
ALA. 2.3
GA. 2.7
S.C. 2.2
N.C. 1.5
VA. 2.5
W. VA. 0.8
PA. 4.3
N.Y. 1.9
FLA. 1.4
VT. 15.8
N.H. 7.5
ME. 7.2
MASS. 1.2
R.I. 1.2
CONN. 1.4
N.J. 2.0
DEL. 3.3
MD. 1.0
HAWAII 0.3
ALASKA 2.3

MILES 0 100 200
MILES 0 200 400
MILES 0 200 400

ment cries out for a streamlined organization conducive to coordinated, planned action.

Over two-thirds of the nation's population now lives in 233 so-called "standard metropolitan statistical areas." These economically and socially interdependent areas "with a recognized large population nucleus" account for most of the recent increase in population. Within these areas nearly half the people still live in the central metropolitan cities, but the proportion is diminishing because most of the new population growth is on the fringes of the cities.

These 233 metropolitan areas are served by nearly 21,000 governments with about 135,000 popularly elected officials. The average metropolitan county has about 26 separate local governments, but some have many more. The Chicago area has 1,113 separate local governments (186 per county); Philadelphia, 876 (109 per county); Pittsburgh, 704 (176 per county); and New York, 551 (110 per county). Most of these governments are relatively small. Half the municipalities within metropolitan areas cover less than a single square mile. One-fourth of the 5,000 school districts in metropolitan areas have fewer than 300 pupils, and one-third operate only a single school.

LOCAL GOVERNMENTS HAVE LOST THEIR FISCAL VIABILITY

The splintering into many separate governmental entities cripples financing capability. In bygone days, when America's urban population was concentrated in cities with clearly identified perimeters, the city was a viable and fiscally balanced community. Those who worked in the city, lived in the city. The city had rich, medium income, and poor sections; residential, commercial, and industrial areas; white and nonwhite settlements. A city's variety gave it fiscal balance. It collected a relatively large share of its taxes from the sections that had the taxpayers and spent them, as necessary, in the sections with the needs. This permitted many cities to organize superior governmental programs.

All that has changed. The new migrants into metropolitan areas tend to settle in communities inhabited by their own kind. Increasingly each urban area is fragmented into distinct low-income, middle-income, and high-income communities and into industrial and commercial enclaves. Fiscally varied and balanced communities are being replaced by fiscally unbalanced government entities. These specialized settlements, and the old city centers they surround, are characterized increasingly by the absence of any correspondence between their stock of taxable resources and their program needs.

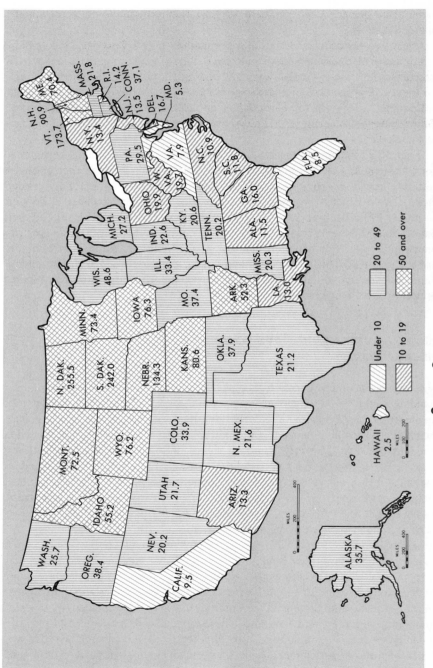

figure 2 Number of Elected Public Officials Per 10,000 Population: 1967

Under 10   20 to 49

10 to 19   50 and over

We have it on the authority of the prestigious Committee for Economic Development that in 1966 over half of America's 30 million poor lived in metropolitan areas, and that nearly two-thirds of these poor lived in central cities. (For purposes of this count a household is "poor" if its annual money income is less than three times the cost of a minimal diet for the persons in that household. The "poverty level" for a four-person household was $3,335 in 1967.) The proportion of poor people in central cities was almost twice as high as in the suburbs. Nearly half of the poor people in metropolitan areas were in households without prospects for becoming economically self-sustaining because they were headed by persons over age 65, by disabled males under 65, or by females with children. Over 40 percent of the poor were children under 18.

THE OLD CITIES ARE ESPECIALLY VULNERABLE

The old cities, frequently at the center of the metropolitan areas, are comprised increasingly of poor homes and abandoned structures that produce the welfare loads, health problems, police and fire calls, but little tax revenue. National economic growth passes by such cities. Their tax bases —property values, retail sales, business volume—are stagnating, in some cases even declining, as middle-income residents and businesses move elsewhere.

State legislatures often make matters worse by shortchanging the cities and favoring the suburbs in the distribution of state aid, particularly for public schools. To stay in office, legislators have to be elected and reelected; and to win elections they must demonstrate allegiance to the pocketbook interests of their constituencies. Increasingly theirs are suburban constituencies, because this is where the people live and vote in growing numbers —and suburbanites do not want their taxes "dissipated" in the cities.

It is not that the people in the residential suburbs are oblivious to the cities' problems. Many spend their daylight hours five days a week earning their living in the city, worrying about their personal safety while they are there. When their business is done, they beat a hasty retreat to their suburban green shrubs and lawns and turn a deaf ear to the city's anguished fiscal cries.

Striving to meet pressing social needs, many old cities have pushed their tax rates substantially above those in neighboring jurisdictions and allowed their physical plants and services to deteriorate—which only encourages more out migration and discourages new settlement.

High incidence of poverty and associated social needs combine with the high cost of providing services to preempt the cities' limited revenues. This leaves relatively less for financing other needs, including public schools, even though theirs are the disadvantaged children with special and expensive educational requirements. Some suburbs, especially the long-established bedroom communities, have comparable problems. Few, however, have social costs comparable to those of the old cities.

The cities, of course, do not have a monopoly on poverty. There are all too many poor families in small towns and rural areas all across the land. Indeed, nearly half the poor live outside the metropolitan areas. Those who live in cities, however, are crowded together in large numbers, visible, audible, and impatient for attention.

URBAN NEEDS ARE MUSHROOMING

The primary burden of providing for the expanding governmental needs of America's population falls on state and local shoulders rather than on the federal government. Their general government expenditures now approach $120 billion. Since World War II, the state and local share of the nation's direct government expenditures for civilian services (as distinguished from national defense and international expenditures) has increased from two-thirds to three-fourths, while the federal share has declined from one-third to one-fourth. State and local employment has increased by about 130 percent; federal employment by only about 40 percent. In the middle 1950's, the state and local governments' share of the nation's output in goods and services (GNP) was less than 8 percent, the federal share 12 percent. By the middle of the 1960's the state-local and federal shares were approximately equal, and the relatively faster growth of the state and local share was halted only by the federal government's Vietnam-connected activities.

Pressures for increased spending converge on state and local governments from all sides. Since 1948, 55 million Americans have been added to the population. More babies are being born, and more are surviving infancy and early childhood. This leads to increased needs for maternal and public health clinics, and for more elementary and secondary schools. In addition, people are demanding more expensive services from their public schools—such as buses, lunches, gyms, auditoriums, foreign-language and other specialized instruction, vocational education, special classes for the gifted, the mentally and physically handicapped, and special school services for poverty-stricken children. More and more communities are providing post-high-school education in junior and four-year community colleges.

At the other end of the population range, people are living longer and retiring earlier. This creates needs for more hospital facilities and medical services, special facilities for the disabled and senile, and community services for the aged who live in their own homes. This growing group of

figure 3

**Government Employment
1948-1968**

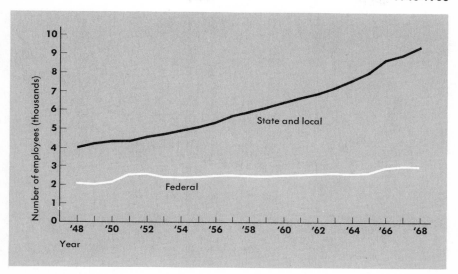

retired persons also increases the need for welfare funds to assist those with inadequate financial security.

The economy is expanding (its output of goods and services has tripled in twenty years) and business needs more municipal facilities and services to enable it to produce and deliver its expanding output. This includes fire and police protection, waste disposal, highway and transportation facilities, and government assistance in fighting air and water pollution by industrial processes. Mechanization, automation, and new technology all create new demands for public services, as symbolized by the effects of food and beverage packaging in disposable containers on trash disposal and highway maintenance costs.

The population is tending to concentrate in cities where the government is obliged to do more things for them, and each service costs more: intensified police and fire protection; comprehensive community sanitation and health services; expressways and parking facilities; and mass transit. In addition, the average city dweller who is without a job must be given financial aid. The small garden plot and a bit of private charity no longer suffice to take care of those without income.

The prosperous suburban population demands more recreational facilities and improved roads as well as a high standard of community services. Disadvantaged groups in the population are restive and militant, and de-

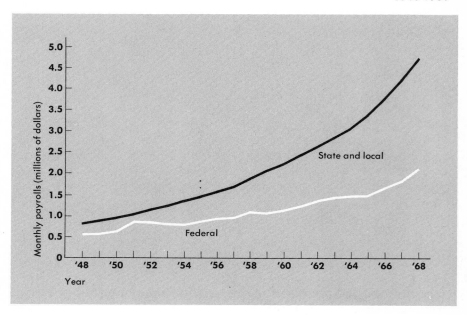

figure 4

Government Payrolls
1948-1968

mand a larger share of the national dividend. Many who participate in national debate encourage them and thus add to the pressure for increased government services. All these pressures are having a profound impact on state and local expenditures.

LITTLE PROGRESS IS BEING MADE

In many respects, state and local governments' recent fiscal performance has been outstanding. They have financed a level of activity with which few would have credited them just a few years ago. Recent performance, however, affords little basis for optimism about the future. With benefit of national prosperity, public pressures, and political ingenuity state and local spending for general government has increased dramatically and was financed largely in conventional ways. Some interpret this to mean that good progress was being made, and that in no time at all Americans can relax on their tax oars. Their vision, however, may prove to be a mirage.

The larger part of the increase in spending since World War II has sufficed to compensate only for the growth and changed characteristics of the population, for price inflation, and for the higher real cost of providing families with services in the city than in the rural areas from which they came. When the statistics on expenditure growth are adjusted for these factors, it becomes clear that the real improvement in the quantity and quality of government services (relative to needs) has been modest, particularly in comparison with the simultaneous improvement in privately purchased goods and services. The quality of shelter, entertainment, and personal transportation, for example, has improved conspicuously more than that of government-provided services. Although some progress has been made in compensating for past neglect, new demands and public expectations have mushroomed and tend to leave an unsatisfied gap as wide as before.

Moreover, such improvement as has been made in programs involved the commitment of new resources and the dissipation of one-time windfall opportunities, and depleted the stock of fiscal reserves. Two-thirds of the states now use both sales and income taxes. Not many unused taxes remain. It has involved also recourse to financing methods—heavy property taxes on shelter and heavy sales taxes on necessities—inimical to the nation's social policy objectives.

Although state and local governments have raised the largest part of their increased revenues by tax-rate increases and new types of tax measures, they have also used debt financing, chiefly for capital facilities. The indebtedness of state and local governments increased from less than $20 billion in the late 1940's to $130 billion by 1968. State and local governments have been helped in the sale of their bonds by the continued exemption of the interest paid on these securities from federal income taxes; but as the volume of their bond offerings has multiplied, the scarcity value of their tax exemption privilege has diminished and the unprecedented rise in interest rates has sharply increased their debt service costs.

The constant pressures on state and local governments to find additional funds to meet their mushrooming needs have been relieved somewhat by increases in federal aid. Federal grants-in-aid to states and localities exceed $20 billion a year as compared with less than $2 billion in 1948. More grants-in-aid have produced more friction in federal-state relationships.

WE HAVE THE KNOW-HOW

A statement of state and local governments' fiscal problem almost suggests its own solutions.

If the nation has the resources, and if the problems stem from excessive political fragmentation that isolates the fragments with the needs from those with the means to alleviate those needs, the logical answer would appear to be larger governmental taxing and spending jurisdictions with better fiscal balance and less vulnerability to interjurisdictional tax competition. If the expenditure pressure on city governments stems from the social problems associated with the heavy concentration of low-income families, funds to pay for welfare payments and services should come from the higher levels of government. The taxes employed for financing these public services ought to concentrate on ability to pay and avoid aggravating poverty by burdening the purchase of life's necessities, including shelter. If it is unfair to require local taxpayers to pay for costly education and social programs, the benefits of which spill over local boundaries to people in other parts of the country, then a larger portion of these costs should be financed from state and federal sources.

Admittedly, America does not want for answers to these problems. A people with the ingenuity to perform miracles in space doubtless possess the capability to shape governmental arrangements to meet daily needs at home. In fact, promising solutions to fiscal problems have been pouring out in volume from innumerable sponsors for years. Much of this book is taken up with the examination of such prescriptions. But American governments' fiscal problems depend on political solutions because popularly elected leaders can make fiscal solutions their own only when their electorate understands them and is ready to suffer them. If state and local governments in a prosperous democracy experience difficulty in financing themselves adequately and in approved ways, the difficulty is likely to be related to how people feel about these governments—about the services they provide, the taxes they collect, and the efficiency of their operations. It is appropriate, therefore, to pause for a closer look at the people's preferences in governmental institutions and institutional arrangements and to probe the basis of their resistance to seemingly sensible fiscal solutions.

chapter 2

political barriers
to rationality

It is paradoxical that in the midst of private plenty and organizational creativity, Americans keep the governments of their own choice in perpetual financial difficulty. Political barriers appear to block the path to fiscal rationality.

PEOPLE'S INTEREST IN GOVERNMENT IS LIMITED

Most of the time, most Americans leave the business of government to others. A few do become involved some of the time, usually because this or that government activity displeases them. It is likely to be a state or local activity because, under our federal system, these are the governments with the primary responsibility for most public services on which Americans depend in their private and business lives.

The fact that the people are not directly involved with government does not mean that they have no views on the subject. At times it almost seems that the less intimate their government contacts, the more critical their views. This attitude is reflected in many ways: in distrust of government and those associated with it; in a disposition to keep government on tight financial reins; in a desire to restrict the powers of public officials; in a selfish, paro-

15

chial response to government issues and social programs that is difficult to reconcile with Americans' habitually generous response to private appeals on behalf of social needs.

SOME THINK GOVERNMENT IS DOING TOO MUCH

Americans come from different backgrounds, with different traditions and different sets of values. There are some who underestimate the contribution government makes to their well-being and resent being obliged to contribute to its support. They think that government is at its best when it governs least. Americans respect material success, particularly those who share in it, and admire the man who "makes good." They tend to disdain those who fail and become public charges, and they resent government "rewarding failures" by looking after them with welfare and other social programs.

To be sure, it is difficult at best to keep government in a favorable light. Most of the things government does go unnoticed except by the relatively few who are directly affected, and the services are not always evident even to them. Much of what government does is of a personal service nature and, when accomplished, leaves no physical evidence behind. Much of it is preventive in character, producing nothing tangible for people to see. People have come to expect improving productivity per worker as a result of automation, but personal services afford relatively little opportunity for it. They think that their own share of taxes should decline as the country grows and there are more people to share the tax bill. They do not understand that population and economic growth almost of necessity increase society's need for government services.

In a very real sense, government is at its best when it plans for the future and anticipates problems before they develop. An expanding economy, a growing population, rising living standard, progressive urbanization, an advancing technology—each contributes to society's dependence on more and more complex public facilities. And the more complex the facility —be it a school structure or a sewage treatment plant—the longer the lead time required to put it in place on time and the greater the need for advance planning. But those who anticipate future municipal needs and prevent problems from developing do not enjoy public approval. Few voters appreciate future needs, and political leaders dare to anticipate them only as the public recognizes the need for doing so. They dare not prevent long-run problems at the expense of short-run inconvenience (including higher taxes) to the voters lest it reduce the likelihood that they will still be on deck after the next election. Officials in advance of their time, out of step with their people, do not long survive.

Government is a large, steadily expanding enterprise, and, in common with all large organizations, it tends to become impersonal—the captive of bureaucratic inflexibility. Most people can and like to relate a personal (or a friend's) encounter with government inefficiency and senseless inflexibility, and this encourages them to credit the kind of infamy about government that Parkinson unfortunately has so successfully popularized. Bureaucracy is a problem in both private and government enterprise. Government is large, and the citizen with a problem is often frustrated and does not know where to go with his complaint. Although this also happens in private enterprise it bothers people less, perhaps because they can usually take their future patronage to another tradesman.

Americans have the resources, but some begrudge the share they have to give to government. All too many believe that government is already overdoing it; that it is taking too much of their income in taxes, dissipating their dollars in bureaucratic inefficiencies, and encouraging millions to live on government handouts.

SOME THINK GOVERNMENT IS NOT DOING ENOUGH

On occasion—one cannot say how often—the displeasure with government stems from an inadequacy in some particular service such as trash collection, police protection, education, traffic control. Most of us are not familiar with all of government's many responsibilities. We think only of those government activities that affect us personally and visibly in an affirmative manner. We expect that the taxes we personally pay will buy the services we personally want, in the quantity and quality we expect. The problem may stem from an insufficiency of public funds. For example, the city does not provide a good enough or frequent enough trash collection service because the council has not appropriated enough money. This puzzles the individual, because the service in question is likely to be one which he believes to be critically important. He would not have noticed the deficiency if it had been a service that did not reach him directly. How can government be short of funds when his own taxes grow year by year? How can government be short of funds in this land of affluence where so many billions can be spared to help other lands and to indulge in unmatched private waste, extravagance, and conspicuous spending? The simple assumption that government is wasteful has widespread appeal.

Another and apparently much smaller group is perplexed by the contradictions in our society's values. It sees a contradiction in our rushing headlong into urban concentrations, crowding most of the nation's population into a tiny fraction of the available land (less than two percent) and then standing by as our great cities deteriorate into islands of poverty, deprivation, and social shame while city governments plunge from one fiscal crisis into another. The plight of the cities is particularly perplexing because the world associates them with American wealth and strength, and the cities are the custodians of our cultural heritage.

There is a contradiction in our national commitment to provide all young people with the educational opportunity to develop their latent potential to the maximum, and then spend the least on the children of the underprivileged families who most need education; in a national commitment to banish poverty, and then oblige state and local governments to depend largely on taxes particularly burdensome on shelter and other necessities.

SOME HAVE OTHER COMPLAINTS

Not infrequently the public is confused by conflicting professional judgments. Economists bear a share of the responsibility. Although most economists have built the framework of their government finance philosophy on a common set of values—on the need for government intervention to help the poor, the virtues of progressive ability-to-pay taxation, and the need to safeguard taxpayers' convenience and ease of tax administration—when it comes to the espousal of policy positions in which taxation or spending play a part, each feels free to compromise one or the other of his economic principles in the interests of political reality. Policy positions reflect subjective judgments, and those engaged in professions cannot be expected to deny themselves the privilege of expressing personal views on public issues. The problem is that few economists reach identical subjective judgments. Those in agreement on one issue one day, are likely to disagree on a related one the next day. As a result the people are confused, and increasingly so as the economists they recognize venture into more and more public policy fields.

Moreover, the way we have assigned responsibilities for financing government does not help people to like it. Since the public school is a local responsibility, for example, the community that wants a strong school program has to foot a large part of the bill despite the likelihood that a substantial portion of the children it educates will spend their productive years in another community. A school system that undertakes to care for the handicapped or brain-damaged child—a relatively very costly effort—quickly finds itself burdened with an overload of families who move into the community to take advantage of its special facilities. We hold local taxpayers responsible for a large part of the cost of taking care of even those among the poor who are newcomers to the community, forced into poverty through neglect in other communities. Local taxpayers aware of these arrangements believe themselves misused.

The people negatively inclined toward government are extremely vocal; and the fact that the gap between the need for government services and the performance grows wider while the nation prospers suggests that they are also quite persuasive. It is possible, of course, that they are only more audible and that the satisfied among the people keep their own counsel.

We are inclined to associate negative attitudes toward government activity with conservatism, and that in turn with wealth and affluence. But such generalizations are overdrawn. Although spokesmen for organizations of business—particularly the hired help under constant pressure to demonstrate loyalty to the interests of its employers—all too often oppose budget and tax increases for the introduction of new government programs and the expansion of old ones, some of the more effective and dynamic leadership on behalf of responsible public policies has come from the nation's business executives and from men and women of wealth. In any event, middle-income professionals in both public and private enterprise have not been particularly conspicuous in their espousal of liberal public spending programs.

THE PEOPLE'S ATTITUDES IMPOSE CONSTRAINTS ON POLICYMAKERS

The contradictions in the attitudes of Americans toward government are not easily explained because their genesis lies buried in the intangibles which comprise American political institutions and their processes. Much of what happens on capitol hills and in city halls is inexplicable—except in terms of the ground rules imposed by the political process on public officials, and the compulsion experienced by these officials, in the interest of political longevity, to conform to people's likes and dislikes.

Those elected to formulate tax and expenditure policies function under a variety of constraints. Public officials feel a strong compulsion to keep voters' taxes low, and to this end they are eager to attract taxpayers and to keep away taxeaters (those who require expensive services). They strive to foster the image of low taxes in their jurisdiction in the belief that a favorable tax climate stimulates economic development. The objective is to establish a reputation for a favorable business climate and at all costs avoid a contrary reputation because an unfavorable tax reputation is difficult to live down.

It is widely alleged that taxes play an important role in the wealthy person's choice of residence and the businessman's decision where to locate his new plant. The allegation persists, although study after study has failed to confirm it. There is considerable evidence that taxes rank relatively low among the factors which influence these decisions.

Wealthy people's choice of the location of their homes appears to be influenced by proximity to their place of business activity, by family and friendship ties, by personal amenities (even golf courses) and other subjective priorities. Business appears to locate its plants with an eye to the availability of labor, materials, transportation, and space, the accessibility to markets and to other business firms with which frequent contacts are required, and a host of other variables. Increasingly location decisions by business are importantly influenced also by the quality of government services provided to business itself and to the families of the employees.

There is also some basis for the view that businessmen's preference for a community with a favorable tax climate may not be motivated so much by tax savings as it is by the inference drawn from kindly tax treatment. A community which consciously pursues tax policies favorable to business is believed to be one to which business would be welcome. Like the rest of us, business likes to be wanted.

If opinions differ on how taxes affect economic development, there is little doubt that what is believed to be true is no less important than what actually *is* true. Policymakers in state legislatures and city halls yearn for trade and industry and tend to credit the repeated assertions of their business constituents that taxes are influential in business decisions. Officeholders are eager for a share in business prosperity and national economic growth because they know that additions to the local tax and employment base will make their financial problems more manageable and their political fortunes less vulnerable. When more revenue is needed, they would much rather that it came, say, from a 25 percent increase in the volume of retail sales with existing tax rates than from an increase in the 4 percent sales tax to 5 percent—two equally lucrative paths to an increase in tax collections.

OVERLAPPING TAXES ADD TO CONSTRAINTS

The fact that others are also taxing the same citizens and businesses imposes still another constraint on tax policymakers. Local, state, and federal governments all fish in the same tax pond, frequently with identical lures, and the practice of one necessarily affects the success and the maneuverability of all the others. Those at the lower governmental levels are inclined to blame their financial troubles on the avariciousness of other, often higher, government authority. Mayors complain that the good taxes have been preempted by the states; the states complain that they have been preempted by the federal government; town and county governing boards complain that the property tax has been monopolized by the school districts, and so on.

Scapegoats are essential stage props in politics, and the government in Washington is always fair game. However, the preemption argument has some basis in fact. It cannot be gainsaid, for example, that the federal government's heavy use of the income tax limits the states' freedom of movement in that taxing area (even though the deductibility of state taxes for federal income purposes means that part of the take of the state income tax comes out of the U.S. Treasury's share since it reduces federal tax bills). It is true also that the federal government has a great advantage because the larger a government's territorial dimensions the less its concern that taxpayers will move elsewhere to escape taxes, and the greater its opportunities to benefit from the economies of large-scale operations. The other side of the argument is that cities and states create their own problems by engaging in self-defeating competition with one another, and that they have substantial untapped taxing potential, if they would but use it.

Spokesmen for state and local governments are wont to crusade for the reduction in this or that federal tax in the hope that they can then move into the area vacated. Generally, this is a vain hope. The special interests that succeed in persuading Congress to reduce their taxes are quick to argue that Congress has strong economic or equity reasons for reducing or repealing their particular tax and that it would be unseemly for states to undo what Congress, at an expense to federal revenues, deemed essential in the national interest. Interest groups with enough political muscle to persuade Congress to give up a tax are generally capable of stopping state legislatures or city councils from reimposing it. That, at least, was the experience when Congress repealed federal taxes on electrical energy and on admissions to places of amusement.

Those who are so inclined are quick to see conflict and rivalry among federal, state, and local taxing jurisdictions. News dispatches, particularly those reporting on political activities, nurture the impression. The progressive increase in the relative fiscal strength of the federal government lends itself to the image of a dominating monolith. It is popular to complain about the federal government's monopoly, the overbearing bureaucratic attitudes of federal officials, and the mountains of governmental red tape. The coin, however, also has another side.

The federal government helps state governments, and the states help local governments in the administration of their taxes. Governments also help one another indirectly. Perhaps the greatest assistance the national administration has given the states toward more effective use of income taxes, for example, is its continued emphasis in public statements on the fairness of these compared with other taxes, and by demonstrating the revenue growth capability of income taxes in a prospering economy even in the face of tax rate reductions.

Moreover, there is a sense of professional solidarity among federal, state, and local officials engaged in a common mission that binds them together. City, state, and federal public health or school officials, for example, all share a dedication to a common objective, to a common professional purpose, and strive for one another's high regard. Frequently their first loyalty is to their professional mission rather than to one or the other governmental level.

It is possible, too, that the political utterances of mayors and governors overstate their true feelings about higher levels of government and that each example of disregard of one another's interest among governmental levels can be matched by less dramatic examples of conscious mutual for-bearance unnoticed by the public: Congress seeking to avoid infringing on state taxing freedom, and the states exhibiting similar regard for the taxing freedom of their local governments.

Mutual forbearance, however, may be less characteristic of interlocal and interstate relations. Rivalry among cities and among states, success in looting one another's businesses and in dumping the poor on one an-other's welfare rolls appears to have been elevated to the status of political virtue.

THE PEOPLE'S ATTITUDE SHAPES TAX PRACTICES

Democracies and sound tax policies make uncomfortable bedfellows. The public's aversion to paying taxes obliges legislators and others in leadership positions dependent on elector approval to avoid overt associa-tion with tax increases even at the cost of imprudent fiscal policies.

Bypassing urgent public needs, postponing the orderly maintenance of plants and equipment, diverting funds from purposes for which they had been accumulated, and even borrowing for projects which should be paid for out of current income, are considered lesser evils than tax increases. And when the need for more revenue can no longer be ignored, it is politically wise to raise it in ways that will attract little attention and affect as few voters as possible.

For long years the out-of-state business firm with few, if any, local votes was the favorite game of revenue hunters. This is changing (except possibly with respect to utilities not free to move elsewhere) because, as already noted, state and local governments compete with one another for new business and are eager to keep their old business.

The compulsion to avoid general tax increases drives policymakers into ingenious and frequently one-shot affairs. As a result of the public's pre-occupation with the relationship of smoking to lung cancer, the cigarette tax has become eminently acceptable although it is an especially heavy tax burden on low-income people. In a relatively short time all states adopted it, and those that already had it doubled and tripled their tax rate. One should list here also the inclination to exploit such opportunities as taxes on liquor, wagering, pari-mutuel betting and, perhaps, even lotteries.

The policy of catch-as-catch-can, picking up dollars where the inventive finance officer can help politically responsible leadership to find it with a minimum of political displeasure and loss of voter support, has its appeal at the local as well as the state level. It explains why, in some parts of the country, the landscape is cluttered with nuisance taxes that produce only little revenue and with taxes that cannot be enforced effectively at the local level.

Another objective avidly pursued by political leaders is to make maximum use of exportable tax burdens. These are the hidden taxes paid by the out-of-state consumers of exported products. Out-of-state consumers do not vote! Severance taxes on lumber and petroleum products, and special taxes on tourist accommodations are examples. To the regret of tax policymakers, most of these tax devices are chiefly useful in connection with commodities and services in which the taxing state has a monopoly or a strong competitive position. Nevada is able to take a substantial cut from the gambling tables without jeopardizing its preeminence in this field. Michigan's freedom to tax the automobile industry, on the other hand, has been progressively restricted as the industry has been decentralized to several states. In Texas, opportunity to exploit the extraction of petroleum was gradually restricted as numerous other states began to compete for the business.

Their relatively short terms of office oblige elected officials to prefer tax changes that promise quick payoffs, even one-time windfalls, provided they are within immediate reach. They cannot afford the luxury of inviting voter displeasure with tax measures whose benefits are delayed beyond their own terms of office (unless the burdens also are deferred). During World War II, the federal government demonstrated that withholding of income taxes could be sold to the people as a device to serve working people's convenience and improve the quality of tax enforcement at the same time that it increased immediate tax collections. This was quick to attract the states' attention. Most states now collect their income taxes through a system of withholding by employers. Before the introduction of withholding, the final income tax payment on the year's income often occurred only toward the end of the following year. Withholding accelerated the final tax accounting, and enabled all or part of two years' tax collections to be crowded into one year. Although the ploy could not be repeated, its lesson was not lost. It was only a question of time before the technique was adapted to accelerate corporation income tax payments.

However much political officeholders avoid association with tax increases, they seem quite willing to speed the need for new taxes in the future by dissipating the revenue capability of existing taxes. They show all too little reluctance, for example, to reward groups of voters or businesses with tax exemptions, tax credits, or other tax favors. The tax-exemption route to social and other policy ends is particularly attractive when accomplished at the expense of another jurisdiction, such as when the state legislature mandates homestead or veterans' property tax exemptions at the expense of local governments. Preferential tax provisions accomplish the political objective sought and do not necessitate appropriations which have to be explained, even though their impact on finances may be as great as, if not greater than, that of direct appropriations. The cost of such tax exemptions can be understated with little fear of being proved wrong. In any event, the integrity of the tax system has few public defenders other than the tax commissioner, the college professor, and occasionally the organized champions of "good government." Even some of them can be neutralized.

The dissipation of revenue resources through preferential tax provisions and avoiding increases in broadly based taxes can work only for a time. Ultimately the cupboard is left bare, and politically unpopular revenue legislation can no longer be avoided.

IT INFLUENCES THE TIMING OF TAX INCREASES

Although many state legislatures convene only in alternate years, it was a rare year in the 1950's and 1960's when the volume of tax legislation failed to provide enough substance for lengthy press accounts and professional journal articles. Each of the past two score years found a number of states in need of more taxes.

The logs of annual state tax increases are typically dominated by legislation of the "bits and pieces" variety. The number of major pieces of state tax legislation in any year is relatively small, for a major tax bill becomes politically tolerable only when further disregard of expenditure pressures has become politically even more hazardous than the sponsorship of tax increases. This occurs at different times in different states, and is not likely to come in any one place more often than once or twice during the same decade. It is not likely to follow immediately upon a change in political party control because, regardless of party, a new administration is likely to be committed to solving the state's financial needs through economy, improved administrative efficiency, and without new taxes—unless it can charge gross financial mismanagement to the preceding administration and do it convincingly.

Tax increases tend to follow in the wake of pessimistic business forecasts. At such times the need for more revenue appears to be particularly pressing because estimated collections from existing taxes are likely to be low, and estimated budget needs for social programs high. Conversely, when the economic outlook is bright, the inclination is to postpone the evil day in the hope that social program costs will decline and revenues increase, particularly if the state has an effective income tax.

Governors with four-year terms have more latitude in the timing of tax increases than their two-year term colleagues, for the objective is to avoid association with a tax increase just before a bid for reelection. One Eastern four-year-term governor had the rare fortune of sponsoring a tax increase based on a pessimistic economic forecast, only to experience a quick turnaround in the economy and an unexpected revenue windfall large enough to justify a small tax reduction in the very next year. By the time of his campaign for reelection, the voters were encouraged to forget the large tax increase and to remember the more recent small tax decrease. Most governors are less fortunate.

The timing of tax increases is affected also by the ground swell of public opinion in support of one or another public program that periodically overtakes Americans. In recent years, as during the Depression of the 1930's, widespread support for property-tax relief to farmers and homeowners improved the acceptability of state tax increases to provide replacement revenue. The national emphasis on education following Sputnik created a favorable climate for tax increases to finance increased state aid to local schools. Although these movements come in cycles that approximate national fashions, the compulsion to recognize them comes at different times in different states.

At the local level, political leadership has a somewhat easier time of it. In most local communities the major tax source is the property tax, and over a period of years sizable additions to revenues can be effected by small annual increases in millage rates. A city with a $1.60 tax rate can raise its tax-supported budget by 25 percent with four successive 10-cent increases in the millage rate. The effect on the average property tax bill is not likely to be overly alarming, particularly if the taxes are collected monthly by the financial institutions which hold the mortgages, and if the tax increase is associated with an improvement in a popular program such as public schools. Contrast this with a corresponding 25 percent increase in the state's tax budget. A state tax system with a 3 percent sales tax that now accounts for 25 percent of total tax revenues will serve as an illustration. A 25 percent increase in that state's tax revenues would require an increase in the 3 percent sales tax to 6 percent. That corresponds to a 100 percent sales tax increase, and voters would be reminded of it each time they visited a store. No governor would want to try it.

IT INFLUENCES TAX RATE LEVELS

Political leadership is restricted also by tax rate levels in other, particularly nearby places. In taxation the objective is to lag, not to lead. North Carolina has long prided itself on being the only state without a tax on cigarettes. New Hampshire boasts that it is the only state with neither an income nor a sales tax. Nevada is proud of being the only place where one can die free of state inheritance tax even though Nevadans derive no benefits from the distinction. Since taxes paid to states are credited against federal estate tax, if Nevadans paid a state tax they would owe correspondingly less in federal taxes.

States that cannot stay below their neighbors' tax rates strive to avoid rising too far above them. As will be noted in subsequent discussions on taxes, state tax rates at all times tend to cluster around specific levels; each state hoping that another will be the first in going to a new high, each wanting to avoid a tax increase long enough to become conspicuous with a low tax rate.

Politicians' prayers notwithstanding, tax rate levels have drifted upward over the years and are expected to continue in that direction. The skillful politician follows the trend; he avoids leading it. The political graveyards are filled with one-time state and local leaders whose promising careers abruptly ended because they did not or could not avoid association with tax increases.

COUNTERVAILING PRESSURES

The political pressures that handicap tax enactments also oblige legislatures to respond to the people's demand for services—for public expenditures. Politically popular and effective pressure groups, whether "old folks," veterans, educators, homeowners, or "the poor," have to be satisfied by those who would continue to serve them. Each legislator makes his own calculation of the political implication of supporting or rejecting demands. All can manage to resist all pressure some of the time, but none survives long if he resists them all the time. There are always some with political courage or strength to respond to the pressures solely on the basis of their public policy merits, although the number of such lawmakers is rarely large enough to determine the outcome of roll-call votes in legislatures.

Those who are perplexed by the frequency of state and local fiscal crises in this most prosperous of popular democracies are likely to find some of their answers in the perverse impact of political pressures on the outgo side of the budget on the one hand and on the income side on the other, in the bias to keep spending high and taxes low. The influence of these dominant forces pervades many of the facets of state and local finance explored in the following chapters, written out of a conviction that political leadership will push toward more constructive fiscal practices as rapidly as voters will accept them and that voters will accept more as they understand better.

part II

GATHERING
OUR TAX DOLLARS

chapter 3

our tax
institutions

Ours is a country in which, in addition to the federal government and the 50 states, over 80,000 separate governments levy and collect taxes. Constitutionally, the federal government and the states have wide taxing powers. They are said to be co-sovereign in taxation because both are free to dip into practically any tax pond. Virtually the only tax off limits for the federal government is the one on property; for state governments, on interstate and foreign commerce. Each is free to choose almost any tax it pleases; and many please to choose some of the same taxes, albeit in different shapes.

Some of the states, to be sure, have imposed restrictions on themselves and on their political subdivisions some time in the past by writing prohibitions against certain taxes into their constitutions or statutes. In some cases, these constitutional limitations are quite explicit; in others they have been read into ambiguous constitutional language by the courts in earlier periods. Constitutional limitations, once imposed, are difficult to remove and generally inhibit succeeding generations.

Because local governments—counties, cities, towns, school districts, and so on—are created by states, their taxing powers are circumscribed by the states. Some give their cities and counties wide taxing latitude; most keep them on tight reins. Quite frequently they prohibit local use of such taxes as those on incomes or sales and place ceilings on tax rates local governments may impose on other objects of taxation, notably property.

Although states enjoy great taxing freedom under the U. S. Constitution, they do not have much freedom in fact. The things that states may and may not do in taxation are influenced by many considerations, including local and federal tax practices, tax competition with other states, problems of tax enforcement and, as earlier noted, voters' attitudes. Taxes acceptable to the people in one state may be anathema to those in another state.

GOVERNMENTS PRACTICE TAX SPECIALIZATION

In view of the latitude afforded by the U. S. Constitution and man's ingenuity in inventing different ways of doing things, one would expect the tax system of America's thousands of governments to exhibit great variety. In the main, this is not so. The governments at the several levels —federal, state, local—have developed tax specialization, with major reliance on one or two types of taxes at each level.

A checklist of the levels of governments which use each kind of tax would indeed have two or more checkmarks opposite most taxes. Income taxes, for example, are used by the federal government, states, and increasingly by local governments; motor fuel taxes by the federal government, all states, and some local governments; taxes on retail sales by states and many local governments. But the frequency of checkmarks tells an incomplete story.

Governments at each level have one workhorse, one type of tax on which they generally rely for most of their tax revenue. Although there is duplication or tax overlapping, as it is called, it involves only a small share of the tax collections at each level of government. The federal government, for example, derives 83 percent of its tax revenue from income taxes; the states almost 65 percent of theirs from consumer taxes; the local governments about 87 percent of theirs from property taxes. These are the three principal taxing methods and produce most of the 80,000 governments' revenues. The federal government, and all states except Nevada, also tax inheritances, and state and local governments tax various kinds of business activities, but these are secondary producers. Annual wealth taxes, common in many other countries, are unknown here except as represented by property taxes.

As a result of specialization, each of the three major families of taxes tends to be the monopoly of one level of government. Over 90 percent of all income taxes paid by the American people go to the federal government;

figure 5

**Federal, State, and Local Tax
Revenue, 1968: Distribution among
Broad Tax Categories**

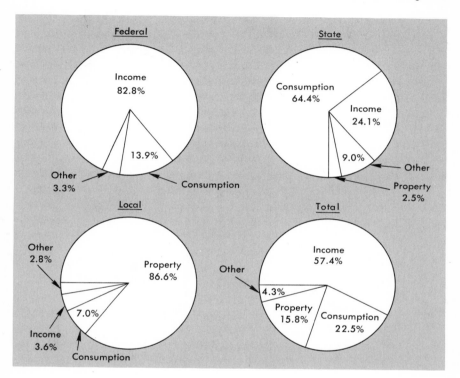

88 percent of all general sales taxes to the states; 97 percent of all property taxes to local governments. The federal government also takes almost 80 percent of the taxes assessed against inherited wealth. This means that the tax overlapping that prevails pertains to only a small part of the collections from each tax. This was even more true a few years ago, before persistent revenue pressures obliged state and local governments to reach out for taxes they had formerly disdained. It remains true, however, that if federal, state, and local tax collections could each be cut about one-fifth, this could be done in such a way—if it were so desired—that virtually all tax overlapping would be eliminated.

Tax specialization at each governmental level is the product of history, economics, and politics.

Local governments have always specialized in property taxes as a matter

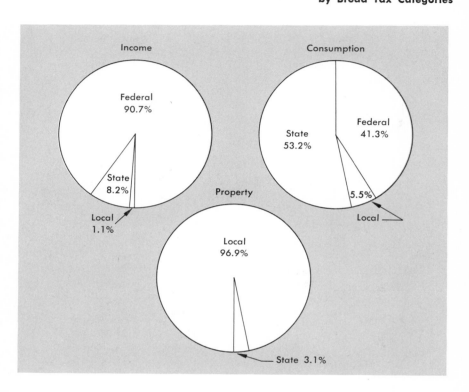

of necessity. This is the only major tax, if any, that can be readily administered locally and that is also capable of producing large amounts of revenue. When originally developed, it was also an acceptable gauge of taxpaying ability and of benefits derived from local government activity. Although the vast majority of local governments continue to rely almost exclusively on property taxes, some municipalities and counties are urgently trying to develop other taxes—notably on sales and payrolls. In a very few places these nonproperty taxes already outproduce property taxes.

There was a time when states also depended on the property tax. In recent decades, however, the states have largely vacated this area and left it for the exclusive use of local governments partly because they developed other revenue sources, but primarily because local revenue needs alone resulted in tax burdens as heavy as they wanted property to bear.

As states stopped levying property taxes, a few came to rely on income taxes, most on different kinds of consumer taxes, but chiefly on retail sales and on selected commodities. Also they are increasingly lending their tax collection capability to collect these taxes for their local governments. Most states abstained from income taxes because the federal government was in that field, business interests opposed it, consumer taxation appeared to hold more revenue promise for the less prosperous of them, and some believed that state constitutional restrictions blocked their way.

Although state taxation is typified by consumer taxation there are exceptions, and changes are under way. A very few rely heavily on income taxes, and one or two even on property taxes. Not infrequently these contrasts involve adjoining states. Washington, for example, still depends almost exclusively on consumer taxes; Oregon on income taxes. Delaware uses income taxes; Pennsylvania, sales taxes. These contrasts are beginning to fade, however, as persistent revenue pressures push increasingly more states into both income and consumer taxes. Moreover, consumer taxation means different things in different states; most concentrate on the taxation of the sale of commodities at retail, but a few tax also manufacturers' and wholesalers' sales; virtually all tax some services and supplement their general sales tax with special taxes on selected consumption items such as liquor, tobacco, or gasoline, and with licensing requirements which often are essentially consumer taxes (such as, for example, motor vehicle licenses). The taxation of property and income also takes varied forms, but not to the extent true of consumer taxes.

The type of taxes that states use is affected also by the increasing mobility of people and businesses and their assets. About one-fifth of Americans change their homes each year, although most stay in the same county. Theoretically, at least, they have an opportunity to take tax considerations into account in deciding where they will settle, or whether they will move at all.

Improved transportation and communication has given business more freedom in the selection of sites from which it can serve its customers. This increased mobility tends to curtail the freedom of states to embark on new types of taxes, and has helped to shift the balance against income and in favor of sales taxes in the belief that the latter is less detrimental to business growth and economic development. This also is the principal reason why the states feel obliged to deemphasize property taxes on business inventories and machinery. No state wants to risk losing residents and businesses, or weaken its attraction for new ones.

It was earlier noted that federal use of the income tax has tended to steer the states away from that tax. In fairness it should be recognized that the federal government, mindful of the limitations on the revenue-raising capability of state and local governments, has sought to avoid encroaching

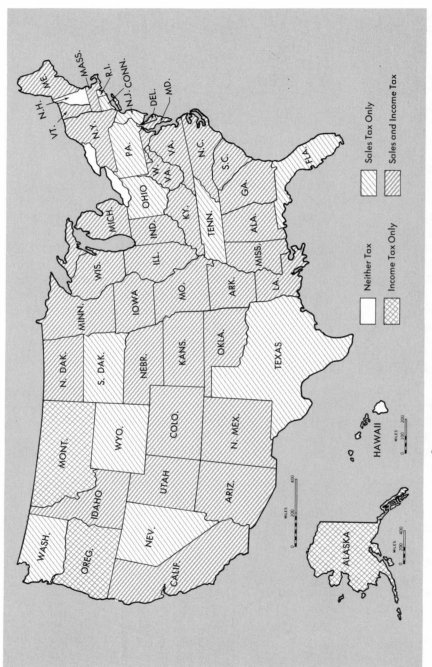

figure 7 Use of Personal Income and General Sales Taxes: by States, mid-1969

Neither Tax

Income Tax Only

Sales Tax Only

Sales and Income Tax

on their taxing preserves, and its ability to do so has significantly improved with the spectacular revenue response of its income tax to continued national prosperity and rising personal and corporation incomes. This has enabled the federal government to reduce its relative reliance on other taxes, and particularly on consumer taxes.

On two or three occasions in the past, when national emergencies prompted serious consideration of a federal sales tax, it was taken for granted that it would need to be a tax at the wholesale or manufacturing level because the states already occupied the tax on retail sales. It was taken for granted, too, that the federal government would go to general consumer taxation only as a last resort. During the Depression and the two world wars, the federal government imposed a wide variety of excise taxes on commodities and services. When budgetary conditions permitted some tax reduction, it was partly directed to excise taxes, among other reasons, in order to clear this area for state and local use.

Tax specialization at the three governmental levels—federal, state, and local—does not mean, however, that taxes at each level are uniform. Individual jurisdictions at each level have managed to develop substantial— even bewildering—variations in all the major types of taxes, reflecting varying political attitudes and pressures. Although all state sales, income, and inheritance taxes, for example, have common characteristics, differences in detail are sufficiently numerous to create a national market for several voluminous commercial publications devoted to keeping subscribers abreast of changing state tax provisions.

Despite tax specialization at the three levels of American government, tax overlapping occurs frequently enough to give people concern. It concerns them for diverse reasons, some profound, others are less so.

TAX OVERLAPPING IS UNAVOIDABLE

We have an aversion to two or more governments using the same tax. To put it another way, we dislike paying two taxes on the same income, on the same transaction, or on the same piece of property, and our dislike is not wholly because the combined tax bill is too large.

Tax overlapping generally requires the preparation of separate income, inheritance, or sales tax returns for two or more separate tax administrations and we believe this is wasteful. Tax overlapping often means also a duplication of publicly supported tax assessors and collectors, and that is costly. When it involves two or more sets of auditors who interrupt office routines while each reviews identical records for identical purposes, the waste seems compounded.

Because of this aversion to overlapping taxes we have evolved the image of a utopia in which each level of government would be assigned its own private tax domain, and governments would be enjoined to keep out of one another's preserve. Technicians call it separation of revenue resources. It is a pleasant kind of tax utopia to contemplate. It caters to man's love for symmetry and simplicity. Unhappily, an idle dream is all that it can ever be in our kind of federal system. This must have been the conclusion also of scores of scholars and practitioners who labored diligently for over two decades after the middle 1920's on behalf of reduced tax overlapping with little discernible impact on the country's tax structure. Man's ingenuity has devised only so many kinds of taxes, and there are not nearly enough good revenue producers to go around and to meet the needs of the different kinds of governments we support.

There is another compelling reason. It would be a necessary objective of any revenue separation plan to give each level of government a tax that would yield enough to match its revenue needs at the same time that the weights of the different taxes levied by the several governments maintained an acceptable relationship to one another. Presumably those striving for revenue separation would also strive for a particular pattern of distribution among types of taxes (consumption, income, inheritance, property, and so on) and among different groups in the population. But needs change over time, not only because the relative importance of the different governmental functions changes but also because the state and federal contributions to the financing of some of the functions tend to increase. Also the relative yields of the different taxes alter with short- and long-run economic changes. In the face of these changes any revenue separation plan would be obsolete before it could be presented, not to say implemented.

It may be, too, that tax overlapping is a political necessity. State and local legislators, mindful of voters' antipathy to taxes, generally prefer to spread the load over several taxes rather than concentrate it conspicuously on a single tax. They are also attracted to taxes used successfully elsewhere. Add to this the public's preference for paying small amounts of taxes under several different tax labels at different times of the year rather than the same amount under one label all at once, and you have the makings of tax overlapping.

TAXES SERVE SEVERAL PUBLIC POLICY PURPOSES

Our concern with the ways in which state-local governments gather their tax dollars focuses on several objectives. These objectives have been in process of development at least since Adam Smith turned his attention to formulating "canons of taxation" over two centuries ago. Although no two persons are likely to give the several criteria identical weights, each of them enters into most people's selection among alternative taxes.

Quite obviously, high on the list is *productivity*. The quest is for taxes which suffice to meet the jurisdictions' revenue requirements without excessive reliance on financial aid from higher levels of government. Our federal system lays stress on each governmental unit taking primary responsibility for the support of its own functions, and local governments are sorely pressed to find adequate revenue to meet the demands of their residents and businesses for increased services.

Closely related to the objective of productivity is *revenue elasticity,* a technical term for the revenue responsiveness of a tax to changing economic conditions. Revenue elasticity has acquired increasing importance in the ranking of taxes as a result of the rapid expenditure increases since World War II and the public's resistance to tax increases against the background of steady economic growth.

The yield of a tax that has a relatively high income elasticity increases faster than income. This characteristic is especially appreciated by those charged with policy responsibility, for it reduces the frequency of unavoidable tax rate increases. Of course if incomes declined, tax collections would fall more than proportionately; but the country has enjoyed economic growth for so many years that the possibility of another severe depression has receded to the background in people's calculations.

Some taxes have a low, some a proportional, and some a high elasticity. A cigarette tax, for example, has a low elasticity because the tax is based on the number and not on the price of cigarettes, and the number of cigarettes people buy and smoke does not significantly increase when their incomes rise. When incomes rise 10 percent, the volume of smoking, and therefore the yield of the cigarette tax, appears to increase only about 4 percent—less than half as fast. The income elasticity of the cigarette tax is said to be 0.4.

The general sales tax has a higher elasticity, but probably not quite 1.0 because as people's prosperity increases they tend to save a larger share and spend a smaller share of their income. If all increases in incomes were spent on items subject to sales tax, the elasticity of this tax would be unity or 1.0.

The elasticity of the property tax appears to be around 1.0, perhaps somewhat higher. Apparently economic growth is now accompanied by enough new construction and increases in property values and these, in turn, are reflected on the tax assessors' lists quickly enough to produce a corresponding rise in assessed values and therefore in tax yields.

The one tax with a conspicuously high revenue elasticity is the graduated income tax. This is because additions to people's incomes frequently throw them into higher tax rate brackets.

Another objective of tax policy is to distribute the tax load among taxpayers as *fairly* as possible. We would like to arrange the total burden of taxation so that neither the rich nor the poor, neither the farmer nor the laborer, nor any other citizen pays more or less than his fair share. But tax fairness is an elusive, widely debated concept. Cynics like to say that the only fair tax is one paid by the other fellow. However, this generation is believed to have come to accept the idea, at least as a generality, that tax fairness requires people to be taxed on the basis of their incomes and family circumstances, and that their bills ought to increase more than in proportion as their incomes rise. This is called progressive taxation. But agreement on the principle leaves wide room for disagreement on what is included and excluded from "income" for tax purposes.

Progression requires that at any income level those with larger incomes be subjected to higher rates, and those with smaller incomes to lower tax rates, and that the rate at which tax rates progress have some semblance of orderliness. This means that the rate at which the tax schedule rises should have a rational pattern, as should the size of successive tax brackets. Compassion for taxpayers dictates the avoidance of fractional rates to minimize calculation difficulties. Moreover, to avoid income confiscation, the maximum rate has to be less than 100 percent, and preferably should be substantially less, since excessively high tax rates may impair incentives to work and invest. Some think that the maximum rate should not exceed 50 percent, because the citizen who shares his income with government ought to remain the senior partner.

The outside limits of tax rate graduation are further constricted by the concentration of much of America's income in relatively small individual shares. In 1966, for example, when over 70 million federal income tax returns were filed, 81 percent reported incomes under $10,000 each; but these returns accounted for over half of all the income reported and for over one-third of all the income taxes paid. At the upper end, all those with incomes of over $50,000 produced only 15 percent of the tax revenue. This means that tax rates at the lower end of the income scale have to be substantial to produce the revenue needed.

Present federal income tax rates begin with 14 percent on the first $500 of income above exemptions and deductions, although during war years the starting rate was as high as 23 percent. This necessarily limits the range of tax rates between the starting rate prescribed by revenue needs and the maximum (now 70 percent). Moreover, this limited range (14 to 70 percent) has to accommodate a very wide range in incomes. Although most Americans have incomes below $10,000, several hundred regularly report incomes in excess of a million dollars. To accommodate the wide range in incomes within the beginning tax rate and the top tax rate and still produce the needed revenue, it is necessary to keep the tax brackets narrow at the lower end of the income scale and make them very broad at the upper end. However, very large brackets jeopardize the objective of progression, as when the first dollar of taxable income above $200,000 is subjected to the same tax rate as the second or tenth million.

This seeming digression into federal tax rate-making illuminates the practical limitations on tax rate graduation in state taxes. States typically keep their maximum income tax rates below 15 percent; most below 10 percent. Since the limited number of percentage points between their starting rate (mandated by the revenue objective) and their maximum rate is quickly exhausted in differentiating between low and middle incomes, most states feel obliged to stop their tax rate progression at the $15,000 taxable income bracket, and many below the $10,000 bracket.

Still another objective of tax policy is to make the process of tax collection *efficient and economical* for the government, the taxpayer, and the businessman whom the government requires to act as a supplier of information and sometimes as a tax collector. A related consideration is *certainty,* because the taxpayer should know (or be able to find out) what his tax bill is, and when it is due, and be able to make a reasonably dependable estimate of what he owes as he earns.

The search for efficiency and economy may lead to different types of taxes at different levels of government. A sales tax, for example, may be reasonably efficient and economical for a state government to administer but difficult and expensive for small local government, because many of the merchants with whom consumers trade operate across town or school district boundaries and are beyond the control of local tax administrators.

And finally we would like tax practices to exert a constructive influence on behalf of public policy objectives: economic growth, industrial development, the elimination of poverty and ghetto living conditions, and the maintenance of a congenial natural and social environment for all the people. At the very least, the tax system should not handicap these objectives.

Now let us look at the principal taxes with these considerations in mind. We begin with state taxes on income and consumption, because together they account for over 80 percent of the states' total tax collections; and with the inheritance-estate taxes, because their contribution to state needs falls so conspicuously short of their potential. In subsequent chapters we will examine local revenues: first, the property tax which in productivity and the number of people who pay it is exceeded only by the federal income tax, and then the nonproperty taxes.

The omission of corporation income taxes is not inadvertent. A society in which business is increasingly characterized by the multistate corporation would do well to leave the taxation of corporate income to its national government. Admittedly states are not free to relinquish the $3 billion annual revenue involved. However, it may not be unrealistic to look forward to a time when the federal government deems it both practicable and constructive to "rent" or "buy" the states' equity on this tax area. The economy's gains from removing the influence of these state taxes in ways of doing business would be substantial.

The discussion of state and local taxes in this book is necessarily general. Complete details are published in the Prentice-Hall *State and Local Taxes* service. This is a multi-volume looseleaf service covering all aspects of taxation in every state, and in thousands of local governmental units. Included are charts of every state tax system, tables showing the types of taxes imposed in each state, and calendars noting due dates of reports and returns. The tax statutes and tax agency rulings and regulations in each state are set out in full text; pending legislation and court decisions are reported also. A discussion of each tax by the editorial staff simplifies an understanding of the otherwise complex and confusing mass of official information. Weekly reports keep all information up to date.

chapter 4

personal
income tax

For those who are concerned with state and local finances and ways to strengthen them in quality and productivity, one of the critical issues is what role, if any, the income tax should play. This has been an energetically contested issue for years in many states, though their number is declining.

IT HAS DEVELOPED HALTINGLY

In the half century since Wisconsin first demonstrated the practicability of enforcing an income tax at the state level, the tax has spread in fits and starts to about two-thirds of the states. Even today it is an important revenue producer in only a few. Nationally its share of state and local tax collections did not reach 10 percent until 1968.

The progress of state income taxation contrasts sharply with that of consumer taxes. The general sales tax and the selective sales taxes on liquor, tobacco, and gasoline all had later beginnings than the income tax, yet each has spread faster and farther; the general sales tax to all but five states, the others to virtually all the states.

States had experimented with income taxes as long as a hundred years ago, but these experiments were not successful. The administration of the earlier taxes was entrusted to local property tax officials who had neither the enforcement skill nor the will to make state income taxation a success. Wisconsin solved the problem in 1911 by placing the tax under the direct control of a state tax commission staffed with income tax assessors selected on the basis of professional merit, and by requiring employers and corporations to provide the state with information on their wage and dividend payments.

While Wisconsin was demonstrating an income tax enforcement capability, the federal government was moving in a parallel direction. The success with income taxation did not go unnoticed. By 1930, thirteen other states had followed Wisconsin's lead. With two or three exceptions, these were chiefly agricultural states with relatively limited taxable incomes. They appear to have been attracted by the appeal of imposing progressive taxes on the nonfarming population as much as by the prospect of larger revenues, although the desire to provide tax relief to property had strong popular support. With the collapse of farm prices and incomes during the Great Depression, the need for property tax relief became politically compelling. Between 1931 and 1937, fifteen states joined the income tax ranks. These, too, were chiefly nonindustrial states and, in consequence of the nationwide economic depression, obtained only modest revenue from their new taxes.

After 1937, not another state joined the ranks for a quarter century except that Alaska and Hawaii brought two additional income taxes into the Union. The response of existing and newly enacted consumer and other taxes to national prosperity apparently staved off the kind of financial crisis that is required to overcome political resistance to income taxes in industrial states with relatively numerous high income residents. By the 1960's, however, the accumulated revenue deficiencies became critical again and six states enacted income taxes during the next several years, raising the count by the close of the decade to thirty-seven, not including four states with limited taxes.

As already noted, only a minority of the states make effective use of the income tax. An approximate measure of effectiveness is the ratio of state to federal collections. Another is the relationship of income tax collections to personal incomes.

In the aggregate, state income tax collections correspond to about 14 percent of federal collections within their borders. This average, however, masks substantial interstate variations. In twelve states, state taxes take less than 10 percent as much as the federal; in only six states as much as 25 percent. All state and local governments' income tax collections represent about 1 percent of the American people's personal incomes. In a few states the percentage rises above 2 percent, but in most it is substantially lower. Income taxes of sorts are levied also by an increasing number of local governments.

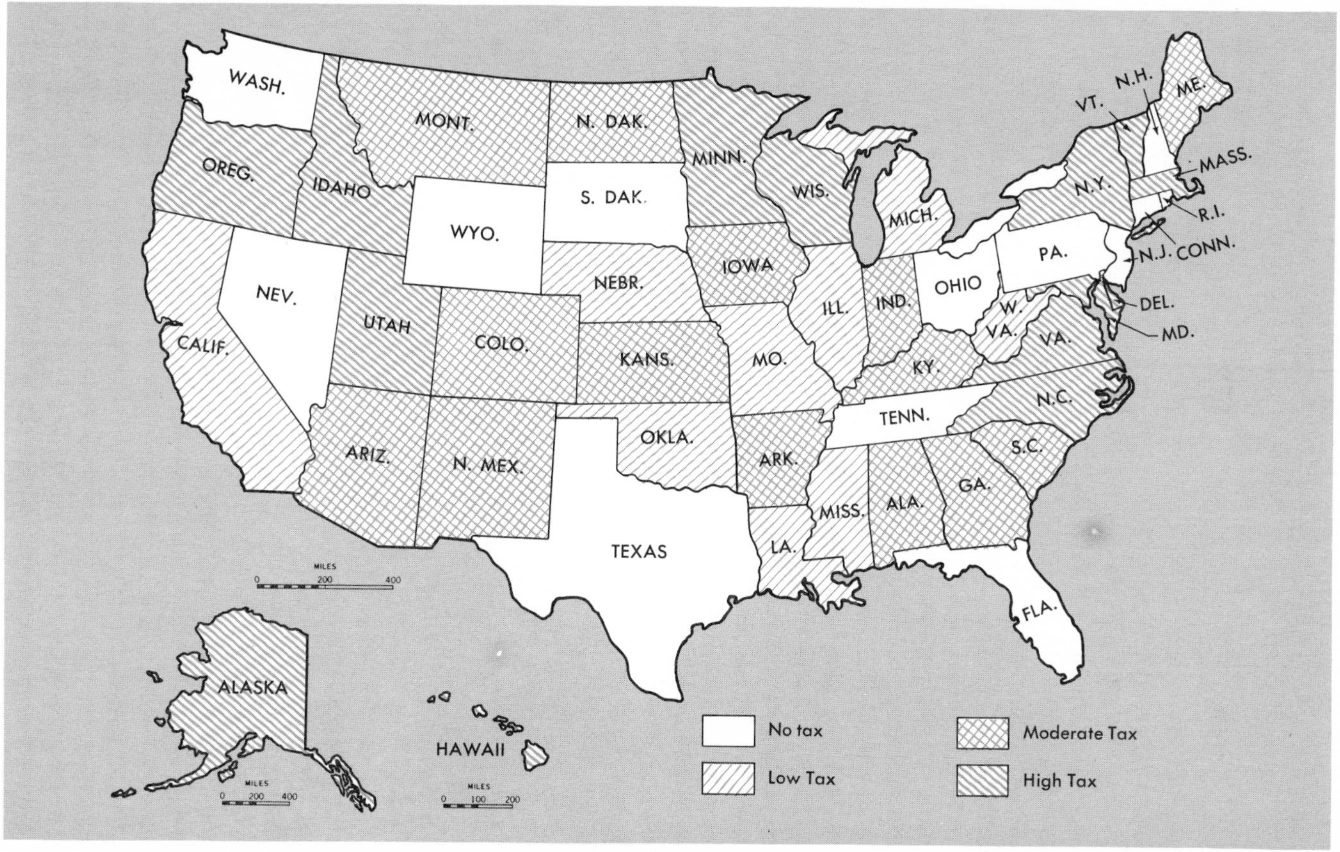

figure 8 States with Broad-Based Personal Income Taxes: mid-1969

Moderate Tax

High Tax

No tax

Low Tax

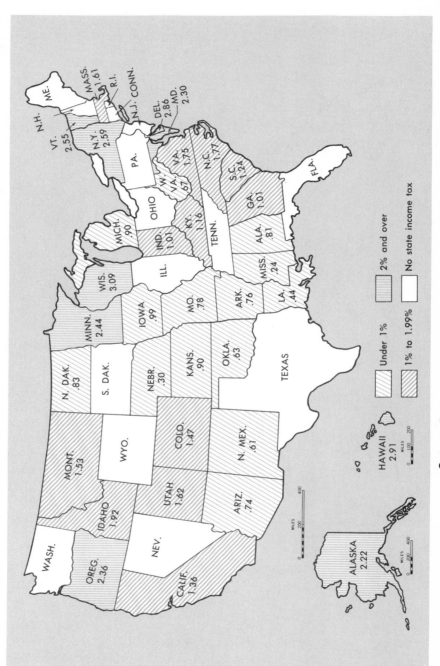

figure 9 State Income Tax Collections as Percent of State Personal Incomes: 1968

IT HAS ATTRACTIVE FEATURES

The distinguishing feature of the income tax—the characteristic that explains the ardor of its advocates and the bitterness of its opponents—is that it can take account of taxpaying ability in distributing its burden among taxpayers. This is accomplished by adjusting the size of the tax bill not only to the amount of the taxpayer's income but also to the size of his family, costs he incurs in acquiring business income, and to some of the other claims on his income, including certain tax and interest payments and contributions to educational, religious, and charitable organizations.

Another attribute of the income tax that is of particular interest to those with fiscal policy responsibilities and interests is its revenue responsiveness to economic prosperity, commonly termed income or gross national product elasticity. The demand for government services and for revenues to pay the bills tends to grow with each passing year. When times are good and the economy is growing, collections from income taxes, unlike those from most other taxes, increase faster than income and national production. This happens because, when incomes are increasing, the incomes of some of the previously nontaxable people are shifted into taxable categories for the first time, and other incomes are lifted into higher tax rate brackets. Recent experience indicates that each 10 percent increase in economic activity automatically increases state income tax collection 15 to 18 percent.

In this respect the states' income taxes are even better performers than the federal government's because of their different tax rate patterns. Hawaii's and the federal government's tax rate schedules both begin with four $500 brackets. The Hawaii rates are respectively 2¼, 3¼, 4½, and 5 percent; the federal rates are 14, 15, 16, and 17 percent. When the taxpayer's income rises above $500, his added income becomes subject to a 3¼ percent rather than a 2¼ percent Hawaii tax rate, or 44 percent higher. For federal tax purposes, the increase in the take is from 14 to 15 percent, or only about 7 percent. The increase from the second to the third bracket is 39 percent in the Hawaii, and 7 percent in the federal schedule. State and local officials value the revenue responsiveness of the income tax because it helps to reduce the frequency with which tax rates have to be increased. This characteristic of the income tax is particularly important in circumstances when budget needs rise faster than income, as they have done in recent years.

The responsiveness of the income tax to economic prosperity is reflected in the spectacular growth of state tax collections, probably substantially less than half of which is accounted for by increased rates and new enactments. In 1948, state income tax collections aggregated $0.5

billion; in 1969 they were approaching $8 billion. During this interval, when aggregate state tax collections increased about fourfold, income tax collections increased fifteenfold.

The invention of tax withholding at the source has eased income tax administration. Before World War II, these taxes typically were payable after the close of the year with enough of a lag (three or four months) to give the taxpayer time to make his final tax calculation. The tax was then payable in one or two installments. With this timetable, the tax on one year's income frequently was not fully paid until the end of the following year. This arrangement worked reasonably well when the income tax was limited to the few relatively well-to-do citizens and tax rates were low. When, however, the income tax became heavier and applied to substantially the entire working population, the lump-sum and delayed-payment system became unworkable. Most people spend their income as they receive it, and do not have enough cash on hand at any one time to cover a full year's tax liability. The arrangement was particularly awkward when the bread-winner died toward the end of a year and left his family with the obligation of paying nearly a full year's tax after the flow of the family's income had stopped.

Withholding enables taxpayers to discharge their tax liability as they earn income, and in a relatively painless fashion. Actually it is paid on their behalf by employers who withhold it from their pay checks. In this respect the income tax is similar to the social security tax and approaches the convenience of a sales tax which is collected day by day as people spend.

In some people's view, to be sure, it is not altogether desirable to make the tax-paying process too painless. They believe that if the individual citizen is made aware of the impact of taxes on his budget and pocketbook, he is likely to become a more responsible citizen and take a more active interest in government issues.

It cannot be gainsaid, however, that withholding has advantages from the standpoint of both the state and the taxpayer. The steady flow of with-holding payments to the state facilitates matching the state's money needs with the flow of tax collections throughout the year. Before withholding, all income tax payments were made at one or two periods during the year and the states frequently had to resort to short-term borrowing in anticipa-tion of income tax collections. Withholding, moreover, shifts part of the job of tax collection to employers and reduces the possibility of tax evasion on earned income. Generally withholding tax is not applied to investment income (interest, dividends, rents, royalties, and so on) except when the recipient is a resident of another state. Employers are willing to accept the burden of the tax collection arrangement because it is a convenience to their employees and they can handle it with relative ease in their payroll operations, especially if these are automated.

Since investment, rental, and business incomes are not subject to withholding, taxpayers generally are required to estimate their anticipated income from these sources at the beginning of each year and make quarterly payments on their tax liabilities. Those who underestimate excessively are penalized, those who overestimate are entitled to refunds.

All withholding plans have a tendency to overwithhold from some people and require a substantial number of refunds after the end of each year. This is unavoidable. The rate of withholding necessarily is based on the assumptions that the taxpayer's earnings will continue throughout the year and that he will be entitled only to an average amount of deductions. If the worker's flow of income is interrupted by a period of unemployment, or if he incurs an abnormal amount of deductible expenses such as medical bills or capital losses, too much will have been withheld from him and necessitate refunds. Some object to the tendency of withholding systems to withhold too much, particularly from low-income persons. Since refunds are made only after the close of the year, low-income wage earners are deprived of their money for a period of up to a year. The government, in effect, borrows the people's money without paying them interest. Nevertheless, most taxpayers who receive refunds seem to consider overwithholding a desirable form of forced saving and the subsequent refunds a pleasant windfall.

In other situations underwithholding occurs because taxpayers receive income from two or more employers, each of whom gives them credit for personal exemptions and deductions; or because tax rates are increased during the year; or the taxpayer underestimates his income from sources not subject to withholding. In these situations he may find himself with large tax liabilities and even with penalties at final settlement time in the following year.

The fact that withholding is an administrative burden on the employer for which he is not reimbursed obliges the government to make the process as simple as possible. At the federal level, and in nearly half of the states, for example, it has necessitated making uniform the personal exemptions for all dependents (generally $600) even though fairness would require a larger exemption for the first than for the fifth or tenth child. Similarly, it has necessitated granting everyone an optional standard deduction (generally 10 percent of income) in lieu of itemized deductions. Those who are entitled to few or no deductions take the standard deduction; those with large deductions itemize them; and many taxpayers go through two calculations to determine which method gives them a better break. Tax simplicity, so highly prized by administrators and many taxpayers, often exacts a cost in tax fairness!

Still another feature of the income tax, and one that is just beginning to be appreciated, is its ability to correct or compensate for the quality weaknesses of sales and property taxes. The property tax on homes at the local level and the sales tax on the purchase of necessities at the state level can impose excessive burdens on people with very low incomes. Some governments have attempted to avoid such hardships by exempting home-steads from the property tax, or food from the sales tax. Such practices, however, are very costly.

Classifications for tax exemption purposes have to be rather broad and typically benefit a great many more people than just those with low incomes and therefore tend to be costly in revenues foregone. As pointed out at some length in the next chapter, credits and refunds administered through the vehicle of the income tax accomplish the objective more efficiently. They can be designed to return the same amount of sales or property taxes to all taxpayers, rich or poor; or, if desired, can be constructed so as to benefit only taxpayers below specified income levels.

IT ALSO HAS DISADVANTAGES

The income tax, however, is not without weaknesses.

In bygone years the instability of income tax collections was deemed to be an argument against major reliance on this tax. Because its yield is responsive to economic conditions, the income tax has the disadvantage of unstable collections: high in good years, low in poor years. These changes in collections could occur fairly rapidly and without much warning—especially since the adoption of withholding—a situation that could pose difficult problems for a state without annual legislative sessions when ad-ditional revenue measures might be considered. Ironically, this has not restrained low-income states from enacting these taxes. The states which have avoided them are typically the industrial states noted for high personal incomes. Meanwhile, the instability-of-revenue argument has lost most of its force as the national administration succeeded in pursuing a policy of economic growth.

Some people continue to object to state use of income taxes because it results in tax duplication since the federal government also taxes incomes. Where the ground rules for state and federal taxation are not identical, the individual taxpayer has the nuisance of complying with two tax report-ing systems which may significantly differ.

FEDERAL AND STATE RULES DIFFER

Since the federal government administers an income tax and does a good job of it, people understandably inquire why the states use different income tax rules so that taxpayers are burdened with two or more sets of computations. (Major variations between state and federal income tax provisions are summarized in the Prentice-Hall tax chart reproduced on page 218).

The question is best considered in installments. Should states be free to design their own income tax laws, defining the rules of the game differently than they are defined for purposes of the federal tax? Should they exercise independence in setting personal exemptions and tax rates? Should the state and federal income taxes be separately collected by separate enforcement organizations?

Taxpayers are especially interested in the first of these questions because the determination of the amount of a person's income subject to tax can be a complex calculation. It involves such questions as: What income is included and excluded? What deductions are allowed? How are capital gains, royalties, pensions, and so on, treated? Ours is a complex economic society and business is done in an infinite variety of ways. Over the years an elaborate set of rules has been developed through federal legislation, regulation, and litigation for handling these variations. Conformity with these provisions can impose a substantial burden on taxpayers as well as on those who must supply information returns. When federal and state ground rules diverge, taxpayers are inconvenienced, particularly those who operate and derive income in more than one state.

To be sure, federal and state laws cannot be made completely identical. The federal government, for example, taxes the interest on its own bonds but exempts state and local bond interest; states reciprocate. The federal government also taxes the appreciation realized on the sale of stocks acquired at any time after 1913, the beginning of federal income taxation. Almost all states are limited to a later beginning date since they introduced income taxation more recently, and retroactive taxation of capital gains would be considered unfair. Some states do not tax capital gains, or use a different period of time (the federal government uses six months) to determine whether a gain or loss is "capital" or ordinary income gain or loss.

State adherence to federal rules would clearly simplify compliance, particularly for those who derive income from sources other than wages and salaries. It would also help tax administrators because the Federal Internal Revenue Service makes its files freely available to state tax administrations; and to the extent that state and federal rules match, federal income tax findings can be readily taken over for state use.

But federal rules are not always good rules. Over the years, a variety of preferential provisions have crept into federal law and the state that operates on the basis of federal rules necessarily takes over the bad with the good. What is a tax incentive to Congress may be a tax loophole to a state legislature.

It will be appreciated that a decision to base their law on the federal comes hard to state legislators. It implies some surrender of their independence, of their states' tax sovereignty; it means foregoing their privilege to shape their state tax policies in accordance with their personal views; it means foregoing their privilege to favor groups of their choice and to discriminate against others.

Practical considerations and compassion for taxpayers appear to be overcoming state reluctance to adhere to federal rules. In fact most of the new state income tax laws of recent years follow federal law, and some states with old laws have scrapped them in whole or in part for the federal model. A recent case is Wisconsin, particularly notable because that state's law actually predates the federal law by a couple of years. Apparently no state that once has conformed its income tax base to the federal has ever abandoned it.

In some cases, state conformity to federal law even raises difficult constitutional questions that a state can resolve only by constitutional amendment. In several states, as in New York, the adoption of federal rules governing the determination of income tax required a constitutional amendment because it had been held that the adoption of federal rules would be an unconstitutional delegation of state legislative authority to Congress.

Some states have limited the extent of conformity with federal law to the determination of the amount of a taxpayer's income subject to tax. They have adopted their own rules to govern exemptions and tax rates. The case for carrying conformity to include these factors is less clear, if for no other reason than because the differences in personal exemptions and in tax rates are easily accommodated on the tax form and the additional arithmetic involved is not particularly burdensome.

Over the years, the $600 federal per capita exemption has become quite insufficient in light of the increased cost of living, and some states may well want to provide a more realistic allowance. The presumed purpose of the exemption is to allow for the essentials of survival free of tax. An identical federal and state personal exemption is probably of more interest to employers than to taxpayers, for it would make the accommodation of tax withholding to employers' payroll computers more simple.

Before the introduction of withholding, the exemptions typically differentiated between single persons, heads of households, and dependents. When the federal government adopted withholding during World War II, it used a $500 per capita exemption and did not increase it to $600 until 1948. Since that time the cost of living has about doubled. It would now require an exemption of about $1,200 to equal the purchasing power of the original per capita exemption. This, however, would be too expensive;

so the federal government devised the minimum standard deduction for the benefit of the most hard-pressed taxpaying group.

THE SIMPLEST IS NOT THE BEST ANSWER

It is often suggested that states should make income tax compliance really simple for taxpayers and employers by expressing their tax as a percentage of the federal tax. Some states have experimented with such a system and found it created problems. Two considerations trouble them:

Federal tax rates are graduated. If the state tax were a uniform percent of the federal tax, the federal graduation would be carried over automatically for state tax purposes. Since the degree of income tax progression is a political decision, governed more by social policy objectives than revenue considerations, states may not wish to commit themselves to following the graduation in federal law.

The degree of graduation in tax rates is a frequent point in controversy in state income taxation. "Liberals" in the state of Washington defeated the income tax in 1967 ostensibly because, as proposed, it had a flat rate. Illinois, Indiana, Massachusetts, and Michigan tax personal income at a uniform rate. Mississippi has only two income-tax brackets, Virginia and Louisiana only three. Those who insist on graduated tax rates overlook the fact that at the lower end of the income scale, where progressivity is particularly important, differentiation among small and large families through personal exemption is far more important than the kind of graduation in rates that is practicable in state income taxes. When the benefits of an income tax with personal exemptions are forfeited (as was done in the state of Washington in 1967 because the proposed tax did not have graduated rates) the important losers are low-income taxpayers, particularly those with large families.

Although a state's attitude toward tax burden graduation remains the important consideration in deciding whether or not to tie state income tax liability to a percentage of the federal tax, recently a more compelling consideration has come to the fore. In 1964, Congress initiated a policy of changing income tax rates in the interest of economic policy objectives. It reduced tax rates, despite a deficit budget, to stimulate the economy in the expectation that the resulting economic growth would compensate for the revenue lost. Its expectation proved to be correct. States, however, unlike the federal government, cannot engage in deficit financing (borrowing) for operating costs and therefore are not free to take revenue losses incident to national economic policy objectives even for short periods. This was the reason Alaska, which for several years had used the federal tax as a base, was obliged to cut loose from a constant relationship to current federal tax liability in 1964 following the federal rate reductions. The Alaska tax is now 16 percent of the amount calculated by using federal tax rates in effect at the end of 1963. In Nebraska, the state rate is annually fixed by the State Board of Equalization and Assessment as a percentage of the current federal tax liability. The 1968 rate was 10 percent of the federal tax. Vermont alone expresses its tax as a legislatively fixed proportion of the amount of the current federal tax. There the state tax is equal to 25 percent of the federal tax on the current year's income from Vermont sources (before the temporary federal surtax enacted in 1968).

So long as states operate on the basis of the federal income tax law, why not entrust the collection of their tax to the federal Internal Revenue Service? We will discuss this question elsewhere in connection with intergovernmental cooperation in tax administration.

chapter 5

consumer taxation

We have been told time after time that consumer taxes burden low-income families excessively because, unlike middle- and high-income families, they typically spend most of their income on taxed commodities. Most of us have some compassion for the poor; and therefore it comes as a shock that taxes on retail sales and those on some widely consumed selected commodities are in almost universal use by the states, and that the rates of these taxes have been rising faster than any of the others.

The pennies and dimes added to our bills as we spend are the mainstay of state governments' revenues. In 1968, when the fifty states collected $36 billion, nearly $21 billion came from consumer taxes. Licenses of various sorts, generally borne by consumers, provided another $4 billion. Together, those two categories accounted for about 70 cents of each tax dollar raised by the states.

The principal consumer tax is the general sales tax. Forty-five states now use it. State collections in 1968 approached $10.5 billion, and this figure does not include the $1.5 billion produced by local sales taxes. By the middle of 1969, the annual rate of combined state and local collections was around $14 billion.

The selected commodity excises are also good producers. The tax on cigarettes, used by every state now that

North Carolina has joined the ranks (1969), contributed $1.9 billion, sales taxes on alcoholic beverages $1.1 billion, and motor fuel taxes $5.2 billion.

This, of course, is only a partial inventory of consumer taxes. A complete list would include also the taxes on electricity, gas, telephone, water, admissions to places of amusement, motels and hotels, and so on. Of course consumers bear also the burden of the federal excises, imposed chiefly on liquor, tobacco, motor fuel, and automobiles, which now produce about $15 billion.

IT IS A RECENT DEVELOPMENT

The rise of state consumer taxes is a relatively recent development. Before the turn of the century, these governments subsisted on property taxes. Consumer taxation was then limited to customs duties and the excises on selected commodities imposed by the federal government.

The advent of the automobile brought the states in quick succession into motor vehicle registration fees. By 1915 every state imposed them. In 1919, Colorado, New Mexico, North Dakota, and Oregon pioneered the gasoline tax, and it proved to be so popular and lucrative—and motorists' pleas for highway improvement so persuasive—that ten years later every state had this tax. State tobacco taxes began to make an appearance at the same time.

The success of selective excises, coupled with uncertainty about the states' constitutional freedom to exercise taxing jurisdiction over transactions affected by interstate commerce, appears to have restrained state use of general sales taxes. The collapse of the property tax during the depression of the 1930's, however, when shrinkage in property values and tax delinquencies cut deeply into collections, proved to be a turning point. Encouraged by the rejection of the general sales tax by Congress, states began to venture into the field. Mississippi led the way in 1932, and within six years half the states had sales taxes.

Although the enactments of the 1930's were for the most part intended as temporary measures, the sales taxes became permanent in most states. They turned to this form of taxation to escape the squeeze of rising relief costs and shrinking property tax collections. The yields of existing taxes were declining, and there was strong opposition to increasing their rates. In addition, stringent limitations on property tax rates were imposed during the Depression period. When economic conditions improved, the states retained the sales tax, partly in response to pressures from local governments that the states withdraw from the property tax field and partly because revenue needs persisted.

Another sales tax surge occurred after World War II when states sought ways to finance the increased level of postwar expenditures. They had fallen behind during the war, when labor and material shortages kept state-local spending to a minimum. Five states enacted the sales tax in 1947 and 1949, and sixteen more have done so since that time, raising the total to forty-five. In 1968, about 98 percent of the country's population lived in states with a sales tax. This includes some of the most industrialized areas, which so far have been able to shun state income taxes (Connecticut, New Jersey, Ohio, Pennsylvania, and—before 1969—Illinois). The more recent sales tax enactments were preceded by a nationwide intensive exploitation of tobacco taxation, stimulated and made acceptable by the publicized association between lung cancer and smoking.

The states, however, do not monopolize consumption taxation. Municipalities are also in the field. A growing number are taxing consumers in diverse ways and employing various collection techniques—and an increasing number of states are helping them.

As a result of these developments, consumers have shouldered a substantial share of the increased state and local revenue requirements since the end of World War II. However, since sales taxes—and particularly the selective excises—respond less than in proportion to economic growth, their strong revenue performance was possible only at the cost of repeated tax rate increases and new enactments. During the 1959-1968 period, for example, when ten states joined the sales tax list, fifteen states with pre-1959 sales taxes increased their rate once; six states twice; and four states three times. During the same period cigarette tax rates were raised once in twelve states, twice in fourteen states, three times in thirteen states, and four times in three states.

IT HAS FRIENDS AND FOES

The states' emphasis on consumer taxes is all the more striking because during most of the postwar period economic development has been rapid, the people have been prosperous, and public concern for the poor has been increasing. Under these conditions one would have expected a preference for income taxes, since they take better account of people's taxpaying abilities and family obligations and spare the very poor.

It is not that Americans like consumer taxes. They dislike taxes in any category. It is rather that when pressure for more revenue can no longer be contained, the resistance to income taxation appears to be more tenacious than to consumer taxes. State legislatures tend to be conservative and turn to income taxes only as a last resort.

The pressure for increased spending emanates from those who want to improve public education, welfare, health, or the other social services. The social consciousness that motivates community leaders to advocate programs of this kind probably propels them also in the direction of ability-to-pay and away from regressive taxes. However, when frustrated in their efforts to increase fair taxes, they tend to acquiesce in consumer taxes because they would rather suffer undesirable taxes than forego increases in social expenditures. Social expenditures especially benefit low-income families, and the worst of the commonly used taxes is not so regressive as to neutralize poor people's benefits from the expenditures it makes possible.

Notwithstanding the forcefulness of the case against consumer taxes, large portions of the electorate, some politically influential, continue to think well of them. This appears to be true not only of the majority of business groups but of a large number of professional groups, and of the more prosperous young people as well. They tend to prefer them to income taxes, and quite forcefully put the case for including sales taxes in state revenue systems.

Sales taxes can produce large amounts of revenue at seemingly low rates. Since Americans tend to maintain their personal expenditures even when incomes decline, the yield of sales taxes is more stable than that of income taxes. The safeguard afforded by consumer taxes against a precipitous decline in collections during a recession is important to states because their authority to borrow for operating costs (unlike that of the federal government) is restricted. Collections from consumer taxes fall more slowly than from income taxes during periods of recession and falling personal income. This is so because, when incomes fall, people do not proportionately curtail their spending. Some of their spending habits (for a family's food and public utility services, for example) may not change at all.

Sales taxes are also favored because they are relatively inexpensive to administer. They are collected in the first instance by merchants as they make sales—and quite willingly, particularly if the state reimburses them for out-of-pocket expenses. In the early years of the sales tax movement, spokesmen for retail merchants fought these taxes; they argued that taxes added to business costs and diverted trade to states which had no sales taxes. We can only conjecture why they widely tend to favor them now: Because sales taxes help to block income taxes? Or because they make a small profit margin on tax collections? Or simply because they want to support improvements in public programs? The fact that sales taxes have relatively little adverse effect on the states' attraction for business and industry, especially now that they are almost nationwide, may also influence merchants' attitudes.

Friends of sales taxation also like to argue that the ultimate measure of people's income position is what they consume, and that therefore the inclusion of consumer taxes in a tax system improves its overall fairness so long as appropriate exemptions are allowed. When they reinforce their case for the sales tax by theorizing that people can always limit or avoid their taxes by controlling their spending, they are not on very solid ground. There is no contesting the fact that, at any income level, the sales tax discriminates against large families because they have to spend a larger share of income on necessities.

A view also widely held is that all people should be made aware of the cost of government by participating to a degree in its support, and that consumer taxes serve this purpose by tapping people who are exempt from income taxes. Another aspect of this argument is the appeal of a multipronged tax system. Since each tax (except the sales tax) catches only some of the people, only with several different taxes is it possible to catch all of the people.

People everywhere appear to appreciate the seeming painlessness of paying taxes in bits and pieces as they spend, and the capability of sales taxes to catch transients and visitors on such expenditure items as restaurant meals, motels, entertainment, motor fuel, and alcoholic beverages.

This formidable defense of consumer taxes has proved to be more than an adequate match for the tax fairness and revenue elasticity arguments, the mainstays of the opponents. It is incontrovertible that sales taxes take a larger share of the income of low-income families, the smaller their total income and the larger the family. This is so because low-income families tend to spend everything they get for taxed commodities and services, and save little if anything. Where the opportunity is available to them, they spend additional amounts by buying on credit.

Admittedly the weight of this consideration diminishes as the general level of real income rises and the number of the poor declines. A society made up exclusively of families with "good" incomes would not be overly disturbed by tax regressivity. But today's America, alas! is not that kind of happy society. Millions of families are still poor; many are very poor; and the typical sales tax applies to every dollar of expenditure, whether financed from savings, earnings, credit, or from public relief, social security, unemployment insurance, or a friend's charity.

REGRESSIVITY OF TAX BURDEN CAN BE RELIEVED

The most widespread technique for mitigating the sales tax burden on low-income families is to exempt food and medicines. Because these items loom relatively large in low-income budgets, their exemption does indeed work in this direction. A calculation prepared for a committee of the Indiana senate estimated that a 2 percent sales tax without exemptions takes 2.1 percent from the group with incomes under $1,000, 1.3 percent from those with incomes between $5,000 and $6,000, and only 0.9 percent from those with incomes over $15,000. If food is exempted, these burdens are significantly reduced. However, the tax relief is obtained at the expense of a substantial amount of revenue.

On the average, food exemption entails the loss of about a fifth to a fourth of collections—a larger proportion than one would anticipate on the basis of consumer expenditures on food. This occurs, in part, because the food exemption benefits the rich as well as the poor, and because the rich buy more expensive brands and more of them. It occurs also, perhaps primarily, because exemptions substantially increase the cost of effective administration by opening avenues of tax evasion.

When a merchant handles both taxable and exempt items, opportunities for manipulation are increased and can be controlled only by detailed audits of business records. Such tax audits are not practicable on an extensive scale. In the absence of exemptions, tax enforcement can be keyed to the establishment's gross receipts which can be checked against amounts reported for federal or state income tax purposes. Exemptions make the auditing task much more time-consuming. Nevertheless, fifteen of the forty-five sales-tax states exempt food. The exemption of food, to be sure, substantially reduces the sales tax discrimination against low-income families, particularly those with several dependents.

The desire to relieve low-income families without losing too much revenue led to the invention of a tax credit and refund device already in use in half a dozen states. Under this arrangement (pioneered by Indiana in 1963) food is taxed, but taxpayers are allowed a credit against their income tax in amounts computed by applying the sales-tax rate to a presumed amount of food purchased per head. Indiana allows $8.00 credit per capita on the assumption that, on the average, people pay its 2 percent sales tax on $400 of food purchased per person per year. Those who do not pay an income tax are entitled to a corresponding cash refund at the end of the year.

In Massachusetts this device is refined by reducing the amount of the credit as the taxpayer's and the spouse's combined income increases, allowing no credit (vanishing credit) to those with incomes in excess of $5,000. The burden of a 2 percent sales tax on the group with less than $1,000 income can be reduced from 2.1 percent to 1.1 percent by a flat tax credit and to 0.4 percent by a vanishing credit. Indeed, these credit arrangements can go a long way toward converting a regressive sales tax into a progressive tax in the lower ranges of the income scale.

The one respect in which such a credit-refund arrangement is less helpful to low-income families than an outright food exemption is that they are obliged to wait for their refunds until the end of the year. The poor can ill afford to make interest-free loans to the government even for short periods. Some of the poor, moreover, may not be familiar with the procedure for claiming tax refunds. States can mitigate these weaknesses by making more frequent refunds, and by requesting the public information media to inform the poor of their right to refunds.

THE TAX REACH CAN BE WIDE

While state sales taxes apply mainly to retail sales of tangible property, inclusion of some services in the sales tax base is quite common; and, as has been noted, this tendency appears to be gaining momentum. One or more public utility services are subject to tax in two-thirds of the states. Twenty-seven tax intrastate telephone and telegraph services; thirty include sales of gas and electricity under the general sales tax. Only sixteen apply their tax to water sales; even fewer to intrastate transportation services. Printing, publishing, advertising, photography, laundry, dry cleaning, storage, and repair services to tangible personal property are also taxed in a small but increasing number of states. Twenty-five states tax admissions; thirty-nine states tax transient lodging; and all forty-five states tax meals served in restaurants.

The case for including services in the base of the sales tax is good. It makes the tax less regressive because expenditures for services tend to rise as incomes rise. It makes sales tax revenues more responsive to economic growth because as people move up the income ladder their expenditures for services increase faster than for commodities.

The inclusion of services eases the compliance burden for those businesses which render services in conjunction with the sale of parts or other commodities. For example, under prevailing practice, a part used in repairing an appliance is taxable, but the labor cost is not. Therefore separate billing may be involved.

If the usual sales taxes were broadened to apply to personal, business, automobile, contractor, and repair services, revenue yields could possibly be increased by as much as one-sixth.

Although a case can be made for extending the sales tax also to professional services (accountants, architects, dentists, doctors, economists, lawyers, consultants of various sorts, and so on) the effort to do so is likely to encounter strong opposition. Most of these professions are organized and represented by articulate spokesmen who can be expected to make the most of such emotional arguments as increasing the cost of medical and dental care, or adding to the price of a divorce.

Certain types of sales, such as those of a material that becomes a constituent part of a final product, machinery and other items used directly in production, and fuel consumed in manufacturing processes are often exempted from taxation to minimize tax duplication. Sales of feed, seed, and fertilizer are exempt in almost all states, as are agricultural products sold by farmers, reflecting the political strength of this group. Alcoholic beverages and tobacco products subject to selective excises are also taxed in most states, but motor fuel is generally exempted.

Since sales taxes are enforced through merchants, special arrangements are required with respect to merchandise bought from out-of-state merchants and used within the state. This is accomplished through the use tax—a tax levied on the privilege of using commodities purchased outside the state. Its purpose is to reduce tax avoidance by importations from other jurisdictions and to protect merchants against out-of-state competition. The collection of use taxes, however, is difficult except in the case of automobiles. The use tax on automobiles can be enforced by requiring evidence that the tax has been paid before the motor vehicle is allowed to be registered.

States try to enforce the use tax by requiring out-of-state merchants to collect it. They can do so in those cases where an out-of-state firm also maintains a place of business within the state. It is difficult in other situations. For several years Congress has had under consideration legislation to regulate the sales tax treatment of out-of-state sales, but the conflict of interest between the business community and state tax administrators has been difficult to resolve and has delayed enactment.

TAXATION AT THE RETAIL LEVEL IS PREFERRED

Some of the pro-sales tax arguments enumerated above apply primarily to a sales tax imposed at the retail level at the time of sale to final consumer. This is the prevalent American form, and we are familiar with it. Sales taxation is practiced the world over, but some foreign countries prefer other forms. In Canada, the tax is applied at the manufacturing stage; in England, at the wholesaling stage. Some countries (Germany) tax sales at all stages of distribution—manufacturing and wholesaling as well as retailing. These so-called turnover taxes differ only in degree from the multiple-stage sales taxes used by Hawaii and Mississippi, where manufacturers' and wholesalers' sales are taxed at a fraction of the rates applicable to retail sales.

The objection to imposing sales taxes at the early stages of distribution, especially in manufacturing, is that the taxes are added to price and provide a base for taxes upon taxes; for the manufacturer's tax is passed on to wholesalers, and the wholesaler's tax to the retailers. Where the tax applies at the manufacturing level, the manufacturer simply adds it to the price he

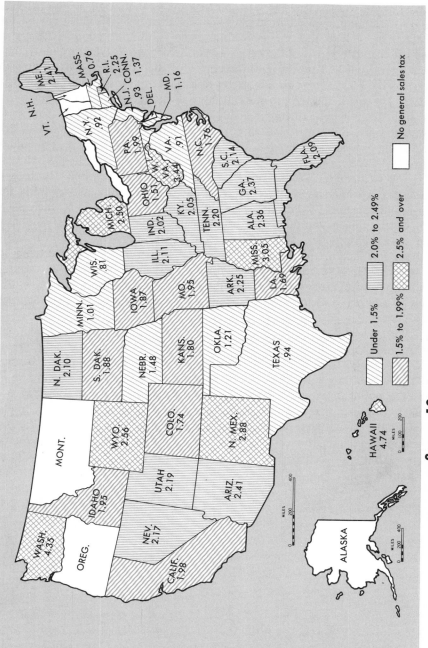

figure 10 State Sales Tax Collections as Percent of State Personal Incomes : 1968

charges the wholesaler. The latter in turn adds his markup to the price he pays the manufacturer (including tax) and then adds his sales tax on top of it. The retailer does the same thing. The consuming purchaser pays an added cost as a result of the turnover tax, which is considerably more than the sums collected by the government. This, the so-called pyramiding effect, is the reason most people prefer sales taxes to be imposed at the retail level. However, the manufacturer's tax has the advantage of cheaper and more effective enforcement because there are many fewer taxpayers to watch. Some think it is also an advantage that a tax at the manufacturer's or at the wholesaler's level is incorporated in the retail price and hidden from taxpayers.

The value-added tax used in France and in other European countries—and, for a while, in a very compromised form in Michigan—reduces the pyramiding effect. It accomplishes this by limiting the tax at each stage of distribution to the difference between the firm's sales and its purchases of material, supplies, and services from other firms. We will hear more about this tax in the future, because economists are impressed with its usefulness for the comprehensive taxation of goods and services with a minimum of pyramiding, discrimination among industries, and competitive disadvantages to export trade. However, it is less suitable for state than for federal use.

We leave the subject of consumer taxes reconciled to their survival and continued expansion because state and local governments could not function without them. Even if states manage to make more effective use of income taxation, as they undoubtedly will be obliged to do in the coming years by the political compulsion to respond to social program needs, they will need consumer taxes. The low-income groups' increasing stake in public expenditures, coupled with new techniques for relieving the more disadvantaged among them from excessive tax burdens, is likely to improve the acceptability of consumer taxes even to the partisans of ability-to-pay taxation.

chapter 6

inheritance and
estate taxes

Inheritance and estate taxes are among our oldest and also our most neglected taxes, neglected alike by legislators, administrators, and the public. Sales, income, property, and some of the other taxes figure almost daily in public discussions; but literally years can pass without a single press reference to the taxes on inherited wealth.

Although the present federal estate tax is over fifty years old, Congress has looked at this tax (even perfunctorily) only once during the last quarter century. At that time (1948) it reduced it substantially by legislating the marital deduction to exempt up to half of any estate so long as it is neglect at the state level, where death taxes have been in existence for a century. Even in recent years, when virtually every state has had to enact several major revenue measures, one would be hard pressed to find two or three states where inheritance taxes received more than cursory mention.

The neglect of these taxes ought to be corrected. In a nation with the world's largest accumulation of private wealth, and where the number of millionaires grows by the score year after year, taxes on inherited wealth are capable of making a substantial revenue contribution—

particularly at a time when the tax burdens on low- and middle-income groups are being pushed steadily to higher levels.

THEY APPEAR IN DIFFERENT FORMS

Most of us have no personal acquaintance with these taxes, so it might be well to begin with an explanation of two or three terms.

The family of taxes that focus on inherited wealth is known as the property transfer tax system. It includes, in addition to the estate tax and the inheritance tax, the gift tax.

The estate tax is levied on the right to bequeath property at death. It applies to the decedent's total estate, after a variety of exemptions (or subtractions) and is imposed at graduated rates. The estate tax is used by the federal government and by some of the states. The federal government allows a $60,000 exemption and taxes the remainder of the net estate, after various allowable subtractions, at rates ranging from 3 percent on the first $5,000 to 77 percent on the portion of an estate in excess of $10,000,000.

The predominant state tax on inherited wealth is the inheritance tax which, unlike the estate tax, is levied on the beneficiaries of the estate on their privilege to inherit property. Each heir is treated as a separate taxpayer. Each is allowed a separate exemption, and the size of the exemption varies, as do the applicable tax rates, with the relationship of the heir to the decedent. Generally, the closer that relationship (spouse, child, or parent), the higher the exemption and the lower the tax rate. A widow may be taxed at rates ranging from 1 percent to 5 percent after a $25,000 exemption, while an unrelated friend may be allowed no exemption and be taxed at rates ranging from 5 to 30 percent.

States also use estate taxes, but these do not lend themselves to ready generalization. The simplest of these state taxes is known as the "pick-up" tax. Because the federal government allows a limited amount of state taxes as an offset against its estate tax, a handful of states follows the simple route of levying an estate tax "equal to the maximum" allowable offset against the federal tax. In other words, these states pick up the offset and nothing more. Other states rely principally on inheritance taxes and then add a supplemental "catchall" pick-up tax just in case, in some situation, their regular tax falls short of the maximum allowable offset. Since inheritance taxes, particularly in the lower brackets, generally exceed the allowable offset, these catchall estate taxes come into play mostly on large estates.

The two taxes—estate and inheritance—are also known as death taxes. The third tax in the property transfer tax system is the gift tax. It was invented to prevent avoidance of the first two by transferring property before death. Without a gift tax, estate taxes could be avoided by gifts before death. The federal gift tax is the liability of the person who makes the gift, and for this purpose a running record is kept of all gifts he makes during his lifetime and provision is made for various exemptions. The tax rates are approximately two-thirds of the estate tax rates (2¼ percent to 57¾ percent). This encourages distribution before death, and caters to the view that children should be afforded an opportunity to acquire experience in handling wealth.

To exclude small gifts, the taxpayer and his spouse are each permitted to disregard the first $3,000 given to any individual during each year without limit on the number of different individuals. In other words, a couple can give, free of tax, $6,000 each year to each of their relatives and friends and repeat this yearly throughout their lifetime. In addition, each is allowed a one-time $30,000 exemption. To the extent that their gifts exceed the yearly and the "one-time" exemption, the amount of gifts is cumulated, a tax is computed under a graduated tax rate schedule, and a credit is allowed for gift taxes that would be payable at current tax rates on prior years' gifts. The difference is the federal tax payable on the current year's gifts.

Only thirteen states make use of the gift tax. The others ignore it because it would not produce appreciable amounts of revenue and is difficult to enforce. Assets, particularly stocks and bonds, are often kept outside the state and beyond the view of the state tax administrators.

THEY ARE UNIVERSAL AND OLD TAXES

Death taxes are in use virtually the world over. They enjoy support because they apply only where there is taxpaying ability and, unlike most other taxes, have little if any deterrent effect on working and saving.

To most of us, wealth symbolizes taxpaying ability—perhaps even more so than income. We think of income as a flow that fluctuates from year to year and may stop at any time. Wealth handled with care can last into perpetuity and produce income all the while. This is the reason that taxing wealth squares with taxpaying ability, and the reason why some countries, such as Sweden, Denmark, and Germany, tax wealth annually much as we tax income. In a sense, these wealth taxes are adjuncts to the income tax.

The case for taxing inherited wealth is especially strong in the United States because it helps to compensate for the imperfections of the income tax, such as the fact that sizable increases in wealth are not taken into account in determining taxable income. An increase in the value of securities or real estate is recognized for income tax purposes only after the gain is realized through sale; and even then the capital gain is taxed only at half or less of the tax rate applicable to wages, salaries, or most other income sources. Moreover, those who can avoid "realizing" their gains by holding on to their appreciated assets until they die, instead of selling them, can escape the tax permanently. Once the appreciated stock or real estate is in the hands of the heirs it is treated for tax purposes as if the heirs had paid for it what it was worth on the day they inherited. Thus, in a sense, the taxation of inherited wealth can be said to supplement the ability-to-pay mission of the income tax.

Death taxes are quite old. Some states began using them over a century ago, but they remained neglected until after the turn of this century when public interest and the concentration of wealth associated with "robber barons" focused legislative attention on them. They were on the statute books of all but six states by the time of the introduction of the present federal estate tax in 1916.

The federal government had made use of death taxes even earlier than in 1916 (first in 1798) but only for short periods at a time to help finance war emergencies. The tax enacted in 1916 was part of the World War I tax program. Its enactment was allegedly on a temporary basis and over the objections of the states which considered death taxes their province. After the war, the sentiment in Congress and the administration was to repeal this tax, and legislation to this effect was actively considered.

STATES NEED FEDERAL HELP TO ENFORCE THEM

The processing of the legislation to repeal the wartime federal estate tax happened to coincide with the emergence of interstate tax competition for wealthy residents. Some states were actually advertising in national journals that they would give immunity from death taxes to those who settled within their borders. Two amended their constitutions to guarantee freedom from death taxes. State leadership was quick to recognize that interstate tax competition, if left unchecked, would destroy death taxation for them all.

Heeding the plea of state leaders, Congress agreed to substitute tax reduction and a federal tax credit (a new kind of tax reduction) for repeal of the federal estate tax. Specifically, it permitted 80 percent of the reduced federal estate tax liability to be offset, dollar for dollar, with receipts for death taxes paid to states. The import of the credit was that it put a floor under state taxes. It became a matter of indifference to people of wealth that a state reduced its tax below the federal credit; for if the tax was not payable to the state, it had to be paid to the federal government. Most people prefer that the taxes they pay remain in their home state.

This arrangement, if continued, would have split the death tax revenue in the ratio of 80 percent for the states and 20 percent for the national government. But the arrangement did not survive. During the next fifteen years Congress increased the federal estate tax several times by reducing exemptions and raising rates, but retained all the new revenue for the federal government by allowing no state taxes to be credited against the increases.

Another factor that contributed to the reduction in the states' relative share of death tax revenues was the enactment of a permanent federal gift tax in 1932. Since there are substantial tax savings by putting property transfers through the gift tax rather than the estate tax mill, the gift tax encourages property distributions during life and correspondingly reduces the size of estates subject to taxation at death, when state taxes apply. The federal government allows no credit for gift taxes to the thirteen states which use them.

These developments—allowing no credit for state taxes against the increases in the federal estate tax and against the gift tax—have cut the states' relative share in the revenues from these taxes to about one-fifth. The credit still provides a floor under state taxes and to this extent prevents interstate tax competition. It does not, however, prevent wide variations in state liabilities above the credit. Moreover, the prospect that some day Congress will get around to revising the credit arrangement to give the states a more adequate share of the revenues has provided opponents with a ready-made argument against increases in state death taxes.

INTEREST IN THEM IS LACKING

Collection statistics reflect the reluctance of the states and federal government to fully exploit the revenue possibilities of the property transfer tax system. In 1967, when America's tax collections at all levels of government exceeded $176 billion, the contribution of all property transfer taxes —those occasioned by death as well as those on gifts—aggregated less than $3.8 billion. That was actually a banner year for these taxes. Rising property values and the accelerating accumulation of private fortunes more than doubled these tax yields between 1950 and 1960, and nearly doubled them again after 1960. The states' share in the $3.8 billion aggregate was $800 million.

Although most of those who have thought about it are agreed that the contribution of these taxes to the American revenue system can and should be increased substantially, there is no consensus on what the states can do about it. Their freedom is circumscribed by the dominating position of the federal tax. The relative state and federal roles in death taxation has been an issue for years; and though repeatedly urged to do so (most recently by the Advisory Commission on Intergovernmental Relations) neither Congress nor the Administration has as yet focused on it.

There is no telling when Congress can turn its attention to updating federal-state death tax relationships. In times of war, legislatures avoid increasing estate taxes because it would be unfair to penalize those who chance to die during the wartime emergency. In times of peace they disdain consideration of them because, as they are wont to say, these taxes pose complex issues which can be explored only when adequate time is available.

The reluctance to tap this potential source of revenue appears to be associated in an unarticulated way with the view that those astute enough to make a fortune should be rewarded and certainly not penalized. Another factor is the sensitivity of the leadership of legislative tax committees to death tax considerations, since they tend to be men of advanced years as a result of the seniority principle. In the meantime, states are foregoing revenue they could use to meet pressing needs. Although handicapped by the uncertainty about the direction of future federal action, they have some freedom to act on those aspects of the problem where the direction of congressional action is relatively clear or in which Congress has relatively little interest. Clearly, then, states would not be well advised to try to influence the way in which people of wealth arrange their property dispositions because, in this respect, the much larger federal tax is in control.

THE ESTATE TAX IS PREFERABLE

The rearrangement of federal-state tax relationships is likely to involve the issue of inheritance *vs.* estate taxes. As noted, a few states rely on the estate tax; but most use inheritance taxes, and rely on the estate tax solely for the purpose of absorbing any part of the federal credit that might otherwise be lost. After imposing its separate inheritance taxes, the state adds up the inheritance tax pieces emanating from each estate. If the sum of the several inheritance taxes falls short of the total allowable as a credit against the federal tax for taxes paid to states, it imposes a so-called "pick-up" estate tax to claim the difference.

It should be kept in mind that so long as the taxes imposed by the state qualify for purposes of the federal credit, the state adds nothing to the aggregate tax liability of the estate. However, it does preempt for the state an amount that, in the absence of the state tax, would have to be paid to the U. S. Treasury.

From the viewpoint of ability-to-pay and tax fairness, the inheritance tax has more initial appeal than the estate tax because there is no necessary relationship between the size of an estate and the respective shares of its several heirs. However, the use of "pick-up" taxes by the states generally means that the estate's aggregate burden will tend to be the same under either system. In other words, any differentiation in rates and exemptions based on the relationship between decedent and his heirs tends to be neutralized because the aggregate state tax is ultimately raised (especially for large estates) to the level of the federal credit.

In addition, the inheritance tax ignores the criterion of taxpaying ability in the sense that any one heir may be a beneficiary under a number of wills but is taxed as if he received only one inheritance. Some have proposed a new kind of tax—the accessions tax—to compensate for this weakness of the inheritance tax.

The accessions tax applies gift tax mechanics to the inheritance tax. When a person received a bequest he would add it to the total of gifts and bequests he had previously received, and compute the tax on the total at current tax rates. He would take a credit against this liability for the taxes that would be payable at current rates on the gifts and bequests previously received. The difference would be the tax due and payable on the last inheritance. Although conceptually attractive, because it comes closer to taxing on the basis of ability-to-pay than other types of death taxes, the accessions tax has not progressed much beyond the discussion stage. Japan adopted it in 1950 on the recommendation of an American tax expert, Carl Shoup, but withdrew it three years later pleading administrative difficulty.

The overwhelming argument for state adoption of the estate tax is that the federal government uses it. If the states did likewise, the compliance burdens of taxpayers and the enforcement tasks of state tax administrators would be eased. States, moreover, could make more effective use of audit and related information available from federal Internal Revenue records. Furthermore, the inheritance tax raises more difficult valuation problems, particularly if life estate and remainders are involved. Consider the problems involved in fixing the present value of the share of a cousin's life interest in an estate which is to be activated only when the decedent's widow and two children die. What is involved here is estimating the cousin's age at the time the widow and both children will have died, and then estimating the cousin's life expectancy at that age. This would provide the basis of appraising the probable (actuarial) value of his future share of the estate at the time of the donor's death.

The chief virtue of the inheritance tax—that it recognizes the closeness or remoteness of the relationship between heir and decedent—can be approached also through the estate tax. This can be accomplished by making the size of the estate tax exemption depend on the relationship of the heirs to the decedent, as is presently done in New York. In effect, each heir is allotted an exemption based on his or her relationship to the decedent; but the sum of these exemptions is limited to some stated amount, say $60,000. In this way an estate left entirely to a spouse or a child is given a larger exemption than one going to a cousin, and one shared by a spouse and a cousin is given a larger exemption than one left entirely to one or the other.

ITS REVENUE POTENTIAL REMAINS UNTAPPED

The amounts that states collect from these taxes represent little more than 1 percent of state and local tax collections. The federal government's estate and gift revenues represent about 2½ percent of its tax collections.

We do not have any firm figures on the value of American private wealth. Even on very conservative assumptions, it probably exceeds $2,500 billion. If we assume that this property passes from one generation to the next once every thirty years, the amount involved in yearly transfers is about $80 billion. In other words, the $4 billion death tax collections of the federal and state governments take on the average about 5 percent of private wealth once in a generation. This is very modest compared with other countries' practices, and is a reflection of America's aversion to penalizing those who inherit wealth or have made a financial success of their lives.

There are several ways in which the states might increase their revenue from the property transfer tax system without waiting for the long overdue revision of the federal estate tax with its important implications for state tax policy.

Logically, the states might concentrate more attention on the smaller and middle-sized estates. On the grounds of administrative convenience, the federal exemption for estates tends to be relatively high—$60,000. This frees small estates from federal taxation, and results in relatively low tax burdens on medium-size estates. However, the number of small and moderate-size estates is vast and potentially capable of producing important amounts of revenue.

Although America is noted for its great private fortunes, most of the private wealth is held in relatively modest amounts. Increased state reliance on this portion of the tax base would have several advantages in addition to the added revenue. It would improve the stability of state revenues, because small and medium-size estates are numerous and their number is relatively stable. The present instability of death tax revenues is due to the irregularity and the relative revenue significance of the large estates. The smaller nonindustrialized states, in any event, have only a few if any wealthy residents.

Most states appear to be concerned with the effect of death taxes on their attractiveness for new residents. They choose to disregard the fact that tax considerations are minimal for people with relatively modest estates. In any event, most people are not likely to select their state of residence out of consideration for potential death taxes if only because man tends to proceed on the assumption that death will somehow continue to pass him by. Notice the number of people of advanced age who die without having made a will.

To the extent that estate and gift tax considerations influence the way people dispose of their wealth, federal law with its sharply graduated rates is controlling. The relatively low rates of state taxes mean that these taxes are not particularly influential in how people dispose of their property. A case in point is the unlimited exemption of bequests to educational, charitable, and religious organizations. Federal law grants these exemptions on the theory that these organizations merit public encouragement because they perform socially desirable services, of which at least a part would otherwise be performed at public expense.

The federal exemption exerts a strong pressure in favor of such bequests, particularly for large estates. When the otherwise applicable estate tax rate would be 60 or 70 percent, the charitable bequest is made largely at federal expense even if the donor credits no value to his role as a benefactor. If the bequest were not made, and the property remained in the owner's estate, then on his death 60 or 70 percent of it would pass to the government in estate taxes. In other words, if the bequest were not made, only 30 or 40 percent of the amount involved would actually accrue to the heirs, and they would forego also such benefits—possibly substantial, if intangible —as may redound to them by virtue of their parent's public generosity. Little wonder that the tax-exempt foundation is today a vast national institution, and is growing. In these circumstances, it is doubtful that the presence or absence of a comparable state exemption of bequests from the generally prevailing moderate state tax rates would have any material influence on the size of charitable bequests.

State governments hard pressed for revenue might understandably reach the conclusion that they could make more effective use of the added dollars, from the viewpoint of the public welfare, than the charitable foundation and, accordingly, limit the exemptions they grant to bequests to nonprofit organizations. However, there is no evidence that their thoughts are moving in this direction.

Gift taxes, on the other hand, hold little revenue promise for the states. They would not influence the amount of giving before death (since here federal provisions are controlling) and could not give the gift tax effective enforcement. About the only argument in favor of state use of gift taxes is the possibility that it might improve the states' case for an increased federal estate tax credit—when and if Congress actively turns to consideration of the tax credit question.

chapter 7

property taxation

The one tax in which we all share—whether we are rich or poor, live in town or on a farm, in a house or an apartment, and whether we own or rent—is the property tax. It is America's most pervasive tax because everyone needs a shelter, and buildings are everywhere subject to the property tax unless they are owned by governments, religious bodies, or charitable institutions, or are specifically exempted or chance to be overlooked by the tax assessor.

IT HAD OLD BEGINNINGS

This has been so since America was first settled. In a sense, the tax is even more pervasive now because we are slowly drifting toward a property tax that tends to concentrate its burden on real estate and to de-emphasize other types of property.

For a time the objective was to tax all forms of wealth; not only land and buildings, but also other kinds of property. The tax embraced tangible forms of personal property such as tools, machinery, livestock, inventories, stocks of goods, business and household furnishings, automobiles, musical instruments, and even jewelry. It applied also to such intangibles as stocks, bonds, bank deposits, mortgages, and even money. Some of these movable types of property are easily hidden from tax assessors; others can be more easily reached through other taxes. In consequence, they have tended to drop out of the taxrolls; first through tax assessors' neglect, later by statutory provision. But this trend has made uneven progress in the fifty states. At one extreme, a few states now limit the property tax to real estate; at the other, a number still require (though assessors may not enforce) its application to even the most elusive forms of personal property.

Our attention here is limited to real property taxation, and only to its more common forms, for this is where most—probably over 80 percent— of the property tax dollars are. Elsewhere we discuss two special aspects of this tax: the taxation of land in relation to that of improvements, and of farmland on the urban fringe.

Property tax collections are growing at the rate of about $3 billion per year and now exceed $30 billion. For those in the middle- and lower-income brackets, and that includes most taxpayers, the tax on shelter is often the big tax bill, typically corresponding to somewhere between 10 and 25 percent of the cost of lodging. Part of it is paid in the first instance by landlords, who reimburse themselves from their tenants' rent checks. Homeowners with mortgages generally pay it in their monthly checks to the bank or insurance company. Those who own their homes free and clear of debt (about 40 percent of homeowners) have the pleasure of a single yearly tax bill, although some communities permit payment in semiannual and a few even in quarterly installments.

The property tax is so widespread because it is the only large revenue producer local government can administer and under our governmental system local government has the lion's share of the responsibility for supplying domestic government services. Nationally, it provides about 87 percent of all locally collected tax dollars. This national average has been fairly stable for some years and spans a wide state-by-state range (between 51.2 and 99.6 percent). The percentage is likely to be high where the state provides little financial aid to its local governments and limits their powers to use nonproperty taxes. Communities with relatively high expenditure generally find it necessary to resort to nonproperty taxes. A few cities, mostly the large ones able to make use of local earnings and consumer taxes, obtain as little as half of their tax receipts from property taxes; but they are in the minority. The property tax is almost the sole tax source for school districts and some of the other special purpose districts which dot the landscape in some parts of the country.

IT HAS WEAKNESSES

The property tax is not the best kind of tax; it is not even a good one, and the fact that so much reliance is placed on it is the result of history and necessity rather than of deliberate choice. In the early years of the Republic, when most people lived by agriculture in scattered settlements, government organization was largely based on the community and it was logical for governments to finance themselves by taxes based on property values. An individual's property holding was a fair indication both of his need for public services and of his taxpaying capability. Most property was visible, and tax assessors had little difficulty in locating it. In those days, too, the job of assessing property—fixing its value—was relatively easy. The worth of an acre of land was public knowledge, and prices changed very slowly. In many instances nominal values were assigned by law to land in specified locations.

Property—particularly real property—is, of course, no longer an index of a man's worth, income, or taxpaying ability. Moreover, the assessment of property is no longer simple. However, public institutions, hoary with age, are not easily changed. We cling to them with the tenacity of anti-quarians. Many persons feel that their relative tax contributions would be significantly increased by a major change in the tax system.

Primary reliance on property for municipal financing also has other shortcomings. Local government no longer limits itself to activities which relate to and benefit property. A large share, typically more than half of local government expenditure, is for services that benefit persons rather than properties. Since we now move about freely, the beneficiaries of today's education, health, or welfare expenditures financed by the property owners of one community are tomorrow likely to be the residents of another community. For this reason it is neither logical nor fair to continue to distribute the cost of education and welfare services in proportion to the assessed value of property to which people happen to hold title.

Taxpayers as well as local governments have complaints about the property tax over and beyond an instinctive dislike for paying taxes. The property tax frequently treats like properties unequally and discriminates between different classes of properties. It burdens low-income families heavily, while it exempts certain favored groups entirely. It contributes significantly to business costs, distorts the location decisions of business, and promotes undesirable land use patterns. Taxpayers find it inconvenient to pay a tax of this size in lumpy installments and, when they believe themselves unfairly assessed, find it costly in time and money to obtain relief. They are discouraged, too, that even with the seemingly endless yearly tax increases the property tax never or hardly ever produces enough to provide for their community needs.

Little wonder that scholars, politicians, and property owners indict the property tax as if with one voice. In terms of popular disfavor, it is truly without an equal. This is cause for public concern, for it pertains to the mainstay of local governments' revenue systems. What is to be done about it?

LOCAL GOVERNMENT CANNOT DO WITHOUT IT

Clearly, we cannot abandon the property tax because local government could not survive without it. It would take most of the tax dollars raised by the fifty states to replace it. However, if we are relying too much on it, as almost everyone in high tax rate communities agrees, more funds should be sought from sources other than the property tax. And, as circumstances permit, some of the existing property tax burden ought to be unloaded to other taxes, if this can be done without producing excessive windfalls. Logically the property tax should pay only for property-related (police, fire, sanitation, streets, sidewalks) services. We can leave the job of differentiating among taxpayers on the basis of their taxpaying ability to income and consumer taxes.

Property tax reform is a large subject and has occupied many thoughtful people over the years, as the mountain of literature they have left behind makes abundantly clear. Here we shall consider only how to make the most of the existing property tax system with remedies entitled to immediate consideration. There are ways to improve its more objectionable attributes, to assuage its burdens, and to enhance the taxing freedom of local officials.

THE ALTERNATIVE IS TO IMPROVE IT

Local communities, left to their own devices, are not free agents in property tax reform. What they may and may not do is everywhere laid down in state constitutional and statutory law as interpreted by the courts. No two states are identical, but statewide rules generally determine what kind of property may or may not be taxed, how property is to be valued for tax purposes, and where administrative responsibility is vested. Many states prescribe exemptions and impose tax rate limits. Whatever the faults of the property tax, they stem in no small measure from state legislation and its ineffective administration.

Moreover, since the property tax figures so importantly in intercommunity competition for taxpayers, each community is reluctant to make a move that might react adversely on some of its taxpayers for fear of driving them to another community. The initiative for reform, therefore, must come from another, higher level so that competing local governments are obliged to act together as they move in a constructive direction.

When the states largely vacated the property tax area for exclusive local government use in the 1920's and 1930's, this was hailed as a step toward "separation of tax sources." Before that time, states, too, financed themselves through property taxation. State withdrawal has proved to be a mixed blessing, for it deprived the states of any direct motivation to safeguard and improve the quality of property tax administration. Now ways have to be found to revive state interest, for without state leadership many local communities are condemned to inaction in property tax reform.

The time may be auspicious for constructive action. High tax rates, the restiveness of overburdened groups, and the political constraints against further tax rate increases are combining to stimulate political interest in property tax reform in ways to increase yields without rate increases and to make essential rate increases more acceptable by improving the fairness of the tax. The pressure, to be sure, is not all in this direction because the beneficiaries of underassessments and preferential provisions cling to their favored positions in proportion to the height of the tax rates they otherwise might be paying.

It should be emphasized—with regard to the relationship between the dissatisfaction with the property tax and the pressure to reform it—that the force of complaints increases as the quality of tax administration deteriorates, and diminishes as the quality of the assessor's performance improves.

Property tax administration typically involves the assessor, who determines the value of the property on which the tax is levied; the members of the local governing board who set tax rates (so much per $100 or per $1,000 of assessed value); and the collector of taxes to whom payment is made. Usually there is also some administrative machinery for resolving disagreements between assessors and taxpayers.

It is a complex structure, but workable if some critical requirements are satisfied. It is significant that those who have thought about the problem—tax administrators, tax practitioners, scholars, and even taxpayers—are substantially agreed on the prerequisites of fair quality property taxation.

THE CRITICAL POINT IS THE ASSESSED VALUE

Since the tax rate prescribed by a local governing board applies to the assessed value of property, the determination of assessed value is critical to tax fairness. In most states, the specified value is the current market value; in some states it is a designated percentage of market value. In either case the starting point is market value, the price the property would bring on the open market in a sale between a willing buyer and a willing seller, both conversant with the property and with generally prevailing market values.

Admittedly the determination of market value, the even-handed treatment of thousands of different properties, requires know-how. Business does it regularly, and apparently with sufficient dependability to enable banks and insurance companies to base billions of dollars of mortgage loans on it.

As real property has become more and more specialized, as location has become more and more important in site value, property appraisal has become a task for trained professionals. We have come a long way from the days when the worth of land was common knowledge in the community—so much per acre—and there was little difference of opinion about that value.

Clearly good quality administration requires, first of all, a law the assessor can administer, live and work with, and be honest about. Second, it requires an assessor who is professionally trained and shielded by career status from political pressure. This means selection by appointment, not by election, although in most states the latter system still prevails. Third, it requires a taxing district with enough properties to permit the use of a large enough staff to accommodate all the specialties in appraisal skills required to assess the different kinds of properties found within the taxing district.

The logical assessing unit is the state; but that system prevails only in Hawaii. In some states the assessing unit is the county; but in some the assessing work is splintered among thousands of local governments. Often overlying jurisdictions duplicate one another's work by making separate assessments. However, in most parts of the country special kinds of business properties, notably railroads and other public utilities and, less often, forests, are assessed by state agencies.

Sound assessment administration requires also a state agency, staffed with qualified people who are authorized to supervise local assessors, pass on their qualifications, peer over their shoulders to verify that they are doing a creditable job and, where necessary, help them to improve their performance.

Finally taxpayers must be given speedy, economic, and efficient means of relief from overassessment. For this purpose they need to be supplied with information on the assessment rules followed in their taxing jurisdiction.

This prescription has been incorporated into a group of model laws developed by the Advisory Commission on Intergovernmental Relations, and placed before state legislators and policy officials so that they might have the necessary legislation at hand when and as they are moved to action.

ASSESSED VALUE SHOULD BE ACTUAL VALUE

One of the villains in the property tax piece is the institution of fractional assessment, the common practice of listing property on the tax rolls at only a fraction of its actual value. Since the assessor, after determining the value of a piece of property, goes to the trouble of computing some fraction of it, he is presumed to have a reason for it. He does have a reason, but it is not a good reason!

The practice of fractional assessment apparently developed across the country in the days when both local and state governments taxed property, and the state based its tax on the locally determined assessed value. In this situation, the assessor thought that he was helping his local property owners to reduce their contribution to the state by listing property at less than its value. However, since this was a game which all local assessors could play, it ultimately resulted in competitive underassessing by all jurisdictions and the assessor's good intentions toward his local constituents were frustrated.

The state provided still another motive for fractional assessment when it began to vary its financial assistance to local governments in relation to how poor they were. Considerations of this kind soothed assessors who were taking liberties with the law which, in most cases, provided that property should be assessed at its true, actual, market, or current value.

Citizens were persuaded to go along with fractional assessment, despite overt violation of law, on the argument that reduced assessments improved the local community's financial position vis-à-vis the state without handicapping local finances. The artificially low assessments could be balanced by correspondingly increased tax rates, leaving unchanged the proportionate amounts of taxes paid by different taxpayers in the community. A $1 tax rate on a $100 assessment, it was argued, came to the same tax bill as a 50-cent rate on a $200 assessment.

This, however, is only a part of the story. Once the assessor departs from true value assessment, the rules of the game go by the board because the taxpayer no longer knows whether he is being treated fairly—in comparison with other property owners—unless he is knowledgeable enough in tax principles to inquire about the "assessment ratio" used in his taxing district, and knows how to make the calculations required to compare the assessment rate of his property with that of other properties in his taxing district.

Tax rates cannot be increased at will even on fractional assessments.

Often they are subject to constitutional and statutory limitations. Moreover, the public inclines to view the nominal tax rate as the real tax rate and frequently places too much emphasis on it.

Tax assessors have reason to prefer fractional assessment to 100 percent assessment. It enables them to hide their mistakes. It may give them a strong voice in local budget policies, especially where tax and debt limits are operative. The lower the assessment ratio, the more binding the tax limits, the greater the governing board's dependence on the assessor's willingness to raise the ratio of assessed to market values, and the more frequent the assessor's opportunities to restrict the fiscal power of local jurisdictions by keeping assessments low.

American assessors are prone to argue against full-value assessment on the ground that the market can rarely be perfectly gauged. This is true. But the fact remains that there are countries with good quality assessing where property is assessed on the basis of full market value. The right way to allow for the imperfections of the market is to recognize that the assessor is reasonably entitled to some margin of error, say plus or minus 10 percent. In any event, fractional assessment does not avoid the imperfection of the real estate market; it only obfuscates it.

Studies in depth, both for individual taxing districts and on a nationwide basis, have demonstrated over and over that the lower the ratio of assessed to actual value, the less uniform and the more inconsistent the treatment of properties. Unhappily, the trend toward lower assessment fractions is stronger than that in the opposite direction. In recent years, as the courts have called a halt to assessment discrimination against particular groups of properties, notably the railroads, legislatures have tended to respond by mandating that the assessment of railroad properties be lowered and not that the assessment of other properties be raised. Others are attempting to legalize varying assessments by resorting to classification of properties for differential assessment purposes. The courts have yet to speak the last word on the "reasonableness" of these classifications.

TAX RATE LIMITS ADD TO THE WOES

In some places, concern over property tax increases is reviving interest in and solidifying support for mandatory ceilings on tax rates. In many states, local governments have long labored under restrictions on their property taxing powers. The typical provision imbedded in state constitutions limits the tax rate that counties, cities, school districts, or the group together may levy to, say, 30 mills per $1 of assessed value, i.e., 3 percent. The limitation, it should be noted, is in terms of assessed value and not market value. When property is assessed at 25 percent of actual value, a 3 percent limitation restricts the true tax rate to three-quarters of 1 percent (25 percent of 3 percent).

The present restrictions on property tax rates date from the last century and from the depression years of this century, when they were imposed in the wake of tax and debt defaults and in the fond hope that the recurrence of such defaults could thus be prevented. Experience with these restrictions shows that although they undoubtedly had an initial dampening effect, if for no other reason than because they provided officials in communities operating close to the legal tax limit with an excuse for inaction, they have not slowed property tax increases. They did necessitate the invention of techniques to circumvent them, often with the acquiescence and help of state legislatures. In the process the structure of local governments and property tax systems was distorted, and the integrity of public business impaired.

Inflexible tax rate limits have aggravated the proliferation of local governments by stimulating the creation of special districts for the primary purpose of gaining additional taxing authority. They have necessitated recourse to short-term financing to cover operating deficits which ultimately had to be funded. They have encouraged long-term borrowing for activities that might better have been financed out of current revenue. They have imposed onerous burdens on administrative agencies and have added to the already overcrowded dockets of the courts. They have also necessitated extensive special legislation to relieve individual communities from the limitations.

Where property tax limits are especially rigid and communities are up close to these ceilings, assessors tend to be exposed to conflicting pressures from governing boards and pressure groups for such functions as education and public welfare who want assessments raised to gain additional property tax revenue and borrowing authority and from taxpayers who want assessments reduced to minimize taxes. In the process, assessors have been propelled into policymaking functions with control over the level of local budgets to the detriment of their performance as assessors.

Why, then, do legislatures tolerate and preserve tax limits? What is their motive in denying a community's voters the right to tax themselves and determine their own level of public services? Part of the motivation is political—a desire to play the role of the citizens' defender against the avaricious tax appetites of school, city, and county governing boards. A germ of jealousy may also be involved. State legislators believe that, unlike themselves, local officials are relatively immune to political sanctions for voting tax increases; and there is some truth in the observation. Local officials do have an advantage in that property tax increases come in small bites. A property tax rate increase of 5 to 10 mills is small in comparison with a sales or income tax hike from 3 to 4 percent. Taxpayers, moreover, may be able to see a connection between local taxes and local programs in which they are individually interested, such as schools. A connection of this kind is less apparent at the state level.

Legislatures' inclination to limit local governments' taxing powers is understandable, even if not desirable. Taxpayers like limitations in principle. Legislators enjoy playing the role of their constituents' protectors even against local officials of their choice. The legislators' constituencies, moreover, always include some influential elements who want taxes curbed —for example, homeowners' organizations that espouse tax limits.

For decades the experts have been urging states to remove from constitutions the shackling restrictions on local governments' fiscal powers, but with little result. Indeed, the persistent upward trend of tax rates is awakening interest in such restrictions where none existed before. Yet those who hold with local self-government and believe in keeping public policymaking close to the people should recognize that local governing boards must be left with latitude to solve local problems in their own way, subject only to the will and scrutiny of their respective constituencies.

Constitutional restrictions may have made some sense when imprudence was a frequent characteristic of the conduct of municipal affairs. But today's America bears little resemblance to the environment of those bygone days. The quality of local government leadership today is incomparably better than it was in the 19th century. Standards prescribed for the conduct of municipal affairs and controls established to enforce them are incomparably more effective. Most important of all, the public is more alert to the conduct of its local government affairs and is experienced in holding its public officials accountable at the ballot box.

assuaging the property tax burden

In recent years, as property tax rates climbed to new levels, taxpayer dissatisfaction has become more vocal—especially on behalf of groups, often low-income families and business firms, who believed themselves to be particularly burdened and disadvantaged. Political leadership responded to the clamor by a surge of legislative relief proposals and enactments. In doing so, it has followed a precedent from the Depression of the 1930's still fresh in the minds of the older legislators.

TAX EXEMPTIONS CREATE MANY PROBLEMS

The favored approach to relieving politically influential taxpayer groups from property taxes is tax exemption. State legislators enjoy voting exemptions from local taxes, especially if they are not obliged to vote state taxes to replace lost local revenue. Moreover, it makes grateful friends of the hometown voters who benefit from the exemptions, without displeasing those who do not—as it would if they understood that each exemption increases their own tax bills.

A state-mandated exemption deprives local governments of tax revenue, but does not relieve them of the responsibility for furnishing the favored properties with municipal services. On the contrary, some tax-exempt properties, such as those used for cultural or educational purposes that bring together large crowds, may require an extraordinary number of police and other services.

In the last half dozen years, over half of the states have enacted property tax relief measures. On occasion, these relief measures were packaged in state tax-increase programs because legislatures felt obliged to garner the political support of property owners for the state tax increases. Increasingly legislatures are responding to pressures for property tax relief even at the cost of increases in state taxes to finance property tax reductions. Some states have increased financial aid to local governments explicitly for the purpose of reducing dependence on property taxes; others are compensating local governments for the revenue they lost as a consequence of mandated property tax exemptions.

Over the years, a substantial volume of property has acquired tax-exempt status. We do not know its precise dimensions because most assessors do not price exempted properties. They have no reason to dissipate their all too small staffs in appraising properties which add nothing to tax collections. In any event, the appraisal of some classes of exempt property is extremely difficult. A museum or an ornate organizational headquarters building may have little market value, except to its present occupant; and for a property without resale possibility, valuation on the basis of estimated replacement cost is not meaningful. In consequence, some assessors value it on the basis of its rental value as office space or other possible business use.

The significance of exempt property varies from place to place. It is fairly small in some places, large in others, but increasing almost everywhere as the holdings of tax-exempt organizations grow in value. This is particularly true of the older cities where new construction is minimal and the old mansions, no longer attractive as private homes and unsalable, pass into the hands of educational, charitable, and religious organizations. In the city of Washington, where government holds title to a third of the real estate, half of all property value is on the exempt list. This proportion is probably approached in several of the old cities.

A common feature of property tax exemptions, pertinent when associated with educational or cultural activities and even religious organizations, is that the hoarding of land tends to be encouraged. These institutions are frequently able to hold on to large parcels in rapidly developing and expensive locations in anticipation of land value appreciation because they can do so without contending with the annual property tax bill that necessarily influences private owners. Few are bold enough to suggest that these exemptions be terminated. Some do suggest, with logic, that the nonprofit institutions, including even churches and universitites, might reasonably be required to reimburse municipalities for the cost of services supplied to them.

There are some developments in this direction in a minority of locations where payments have been instituted "voluntarily" by colleges, foundations, and other nonprofit organizations. Voluntary arrangements, however, place an excessive premium on an organization's sense of civic responsibility, and can hardly be viewed as a solution.

EXEMPTION OF PRIVATE PROPERTIES WORKS HAVOC

The list of exempt property categories varies from state to state. Apart from governmental, religious, and nonprofit institution properties, the more frequent are the exemptions of homesteads and those for the benefit of such special groups as the aged, the veteran, and certain businesses. The homestead exemptions for the benefit of homeowners (not renters) and farmers are largely a 1930's depression product, when homeowners in large numbers garnered legislators' sympathies for their plight symbolized by tax and mortgage defaults and threats of foreclosure.

The legislative intent in granting exemptions to these groups is to serve some socially desirable purpose, and in all probability the public approves the objective. It is less likely to understand that the objective could be realized more effectively, more equitably and less expensively, by direct and open appropriations than through tax exemption. This is so because the cost of tax exemption is never understood and is rarely debated on its merits. Moreover, tax laws are necessarily generalized rules applicable to broad categories of people, without regard for the merits of their particular claim on public favor, and frequently without an effective limit on the amount of the exemption. The property tax exemption of animal rescue leagues may apply to a dowager's mansion in a city's most fashionable section, left in trust to provide a home for the dogs and cats that survive her. Such mansions do exist, and continue to operate.

A look at some of these exemptions will illustrate the difficulty of using them to implement public policies.

When the legislature directs local taxing jurisdictions to exempt the first $3,000 of the assessed value of elderly citizens' homesteads, the intent is to bestow a limited benefit on old couples who eke out an existence on small pensions. In the process, however, it is likely to bestow the benefit also on old people with great wealth at the same time that it withholds it from the poor who live in rented quarters. Since the exemption is in terms of assessed valuation, its actual import is likely to be misunderstood. The exemption of $3,000 of assessed value exempts $4,500 of property assessed at 66 percent of its market value, but $15,000 of property assessed at 20 percent of value. Since assessment practices generally vary widely among communities within individual states, and all too often within individual communities, a mandate from the legislature to exempt a dollar amount of assessed value means different things in different places and for different persons.

Vast amounts of property are removed from taxation by these exemptions. The social purpose fostered by the state legislature in granting them could be accomplished more fairly and efficiently by helping low-income older citizens from direct appropriations. Another method is to adjust the amount of tax relief to the older citizen's personal income through refund payments and credits against income taxes, as is the practice in Wisconsin.

Similar logic applies to the exemption of veterans—an act of generosity that cannot possibly differentiate between the veteran whose war duty was a hardship and the man in uniform who sat out the war in a sinecure assignment at home.

In any case, it is incumbent on state legislatures that elect to reward these groups through preferential tax provisions at the expense of local property tax revenues to reimburse the local taxing jurisdiction for taxes lost.

EXEMPTIONS TO BUSINESS ARE ALSO PRESSED

When local governing boards develop their budgets and fix tax rates, they are likely to worry a great deal about the effect of their decisions on the attractiveness of their community to new business and on its holding power for existing business. Most communities prize business growth because it enhances employment opportunities, enlarges the tax base, and symbolizes vitality. Little wonder that the influence of business in state and local councils has never been stronger and is increasingly being reflected in the structure of business taxes.

The relationship between taxes and business location decisions is one of the many unsettled questions in taxation. Clearly, however, if taxes do have an influence on location decisions, the property tax is more likely to be involved than any other levy. For many businesses, this is one of the larger tax costs and a significant business cost. The income tax also takes a sizeable bite, but the businessman troubles about it only when he is privileged to enjoy a profit. Sales and excise taxes concern the businessman only when he has the pleasure of making a sale; and even then he expects to pass it on in his invoice to customers.

The property tax stands out in stark contrast. It is always with the businessman, one of his fixed charges, an overhead cost much like interest on his debt, whether or not he makes a sale or shows a profit. Little wonder that the property tax has troubled the businessman, and increasingly so as tax rates have moved to 2 and 3 percent (and in some places even higher). In some measure he is not troubled so much by the amount of his property tax as by the uncertainty of it—by his vulnerability to annual changes in assessments and tax rates. The businessman likes to keep expenses under control, and stable, and to plan for cost increases so that he can pursue a price policy calculated to maximize profits.

Business is particularly critical of taxes on inventories, machinery, office equipment, and other personal property. The relative importance of these items varies with the type of business and bears little if any relationship to profitability. Some lines of business, such as warehousing or retailing, require large inventories; others little, if any. In consequence, the taxation of inventories can be particularly onerous for some lines of business, especially in poor years. This explains the strong current trend toward the exemption of inventories and other business and personal properties. In recent years, about a dozen states have moved in this direction.

Another focus of business interest is the impact of property taxes on the availability of land for development and on the economics of property improvements. These are discussed below.

Although the businessman complains about high taxes, he usually understands that government cannot provide services without tax collections. Business is an important user of municipal services, and in some circumstances wants them even at the cost of tax increases. A firm's ability to attract employees to its location may be influenced by the availability of good educational and recreational facilities; its ability to expand production may turn on the availability of water and sewage disposal services; and its capability to serve customers may depend on improved roads and modern airport facilities. How to strike a happy medium, and how to balance the desire for services against the distaste for taxes, with appropriate regard for the attitudes of the different blocs of voters, each policymaker is obliged to work out for himself in the light of local circumstances.

Where tax rates are comparatively low, taxes on business personal property, though objectionable as an erratic and irrational cost of doing business, are tolerable. Where, however, tax rates have reached substantial levels, this ceases to be true. Those who have studied this problem—and they include many with no direct interest in business—are agreed that this portion of the property taxes is best de-emphasized. A few states, notably Delaware, Minnesota, New York, Hawaii, Pennsylvania, did so some years ago. Several others are in the process of joining them.

GOVERNMENT PROPERTIES ARE A SPECIAL CASE

Since World War II, chiefly stimulated by the large wartime property acquisitions of the federal government, considerable attention has been given to the exemption of government properties from local taxes. The problem is particularly troublesome where valuable properties were removed from the tax rolls without allowing adequate time for local adjustment to the revenue loss. This occurred not infrequently in the port and industrial cities where the Government acquired plants for shipyards and for defense production, and in outlying areas where it located military posts.

A government, state or federal, cannot entertain the idea of permitting itself to be subjected to local taxation. Governments, however, have acquiesced in the idea of making limited payments in lieu of property taxes. Some states are doing this. So is the federal government, though on a very restricted scale and on a piecemeal basis except in communities where a significant proportion of children who attend school come from homes where the parent lives or works on tax exempt federal property.

Over the years, several unsuccessful efforts have been made to legislate a general federal policy in this field. One approach that holds some promise would differentiate between properties on the basis of the geographic area they serve. It would continue the exemption of properties which perform basic government functions for the benefit of the local population (post office and court buildings) and which therefore are found in most localities. The burden of these exemptions is properly borne by the local population. It would make payments in lieu of taxes on those government properties that serve areas larger than the particular community in which they are located, possibly the entire country. The cost of these facilities, so the thinking runs, is properly chargeable to the national treasury. Industrial and commericial facilities owned by the Department of Defense are clearly of this nature, as are such regional facilities as government warehousing and computer centers. It is thought, too, that these payments in lieu of taxes might be gradually tapered off as a particular community adjusts to the loss of taxes from properties acquired by government.

There is merit in the Canadian approach of making payments in lieu of property taxes only to those communities in which higher levels of government own a disproportionately large amount of property, where their holdings clearly exceed the national average. The payments are calculated to compensate the particular community for exempt government property only to the extent that the ratio of its value to taxable property in the community exceeds the national average.

chapter 9

taxing farmland
on the urban fringe

The absence of any rational relationship between the value of land on the one hand, and taxpaying ability or the value of benefits derived from local government spending on the other, results in heavy property tax burdens on some property-owning groups. Policymakers in many parts of the country are particularly troubled by the problems of farmers whose land is in the path of urban growth.

THE FARMER MAY HAVE A PROBLEM

The pressure of population in areas around cities has resulted in an unprecedented increase in land prices. This is where most of the nation's population growth is occurring. During the past decade, suburban population rose by nearly 50 percent; while central cities increased only 10.7 percent, and rural areas only 7.1 percent. It has been calculated that 75 percent of all Americans already are crowded into less than 2 percent of the country's land area.

Land values are appreciating substantially faster than can be explained by the demand for land for residential and business development. They reflect substantial speculative demands made by investors who anticipate future development, and those who are buying land as a hedge against inflation.

The tax laws aggravate the situation, although some remedial measures are receiving congressional attention. Taxpayers in the high-income brackets and corporations can afford to pay excessive prices for farmland because they are allowed to shift half or more of the losses suffered from farm operations to the U. S. government. They can do this by deducting their farm losses from their business and investment income in calculating federal income taxes. While this is occurring, the appreciation in the value of their land is sheltered from capital gains taxation and to a degree also from property taxation.

Those who assess property for tax purposes are expected to reflect the value of land for its "highest and best use." The duty of the assessor, albeit all too often disregarded, is to approximate the true market value of property: that is the price at which it would be sold by a willing seller to a willing buyer, assuming that both are familiar with market conditions.

The farmer who operates a working farm in the environs of a city is discovering that the property tax levied against his farm is more than farm operation can support. His land is becoming too valuable for use in farming. His situation resembles that of the low-income family trying to hold on to its old homestead located in the path of a commercial or industrial development within the city. The land under the old family home has become too valuable for residential use.

The analogy between the bona fide farmer and the low-income city homeowner cannot be carried too far. The city dweller can move to another part of town without dire consequences. The farmer does not have this option since other farming land generally is not available in his area. His moving, therefore, may entail the loss of his livelihood and his way of life. On the other hand, the farmer has easier access to tax relief because he enjoys considerable political muscle. He enjoys the public's sympathy, and benefits from its nostalgia for the old way of life. People like the idea of preserving farms, if only to enable them to show their children a cow or a horse on a short Sunday afternoon drive.

Many people would like farming continued close to the city, believing it desirable to retain ready access to fresh vegetables and dairy products even where the accelerated speed of transportation and economies of large-scale corporate farming are rapidly depreciating this consideration. The people's compassion for the farmer, together with the political influence of real estate operators and other holders of large tracts of land in the path of urbanization, help to explain why state legislatures in an increasingly urban society are experimenting with different ways of giving property tax relief to the urban fringe farmer at a time when almost everyone else's taxes are increasing.

Admittedly the community's interest in having something done about this problem goes beyond sentiment, compassion for the old farmer, and the desire for freshly picked corn. Continuing urbanization increases the need for preserving open space for recreation, scenic, and breathing purposes. Urban sprawl has to be controlled, if only to preserve some vacant land for future public use.

THE ANSWER IS NOT CLEAR

The issue posed by the farmer in the urban fringe is not easily resolved. It involves the balancing of conflicting considerations. On the one hand, the public has an important interest in preserving some vacant land in areas exposed to urbanization and the impartial application of the property tax to land can conflict with that objective. On the other, the equitable operation of the property tax and local government's revenue needs require that all property be taxed uniformly in proportion to its market value and without regard for what it happens to be used.

A number of legislatures already have compromised property tax principles to relieve homeowners, veterans, older citizens, and selected business firms. They are showing an increasing disposition to relieve the farmer, too. About a third of the states have enacted some legislation. Others are actively considering it. In this context the important question is how the meritorious farmer can be helped with minimum revenue loss and violence to tax fairness.

PREFERENTIAL FARM ASSESSMENT IS A POOR APPROACH

A favored remedy already used by about ten states is to direct the tax assessor to value farmland, and sometimes also forest and open-space land, on the basis of its current *use* instead of its current *value*. Land used in farming is taxed as farmland even where it is surrounded by industrial and commercial structures.

This procedure protects the landowner while he continues to operate a farm and, incidentally, enables him to hold his land for further appreciation without any tax cost to himself. Indeed, if he retains the property until it passes to his heirs, the appreciation in the value of his land also escapes taxation under the income tax. Federal tax laws treat inherited property for income tax-capital gains tax purposes as if the heir had paid the price it was worth when he inherited it. A farm bought years ago for $5,000 but worth $150,000 when inherited, and sold for that price the day after the estate is distributed, is totally free of any federal and state capital gains taxes.

Preferential assessment amounts to complete tax forgiveness of part (often a large part) of the property tax so long as the property continues to qualify as "farm use." Its revenue consequences, therefore, can be very substantial. In Montgomery County, Maryland, a suburb of the national capital, "farm" land that under the general rules would have been assessed at about $150 million in 1967 was assessed under the preferential provisions at less than $15 million. The consequent yearly revenue loss exceeded $6 million.

This, as most preferential tax provisions, is susceptible to abuse and generally *is* abused. Although it may help the occasional bona fide farmer, it enables others to masquerade as farmers. Tax laws are necessarily generalized rules. They cannot be too specific because ways of doing business are varied, and very precise rules would exclude some meritorious cases. Legislatures, in any event, with rare exception, have not seen fit to adopt rules for distinguishing the bona fide farmer, motivated by the need for a livelihood and by a desire for farming as a way of life, from the real estate investor who uses farming as a cloak to help him save taxes while he enjoys appreciation in the value of his land holdings.

In view of the large tax savings involved, a legislative mandate that the tax assessor must value "farm" land on the basis of its value for farming, rather than its best use, encourages land speculators to purchase large tracts of land for future development and to operate them in the meanwhile as token farms. A few head of grazing cattle may qualify a sizable tract as a "farm." Little wonder that farm acreage for purposes of property taxation in one of the fastest growing suburbs of the national capital and with a record volume of new construction is actually increasing from year to year under this kind of preferential tax provision.

Those who are responsible for the financing of cities, counties, and school districts will be quick to observe that some state legislators can "protect" their land-owning constituents by mandating a provision of this kind because they do not feel obliged to find replacement revenue. They can sidestep that responsibility. They are free to give away city, county, and school tax revenues, and leave it for the local governing boards to find replacement revenue or get along with less money.

The preferential assessment of farmland poses two difficult administrative problems: identifying bona fide farm use, and establishing the value of the land for farming use.

The customary criterion of farm use is that the land is cultivated or used for grazing purposes. Generally, token agricultural activities satisfy the requirement. None of the states has attempted to restrict the preferential treatment to those landowners who depend on farming for their livelihood and for whom farming is a way of life, although Alaska is making a start in that direction. This is not surprising, for the measure is not really intended for the benefit of the bulk of the farmers. Working farmers typically are located in the truly rural portions of the state and are not particularly benefited by this kind of law.

If it were the legislative purpose to limit the preferential tax provision to the bona fide farmer, that result could be approached in various ways. For example, it could be limited to those landowners who for a period of years have been deriving 50 percent or 60 percent of their incomes, excluding investment income, from the farm in question. The burden of proof, in the form of duplicates of their income-tax returns, would be on the claimants for tax relief. This is the approach of a 1967 Alaska law. To qualify for treatment of land as agricultural land, Alaska requires that at least one-fourth of the owner's income must be derived from farming.

The determination of "assessed value for farming purposes" poses problems for the tax assessor. All his operations are keyed to market values, checked against sales prices and appraisals, with important emphasis on uniformity among properties within the taxing jurisdiction. Value for "farming" is a fictitious concept, and the assessor is without standards to guide him. He may have no alternative but to fall back on land values that prevailed at some date in the past. This is one of the critical weaknesses of preferential tax treatment of farmland, because the assessor's determination has important consequences for local revenues.

DEFERMENT OF TAXES IS ANOTHER APPROACH

Three or four states handle the tax problem of the urban fringe farmer by allowing him to postpone part of his tax payment until he sells or develops the land. They, too, direct that his land be assessed as agricultural land so long as it is used for farming. However, they require the assessor to determine agricultural use value and market value and to record both on the tax rolls. So long as the land remains in farming use it continues to be taxed on the basis of the lower valuation. However, when the land is sold or converted to nonfarm use, the owner is liable for the difference between taxes based on agricultural value and what they would have been on the basis of market value. The retroactive collection of taxes, commonly called a tax-rollback provision, is generally limited to three or five years and the customary interest charge is added. Some Australian states have used the tax-rollback arrangement for years.

Although this approach involves the same valuation problem as preferential tax treatment, errors in fixing agricultural use value are less critical because only tax postponement (with interest charged) is at stake.

Some object to tax-rollback arrangements because they make the local government a lending agency. This consideration, however, is offset by the convenience of collecting the postponed taxes at the time the land is sold for development, which generally coincides with the need to finance the construction of community capital facilities.

ACQUISITION OF DEVELOPMENT RIGHTS IS STILL ANOTHER APPROACH

Still another approach to the problem of the farmer in the urban fringe is the acquisition of development rights by government. In these arrangements, the landowner sells to the government his right to use his land for anything other than farming. He commits himself to using it for farming in perpetuity. The same result is attained where the government buys the farmer's land, and leases it back to him for use as a farm on lease terms compatible with farming use. At least four states have authorized this approach to the problem.

The purchase of development rights is free of the abuse associated with the preferential assessment of farms, but it is costly; few communities have the large funds needed to acquire control over enough acreage to significantly influence the urban fringe landscape. It is costly because the person who owns a piece of land which is likely to appreciate considerably over the next several years will not willingly sell the nonfarm use rights of that land unless he is paid a price that approximates the discounted future value of that land. Some federal assistance for financing the purchase of development rights is available under Public Law 87–70, which authorizes federal grants to states and local public bodies up to 30 percent of the acquisition cost of titles or other permanent interests in open-space land.

SUMMING IT UP

None of the approaches examined—preferential assessment, tax rollback, public purchase of development rights—affords a satisfactory and satisfying solution to the problem of the bona fide farmer. Nor should such a solution be expected, short of doing away with the property tax altogether.

As earlier noted, the property tax is no longer a satisfactory basis for financing general government expenditures as distinguished from expenditures primarily for the benefit of property. Property has lost its usefulness as a meaningful gauge of peoples' relative abilities to pay taxes for the support of education and social programs that preempt increasing shares of the local government budget. Some people are poor even though they hold title to real property, and many wealthy people own no real property at all. But so long as it falls to the property tax to carry the bulk of the burden of financing local government, tax rates will necessarily be high and raise havoc with business undertakings, such as farming, that are users of relatively large areas of land and for whom, therefore, the property tax is a critical factor in the cost of doing business.

These considerations should help to restrain the legislative impulse to relieve farmers. Failing that, the prudent and practicable course is the technique of tax deferment with retroactive collection of postponed taxes (plus interest) limited to the landowner who has been deriving the larger part of his livelihood from working the particular parcel of farmland accorded the special tax treatment.

taxing land and untaxing improvements

A suggestion heard with increasing frequency these days is that the property tax be changed by de-emphasizing the tax on improvements (buildings, and so on) and by increasing it on land; that it be shifted in the direction of a site value tax. The proposals range all the way from levying a somewhat heavier tax on land, as compared with that on improvements, to limiting the tax to land and completely exempting the improvements.

To tax land more heavily than the buildings which stand on it would be a departure from the system in general use here since colonial times. Most state constitutions and statutes require land and improvements to be assessed at the same percentage of fair market value, and subjected to the same tax rate. Indeed, homeowners generally do not know, and care less, how their tax bills are divided between their land and the house on it.

THE ADVOCATES HAVE DIVERSE MOTIVES

The advocates of change share a common concern over the growing weight of property taxes, but they come to land value taxation from different directions and with differing motivations and rationalizations.

Many are troubled by the rising local government costs associated with population growth and the concentration of more and more people around cities. Those who are aware that this trend is accompanied by rising land values think it would be only fair to tax some of the landowner's windfall to pay for the costlier services. They consider it a windfall, because the owner need do little more than sit back and watch his land appreciate as urbanization progresses.

City planners and public officials troubled by the blight, slums, and ugliness in and around their cities, attribute part of this condition to the working of the real property tax. They reason that it penalizes a man for improving his property because improvement increases values, assessments, and taxes; and, by the same token, it encourages slums because as property deteriorates, values and taxes fall. They also reason that the tax bargain that results from the property tax bias in favor of land typically assessed at less than its "best use" value encourages owners to withhold it from orderly development and to hold it for speculative gain. They see this as a major contribution to urban sprawl. By reversing the property tax bias and concentrating it on land rather than on improvements, they would exert pressures on owners to improve undeveloped and underdeveloped land to its maximum potential and to modernize buildings, and thus clean up slums and produce more orderly land use. They are attracted also by the prospect that higher taxes on land would reduce its value and improve its availability for public projects to house the poor.

The real estate and construction industries are attracted by the removal of what they call a progressive penalty on investment in property improvements and by the promise of more land becoming available for development and redevelopment.

Because mass transportation systems, roads, and other costly public improvements typically increase the value of benefited real estate, often dramatically, the taxation of these "created" increments in land value has special appeal to those who undertake to demonstrate the financial feasibility of the public improvements they sponsor. In some situations, as in new suburbs with large underdeveloped areas, even homeowners are attracted by the thought that heavier taxes on land held out of development or used for industry would keep down the tax bills on their homes.

The reader may recognize the kinship between the rationale of land tax advocates and the teachings of the early English political economists (Ricardo, J. S. Mill) which were later popularized by the American, Henry George, in the development of his case for a "single tax" on land.

EXPERIENCE IS INCONCLUSIVE

Advocates of the land tax like to cite its performance here and abroad to bolster their case.

Taxing land more heavily than improvements is practiced on a limited scale in Pennsylvania and in Hawaii. In 1965 the island state embarked on a ten-year transition to shift more of the tax onto land, but the process has not been allowed to progress beyond the first of the scheduled ten steps. Influential political groups are urging that the program be abandoned because they are critical of the way in which its benefits are distributed among different kinds of properties. Their criticism is receiving favorable reaction in various quarters.

In Pennsylvania, the cities of Scranton and Pittsburgh have operated a "graded property tax" for over forty years with land taxed for city purposes at twice the rate of improvements. However, since city properties are subject also to school and county taxes which make no differentiation between land and improvements, land actually is taxed only slightly higher than improvements. In the 1960's, the total rate on buildings was nearly 90 percent of that on land. Close students of that experience have found little evidence that it stimulated property improvements or urban redevelopment. Apparently, in the complex of considerations which guide men's investment decisions, a 10 percent difference between the property tax rate on land and on buildings is not significant.

Abroad, land value taxation is or has been practiced in Western Canada, Australia, New Zealand, South and East Africa, Jamaica, Trinidad, and Barbados (all countries with British associations); also in several European countries, notably in Denmark.

Perhaps the most successful land tax was one imposed by the Australian federal government during the first half of this century. This was a steeply progressive tax on an individual's total land holdings anywhere in Australia, and was imposed for the explicit purpose of breaking up the vast holdings of rich landowners who were doing nothing to improve their lands but were withholding it from would-be settlers. At their peak, the annual tax rates on large landowners were as high as 5 percent of current values. Since the lands were producing little if any income, the heavy taxes—in effect taxes on capital—succeeded in breaking up large holdings. The experience in New Zealand and in Western Canada was similar.

Today, graduated land taxes are still in use by New Zealand and by the Australian states, and flat rate taxes by the local governments in both countries. Some of these local governments tax only land, although others tax both land and improvements. Where the different systems operate side-by-side, occasionally on opposite sides of a street that separates two jurisdictions, no marked differences in land development are observable. It is significant, however, that some of these governments have found it necessary to provide hardship exemptions for low-income families with homes in neighborhoods where land values were rising as commercial and apartment development began to replace single family homes. They also found it necessary to exempt farmland where urban development was increasing land values. If these hardships were politically compelling enough to oblige legislative relief from land taxes (imposed on full value assessments) it is reasonable to assume that the taxes were indeed penalizing owners who attempted to retain land in less than its optimum use.

If experience in Australia and in New Zealand does not verify the claims of land tax advocates, neither does it disprove them. The absence of visible differences under the two taxing systems can be explained by special circumstances: The hardship exemptions, which in effect estopped the operation of the taxes precisely where they might have been effective; the relatively low municipal tax rates which prevail because local governments have comparatively few responsibilities (education and police, for example, are state functions), with the result that property taxes are secondary in investment decisions; and the fact that the influence of these low rates is further diluted by the simultaneous imposition of taxes based on the total value of the real estate, including improvements, as in this country. This is the practice of overlapping special-purpose bodies responsible for water and sewer services and some specialized functions.

However one interprets past experience here and abroad, the potential of land taxation in this country must necessarily turn on several critical considerations, the first of which is revenue productivity.

REVENUE LOSS WOULD BE PROHIBITIVE

Those who would replace even part of the revenue produced here by the real property tax with an equally productive substitute undertake a herculean task. Annual property tax collections exceed $30 billion, nearly four times those from state and local income taxes, and they are increasing. Agricultural property and personal property may account for as much as 30 percent of the total. The remaining $21 billion is the contribution of nonfarm land and structures. We have only fragmentary information on the share of land in this $21 billion, but it probably lies in the general range of 35 to 40 percent. Assuming the higher figure, the tax on land would have to be increased by at least 150 percent to match the revenue now contributed by buildings and other improvements. Where the effective property tax rate (tax as a percent of current market value) is 3 percent, the tax on land alone would need to be raised to 7.5 percent even if land values remained unchanged.

But obviously land values would not remain unchanged in the face of tax increases of this magnitude. In most instances, a 7.5 percent tax would confiscate all or most of the income yield of the land. Since landowners could not pass the tax forward to consumers, land values would fall drastically to a level where the rate of return on the lower land values would be comparable to that available from alternative investments. Although the stimulation this would provide to building activity would increase the demand for and the price of land, land values would remain far below present levels. This suggests that under tax rate levels now prevailing in urban America, it is unrealistic to even consider replacing the real property tax with a tax on land. It does not preclude, of course, differentially heavier taxation of land, as practiced in Scranton and Pittsburgh and as it was projected for Hawaii.

TAX BURDEN DISTRIBUTION WOULD BE CHANGED

An increase in the tax on land compared with improvements would affect taxpayers in proportion to their relative investments in land versus improvements. Those with a larger than average land-to-building ratio would be taxed more; those with a smaller ratio would pay less. Commercial properties, office buildings, and high-rise apartments would enjoy savings; manufacturing properties would experience tax increases. Modern homes on small inexpensive tracts would tend to benefit, while run-down homes on valuable tracts would be penalized.

The exemption of improvements would bestow windfalls on their owners which perhaps would be most conspicuous in the case of high-rise business and quality residential properties. By the same token, owners of land would suffer losses; most conspicuously those who had bought land relatively recently on the assumption that taxing practices would continue unchanged. The inequities would be compounded by the fact that the municipal services financed by local taxes are more likely to benefit land with improvements than vacant land. In general those who paid most in land taxes would benefit least, and vice versa.

ADMINISTRATION IS NOT A PROBLEM

American assessors are wont to argue that land taxation is impractical because of the difficulty of assessing land apart from the improvements on it. Professionals, with long years of experience in assessing both land taxes and our type of real estate taxes, disagree. They say that although it may be more difficult to appraise the land component of a single improved parcel of property apart from the building on it, the reverse is true when great numbers of properties have to be valued for tax purposes. They prefer land taxes because it is easier to get equitable assessment on land alone, and more economical because it becomes unnecessary to keep detailed records on the characteristics of every building and the changes made on it. They point out that most assessment errors involve buildings, not land, and that a better job can be done when the available staff has fewer and less varied chores to perform. They prefer the land tax also because comparability of adjoining land values enables taxpayers to determine with relative ease whether they are fairly assessed.

WHAT THIS ADDS UP TO

The debate about land value taxation would be more evenhanded in a new, developing country where high tax rates and urbanization are still in the future. This is the kind of underdeveloped country that has been adopting versions of land value taxation in recent years. Here in the United States the choice is not between land taxation and the present property tax on land and improvements. Revenue considerations deny that option to us so long as the lion's share of the local and school tax burden has to be borne by real estate. We have latitude only for a possible increased emphasis on land as compared with improvements, or, alternatively, for supplementing the present property tax with an additional land tax. And because of their limited scope, neither of these alternatives could be expected to have an appreciable effect on land use patterns. However, they could produce some revenue at the expense of those who are enjoying windfalls from rising land values.

Interest in these proposals emanates chiefly from the urban areas, and understandably so. It is here that repeated tax increases are causing concern, revenue pressures are most compelling, costly municipal capital improvements cry out for financing, and profits of land speculators are most conspicuous. It is here that the replacement of run-down buildings needs to be stimulated. But it is precisely in these places that tax rate levels are too high to permit the total property tax burden to be unloaded onto land alone.

This suggests that if site value taxation has any potential it is in communities with relatively low tax rates and not too many skyscrapers, found only in the less urbanized sections of the country. Only where effective tax rates are still relatively low—say, below 1 percent—and the ratio of land to building values is relatively high, is it practicable to consider shifting a substantial part of the property tax burden to land; or, more realistically, concentrating further tax increases on land and sparing the improvements. But even here the prospects are not bright.

Generally those who are economically motivated to push land taxation are not rurally based, while the owners of large tracts of rural land are not politically impotent to safeguard their financial interests. Moreover, those opposed to the change have the benefit of the argument that the real estate tax is too critically important for the financing of public schools and the other locally supported basic government functions to permit the hazards of tax experimentation.

Those who would experiment with differential property taxation in the less developed areas of this country must necessarily weigh its implications for the quality of assessment administration.

The present state of the assessment art as practiced here is not distinguished for its fairness. Inequalities are all too widespread and appear to be particularly conspicuous with respect to undeveloped land. Study after study frequently reveals particularly glaring underassessments in this category. Differentially higher taxation of this kind of property would increase the premium on underassessment at the same time that it made equitable assessment a critical necessity.

It is relevant, too, that the assessing profession here, in contrast with its counterparts in at least some of the other English-speaking countries, continues to hold to the view that assessing land, apart from the improvements on it, entails far more difficulty than the valuation of the two together. A student of the subject wisely observed that, for the present, site value taxation may be one of those places that it is simply impossible to get to from here.

chapter 11

local
nonproperty taxes

Local government, caught in the pincers of persistent expenditure pressures and rising resistance to property tax increases, looks avidly at other tax possibilities: the sales tax, the income tax, and some of the selected commodity and service taxes.

Nationally, local taxes other than those on property produced about $4 billion in 1967, compared with over $25 billion from property taxes. The relationship between the two for the nation as a whole has been stable for some years. Nonproperty taxes have been producing about one out of every eight local tax dollars. However, their role in individual states and communities ranges all the way from virtual nonexistence to major significance. In 1967, for example, the share of local tax collections provided by nonproperty taxes exceeded 25 percent in six states, and 20 percent in eleven states including the six. In selected individual cities within these states the percentage was substantially higher, occasionally even topping the yield of the property tax. In Ohio, ten of the larger cities derived more than 50 percent of their tax collections from local income taxation. In fully a third of the states, on the other hand, the contribution of all nonproperty taxes fell short of 5 percent of total tax collections.

THEY ARE A DEPRESSION INNOVATION

The local nonproperty tax is a large city invention, spawned by the Depression. Since the 1930's, some cities have been supplementing their revenues by retail sales taxes, income or payroll taxes, and taxes on utilities, cigarettes, motor vehicles, and other selected consumer items.

New York City led the way in the use of the local sales tax when it adopted it in 1934; it was followed by New Orleans in 1938. After the war, a local sales tax movement began in California and spread to localities in other states, particularly Alabama, Alaska, Illinois, Louisiana, New York, Texas, Utah, and Virginia. At present, sales taxes are levied by local governments in at least seventeen states. In some of these states virtually all municipalities levy them. In some states these taxes are used also by counties; in Louisiana, even by school districts. Eight of the fifteen largest cities in the United States (New York, Chicago, Los Angeles, Houston, Washington, San Francisco, Dallas, and New Orleans) tax retail sales. In all, about 3,000 local governments now impose general sales taxes with rates ranging from 0.5 percent to 3 percent and their yearly collections are rapidly approaching $1.5 billion.

Local income taxes began in 1939 in Philadelphia. Here the movement rested until 1946, when Ohio cities began experimenting with income taxes. At the present time, there is widespread use of local income taxes in five states (Kentucky, Maryland, Michigan, Ohio, and Pennsylvania). About fifty municipalities (of over 50,000 population) including New York, and more than 3,000 other units of local government use them. Rates range from 0.5 percent to 2 percent of income, except in Maryland where the local rates range from 20 to 50 percent of the state tax liability. Annual local income tax collections are approximately $1 billion.

THEY ARE AT BEST A SECOND CHOICE

Much has been expected of these nonproperty taxes, considerably more than has been or will be realized. Their promise of providing an escape from exclusive reliance on property taxes attracts political leadership. Tax diversification—a version of the adage about not keeping all your eggs in one basket—appeals to even more people. But, as earlier noted, tax diversification necessarily means tax overlapping and duplicate compliance burdens because income is already taxed by the federal government and most states, and consumer expenditures are already taxed by the states. Thus tax diversity can be had only at the expense of tax simplicity, and it, too, is a goal devoutly to be desired. More than one spellbinder has waxed eloquent about a simple tax system under which the local, state, and federal governments, in that order, would subsist exclusively on property, consumer, and income taxes alone.

Both major nonproperty taxes, those on income and sales, are better levied at state than at local levels. When locally levied and administered, their revenue contribution to individual communities bears no relationship to comparative revenue needs. Localities which are employment centers profit from income taxes; those with shopping centers from sales taxes. The larger the taxing jurisdiction, the fewer the resulting distortions to ways of doing business, the fewer the jurisdictional conflicts, the more economical the administration, and the greater the likelihood that collections will bear a reasonable relationship to requirements. From this viewpoint, additions to the income and sales taxes imposed by the states for the purpose of financing more state aid, and to relieve the pressure on property taxes, are very much to be preferred to local imposition of these taxes.

Another consideration that argues against the imposition of local nonproperty taxes is the shadow of competitive business disadvantage (a strong argument for local politicians) even if it is recognized that the improved local government services these taxes would make possible hold strong attractions for business. In addition, there are problems of enforcement as well as the compliance burden on taxpayers and business firms. A frequent barrier is the state legislature itself. It is reluctant to authorize local nonproperty taxes—partly to preserve the state's own taxing freedom, partly out of a concern for the competitive position of business, partly out of a reluctance to give the cities an opportunity to tax nonresidents, and in some measure just out of an aversion to more taxes.

In the past few years these considerations appear to have lost ground as new techniques for use of the nonproperty taxes solved some of the problems of enforcement and lightened compliance burdens. Another important influence in the increasing number of states which recently have consented to the imposition of local nonproperty taxes is the pressing need for more revenues at the local level. Legislatures would like to do without local nonproperty taxes; but even an unsatisfactory local tax may be politically preferable to an increase in a state tax to finance more generous state aid to local governments.

INCOME TAXATION POSES SPECIAL PROBLEMS

Local income taxation labors under the severe handicap that it is a complex tax and requires a skilled and expensive enforcement apparatus. Since local tax rates are necessarily low, typically 1 or 2 percent, and most local jurisdictions are quite small, the cost of establishing an effective local enforcement apparatus is likely to be high in relation to revenue collections. Although this is generally true across the board, the force of the argument diminishes with the size of the city and with the simplicity of its tax law. An income tax limited to wages and salaries, and collected by requiring employers to withhold it from wages, is easier to enforce than a full-fledged income tax applicable to all residents and to their incomes from all sources. New York City apparently is finding it practicable to enforce with acceptable effectiveness a tax graduated from 0.4 to 2.0 percent and applicable to all taxable income because of its large number of taxpayers, larger than that of many states.

When income taxes are imposed and collected at the local level, they are usually limited to payroll taxes withheld by employers from wage and salary checks. Local enforcement of a tax on investment income, easily hidden from local tax collectors, poses serious difficulties. Payroll taxes can be supplemented, however, with taxes on the net incomes from professional and also unincorporated business activities (the self-employed) as in Philadelphia. These taxes are not really income taxes but are levies on those who work in the community, imposed as a charge for community services which will benefit them.

In addition to the consideration of fairness in levying taxes on income from employment but not on investment income, there is the problem of the comparative treatment of those who work in the city and those who work outside. It is a growing problem, particularly difficult if one of the jurisdictions does not employ an income tax. The tax burden of the worker, in the city with a payroll tax, who lives outside in a community without an income tax, may be excessive because in all likelihood the place of residence taxes the worker through a sales tax or a relatively high property tax. The nonresident problem is critical, because frequently municipal income taxes are candidly adopted with the avowed intention of exacting a tax contribution from commuters who benefit from the employment opportunity provided partly at city expense.

In states where local payroll taxes are widespread—when virtually all jurisdictions in a metropolitan area employ them and not much interstate commuting is involved—the problem of the commuting worker can be handled by each jurisdiction imposing half of the tax on account of residence and half on account of employment in the knowledge that the other jurisdiction will collect the second half.

STATES CAN HELP THEIR CITIES AND COUNTIES

Within the past couple of years states have begun to help in the collection of local income taxes by adopting a technique used by some states for collecting local sales taxes. The local tax is "piggybacked" on the state's tax, and the state collects the local tax as it collects its own. This enables the local tax to be imposed on both earned and investment income, minimizes the problems of enforcement by enabling the use of state information and state sanctions in the case of would-be tax evaders, and cuts the cost of administration for local governments and the burden of compliance for taxpayers.

Maryland was the first (1967) to authorize counties to levy local personal income taxes on their residents with the requirement that the local tax be based on the state tax liability (up to 50 percent) and collected by the state when it collects its own tax. Michigan followed by providing that the state could administer city income taxes by mutual agreement, the legislation going into effect in 1970. In contrast, New York City, where the recently enacted tax is graduated and based on income reported for state tax purposes, has not been given this assistance.

These new devices substantially improve the position of the local income tax with respect to enforcement and administration, make it possible for the municipalities to use a true income tax rather than a payroll tax, and increase the yield of the tax. However, they do not overcome the failure of local income taxes to compensate for the unequal distribution of incomes among local communities; which means that the revenue obtained by the individual communities bears no meaningful relationship to their comparative need for it. Such considerations argue for imposing income taxes at state rather than at local levels. If, however, the state legislators seem to prefer even a poor local tax to a new or higher state tax, such local taxes should be levied in the largest possible jurisdictions in order to lessen resulting distortions to ways of doing business, lessen jurisdictional conflict, make feasible more economic administration, and increase the likelihood that collections will bear a reasonable relationship to requirements.

SALES TAXATION IS MORE PRACTICABLE

Sales taxes at the local level do not have some of the handicaps of local income taxes. A local government that has decided to tax retail sales at the risk of competitive disadvantages and possible dislocation to its local business encounters no significant jurisdictional or administrative problems. In addition, local governments in many states have the advantage of various types of state-local and county-municipal coordination. In eleven states (California, Illinois, Nevada, New Mexico, New York, North Carolina, Oklahoma, Tennessee, Texas, Utah, and Virginia) local sales taxes must be administered by the state; in four, state administration is optional.

Where local government revenue needs force recourse to sales taxes, the use of a supplement to the state sales tax has much to recommend it. If legislative authorization of local supplements is permissible and optional, local governments are permitted but not mandated to employ them; and, in theory, local taxing autonomy is not impaired. In fact the invitation tends to be irresistible, and in most states with these arrangements the local tax tends to become statewide. Few jurisdictions, if any, pass it up for long.

The supplement meets the problem of economical administration. The local tax can be collected with little or no additional cost. But the supplement is not without weaknesses. Its principal weakness is that revenues are distributed on the basis of collections, and collections bear no necessary relationship to revenue needs. Here, just as in the local income tax, public policy would be better served if in lieu of authorizing local supplements to state sales taxes legislatures were to increase the state rate and deploy the added revenue to improvements in social programs and in state aid for such programs. In this way the distribution of the new revenue would be more likely to take account of variations in need.

STATES CAN HELP IN OTHER WAYS, TOO

In the case of those states that do not levy a tax onto which the local tax can be attached as a supplement, there is still room for state assistance. The local jurisdictions can benefit from the state's good offices directly by facilitating the pooled administration of separate local taxes either by a state tax-collecting agency, one created jointly by local jurisdictions, or the larger jurisdiction can perform this service for its smaller neighbors or overlapping entities.

As previously mentioned, for economic and administrative reasons the case for most nonproperty taxes is strongest in the large urban places. Even here, these taxes are best imposed cooperatively by a group of economically interdependent jurisdictions. To make this possible, the city and other jurisdictions comprising an economic area need uniform taxing powers and authority for cooperative tax enforcement. This is often lacking because states tend to differentiate between the taxing powers of different kinds of local government, typically between counties, cities, and small incorporated places. Neighboring jurisdictions operate in a competitive atmosphere and require the state's encouragement in pursuing coordinated tax policies and practices.

To minimize needless variety among local nonproperty taxes, the state authorization granted local governments should be accompanied with specifications governing structure (tax base, exemptions, and so on) and administrative features. Michigan, for example, has now provided a uniform statute for localities wishing to employ the income tax. This has substantially eased problems of administration.

It would also be rational to limit local governments to the more productive taxes. They should be discouraged from levying many kinds of different taxes, none of which produces enough to warrant reasonably good enforcement. Extensive tax diversification is not practical at the local level, especially in the smaller jurisdictions.

States can also help their local units by providing them with technical assistance, by serving as a clearinghouse of information on tax experience in other parts of the state and country, by providing training facilities for local tax personnel, and by giving local personnel access to state tax records. They could go even further and employ sanctions against state taxpayers who fail to comply with local tax requirements. An obvious example is the provision that an application for the annual state automobile tag must be accompanied by evidence that any required local tag has been purchased first. Some local governments with personal property taxes on automobiles require evidence that this tax has been paid before issuing the local automobile tag.

State policies governing local use of nonproperty taxes are most constructive if they limit these taxes to local revenue needs which cannot be satisfied with increased state financial aid, provided the permitted taxes are structured to minimize latitude for tax competition among nearby jurisdictions, and if maximum enforcement assistance is afforded in the interests of economical tax administration and ease of taxpayer compliance.

part III

FINANCING ON CREDIT

chapter 12

the role
of borrowing

In addition to taxing people in order to raise the money needed to finance its activities, a government may have the alternative of borrowing some of it. As a rule, state and local governments borrow only to finance capital expenditures. Usually they may not borrow for operating costs, except small amounts for short periods. They may, for example, engage in tax anticipation borrowing before tax collection dates, and repay the loans when the tax monies are in hand.

The possibility of meeting some of our community's capital needs by borrowing is always intriguing because it raises the delightful prospect that we may be able to enjoy the benefits of government projects without first paying taxes for them. Of course current operating expenditures should always be financed out of current revenue. There are, however, sound reasons for state and local borrowing. Capital expenditures can be financed by borrowing to the extent that those who will inhabit our community in the future will benefit from the public facilities acquired with the borrowed funds and can be required to help pay for them.

State and local governments learned from practical experience many years ago that there are hazards in excessive borrowing. As a result, they now operate under stringent (in many instances unduly stringent) constitutional and statutory rules governing the amounts they may borrow, the purposes for which they may borrow, and the ground rules under which they may conduct their credit operations.

In the fashion of most restrictions imposed in an earlier period, limitations on the rights of states and localities to borrow, where they exist, have seriously limited the financial management of the affected governments. Necessity is the mother of invention; when the limitations were too confining, governments have had to find ways to circumvent them and they devised some rather ingenious albeit costly methods for evading the limitations. At the same time they have found it greatly to their advantage that Congress has seen fit to continue to exempt from the federal income tax the interest on their bonds (generally called municipals, whether issued by states or local governments) after withdrawing the same privilege from federal securities. This exemption enables state and local governments to borrow (sell their bonds) at significantly lower interest rates than if they were taxable.

THE BEGINNINGS WERE SORRY

The respect state and local governments have acquired for the pitfalls of imprudent borrowing comes not from an abstract horror of incurring debt but from some rather unhappy experience. The states first experimented with extensive borrowing during the 1820's and 1830's to finance the construction of canals, highways, railroads, and other "internal improvements." Many of these enterprises proved to be less productive in terms of bringing prosperity to the area than anticipated. When the depression of 1837 hit, and persisted for several years, nine states and one territory found themselves unable to meet their commitments to their bondholders. They defaulted on both interest and principal repayments. Four states actually repudiated some of their debt. A general loss of investor confidence in state bonds ensued, and borrowing came to an abrupt halt. To prevent future misuse of borrowing power, state after state amended its constitution to severely restrict borrowing; some forbid it entirely.

The next major episode grew out of the states' borrowing to cover their share of Civil War costs. When the war ended, the national government helped the northern states to pay off their debts. During the Reconstruction period, the carpetbagger governments of several southern states issued considerable amounts of bonds. Eventually nine states were obliged to make extensive adjustments in their debt by repudiating some of it and scaling down the rest. This experience reinforced the view that states should be severely limited in their borrowing and generated another round of constitutional and statutory restrictions on credit operations.

During the 1870's, some of the newly affluent local governments began their own experiments in borrowing, chiefly for the same type of internal improvements that had intrigued the states at the beginning of the century. They, too, encountered difficulties when they found themselves committed to carrying debt service charges beyond their capability; and after 1873, perhaps as much as 20 percent of local debt was in default. States are sovereign, and may repudiate their debt; but local governments are not, and are exposed to legal remedies reminiscent of private bankruptcy proceedings. At this point state legislatures stepped in and undertook to curb further extravagance by imposing limitations on the amount local governments might borrow. Their limitations generally were couched in terms of a specified percentage of the assessed value of locally taxable property: a city's outstanding indebtedness, for example, might at no time exceed 10 percent of the assessed value of property on its tax rolls.

The restrictions on local governments' borrowings succeeded in holding down local debt for a few decades; but the beginning of the twentieth century found local governments—especially the large cities—resorting to extensive borrowing once again, chiefly for the construction of schools and streets. Local debt soon exceeded state debt. By 1932, local governments had accumulated an indebtedness of $16 billion as compared with less than $3 billion of state debt.

The depression of the 1930's had an extremely severe impact on local debt. By mid-decade, about 10 percent of the outstanding municipal bonds were in default—although they represented only about 2 percent of local government jurisdictions. The problem, however, was quickly cleared up with very little loss to investors. During World War II state and local governments borrowed very little, chiefly because public construction for civilian purposes came to a standstill for lack of materials and labor. As revenues picked up in the wake of the full employment generated by the war boom, states and local governments gradually retired some of their outstanding debt and the end of 1946 found them with 18 percent less outstanding debt than in 1938. In addition, as federal income taxes became universal and rates rose, tax-exempt municipal bonds became more attractive to investors, and it was possible to market municipals at comparatively low rates of interest and even to refund outstanding high-interest issues.

THE RECENT RECORD IS BRIGHTER

For a quarter century after World War II, and until the recent rise in interest rates to record levels, a comparatively stable economy with steady rate of growth provided a climate in which it has been possible for both state and local government debt to increase with extreme rapidity. Total

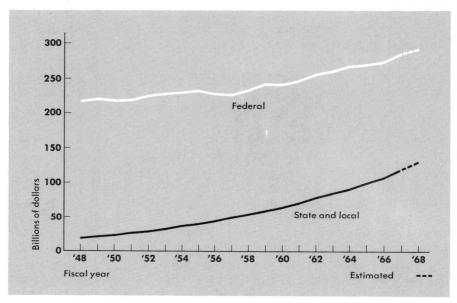

figure 11

**Federal and State-Local Debt
1948-1968**

state and local debt has mounted from $18.7 billion in 1948, and $87.5 billion in 1963, to $130 billion by 1968. Of the debt now outstanding, over 70 percent is local.

In the past quarter century there have been very few serious default episodes. The generally favorable economic situation, cautious debt management, and no major depressions have combined to build a state and local record of sound credit equal to that of the most respected borrowers in private economy. During most of the postdepression years, low interest rates enabled the borrowing governments to cover their annual debt service without undue pressure on their budgets. Most municipal bonds are now serials. A portion of the principal amount is retired each year. This eliminates the temptation to divert funds which otherwise would be accumulated in sinking funds for debt repayment when the bonds become payable at the end of their term.

General public attention has not focused on the growth of state and local debt. Instead it was directed to the larger federal debt. In point of fact, of late the federal government has been the less important borrower. In 1968, the per capita federal debt was not more than it was in 1948. Between these two dates, the per capita state-local debt *increased* from $116 to $648—over $500. In recent years, the volume of new municipal issues nearly equalled state and local debt outstanding at the end of World War II.

BUT WHY BORROW AT ALL?

State and local governments are generally prohibited from borrowing except for capital improvements, and even for this purpose their borrowing is restricted (if not totally prohibited) by state constitutions and statutes.

Since World War II, state and local governments have invested close to $300 billion in capital plant. During this period their net indebtedness (after repayments) increased by over $100 billion. In other words, they covered about two-thirds of their large capital plant acquisitions out of current income and federal aid, and financed only about a third by borrowing—a quality of financing performance not generally appreciated.

Conservative financial practice counsels keeping borrowing to a minimum. This holds down interests costs, exposes the proposed capital investment to the critical test of whether the public is willing to support it to the point of paying taxes for it, and avoids leaving debt service costs to those who come to live in the community in future years. The more conservative its past borrowing record, the more attractive a community's current bond offering to a potential investor. By the same token, a community's credit rating on a particular issue is enhanced as the share of the capital project cost covered out of current income is increased.

In many, if not in most circumstances, however, debt financing of a capital improvement is fully compatible with conservative management. Indeed, fairness to taxpayers requires it. This, for example, is the case when a community urgently needs a relatively costly capital investment (such as a sewer system or a school plant) that will serve the community for a generation or longer. In this situation, it would be unfair to charge the total cost to the taxpayers who happen to live in the community during the year or two when the project is being financed. This would be particularly so if it happened to be a small community making capital investments only at intervals of several years. It would be virtually impossible in a rapidly growing new community.

Recent developments have substantially increased the need for and the justification of debt financing of municipal capital improvements. The increasing mobility of people and the rapid growth of communities (typically suburbs) often confronts these places, particularly in their early years, with the need for costly public facilities—schools, public buildings, sewerage disposal plants, storm sewers, and so on. It would be difficult, perhaps impossible, to finance these investments totally out of tax collections, and it would be grossly unfair to do so even if it were possible.

Borrowing permits the cost of the capital improvement to be shared with those who will be using it in future years. It would be unfair to place the full cost of capital improvements on the jurisdiction's current taxpayers, because some will have emigrated and others will have moved in before the facility is used up. The argument can be overstated, however. Since most places are continually adding to their capital plant, it is possible that those who come to a city will have contributed to capital improvements financed out of current taxes in the place from which they came and in turn will be contributing to capital improvements that will outlast them in the place to which they come.

Municipalities also use debt financing because capital improvements are costly and require more funding than taxpayers are willing to provide immediately. People's tolerance for an expenditure is always more generous when it is not fully reflected in their immediate tax bills, and it would be even more so if they appreciated that local or state government can borrow at lower interest rates than can individuals and even private businesses.

The essential point to note is that borrowing permits the allocation of the cost of capital improvements to those who will benefit from them, thereby facilitating the acquisition of more capital plant than would be possible out of current revenue alone. Also, to the extent that expenditure needs vary annually, financing on credit permits the impact on the budget to be spread more evenly over the years by scheduling repayments (maturity schedule) so that debt service does not fluctuate too radically from year to year.

These considerations apply principally to general obligation bonds, those secured by all of the tax resources of the borrowing community. Other factors come into play in the case of revenue bonds which are payable from the receipts of a particular proprietary enterprise (a water system or a toll road) or from the operating income of a public agency, such as a port authority. The criteria governing revenue bond financing, once the community has elected to employ it, are comparable to those relevant when a private business firm borrows: will the revenue returned by the project, in combination with other resources available for the purpose, suffice to cover repayments as required?

how to fare well
in the bond market

IT IS A HIGHLY SPECIALIZED ACTIVITY

State and local governments now borrow about $15 billion a year, and the proficiency with which the operation is handled has important consequences for taxpayers. The objective is to minimize interest costs, and to schedule commitments for repayment of principal in conformity with an orderly long-term financial plan so as to avoid erratic year-to-year fluctuations. An average saving of only ¼ percent in the interest rate on just one year's state and local borrowing ($15 billion, assuming twenty-year issues) would produce a $750 million saving in total interest costs. This indicates the scope for economy within the competence of those entrusted with the management of the community's borrowing operations. Unfortunately, the municipal bond market is so specialized that most taxpayers are unable to appraise their officials' performance as debt managers.

Except for the large governments that are in the bond market almost continually, the average community cannot afford to have on its payroll the technically competent legal and financial personnel needed to carry a bond issue through the intricacies called for by the statutes and money markets. The finance officers of many small communities are fairly well versed in budgeting, record keeping, and financial reporting, but they enter the money market too infrequently to develop more than a nodding acquaintance with the financial labyrinth through which a bond issue must be guided to fruition. Even such seemingly simple decisions as the time when an issue should be offered, how to time the maturity schedule, or whether to include a call feature contain pitfalls for the uninitiated.

The borrowing terms available to a community are largely influenced by the general condition of the money market at the time it offers its bonds for sale and by its own financial situation. The condition of the money market is shaped by a variety of factors, including the amount of money in the hands of investors and the competing demands for it made not only by other governmental units but also by homeowners looking for mortgage money, and businessmen looking for capital to expand plants and increase inventories. These factors affect interest rates in an overall way—the overall supply and demand situation—and a borrowing government can do nothing about them save exercise its option to stay away from the money market by postponing its borrowing until a more auspicious time.

Within given money market conditions, however, the borrowing governmental unit can do much about affecting the value of its own bonds (its own supply and demand situation) in relation to other bonds. It can control the supply of its own bonds, and influence the demand for them relative to the demand for other securities. The particular supply-demand situation of each community determines the cost of borrowing within the general framework of the market at the particular time.

Specialists are agreed that most communities could reduce their borrowing costs by improving the techniques of merchandising bond issues, and by maintaining and enhancing their underlying fiscal strength. In this way, they influence their credit rating by affecting the judgment of the specialists in the municipal market. These specialists, whose job it is to assess the borrowing community as a credit risk, comprise a sizable group. In addition to underwriters, dealers, and bond counsels, they include the credit analysts who assemble the economic and financial data required for a community's credit rating, and the professionals who manage the investments of banks, insurance companies, mutual funds, and other large investors. The views of these specialists have a major effect on the ability of a community to sell its bonds on favorable interest terms.

REVENUE BONDS ARE FOR SPECIAL NEEDS

Specialists caution communities against indiscriminate use of issues known as revenue bonds. The common form of municipal debt is the general obligation bond that is secured by the full faith and credit of the issuing government, and thus by the community's taxing powers. In contrast, revenue bonds are payable solely from the income of a particular project (say, a toll road) or from the operating income of the borrowing agancy, such a public utility, that lacks power to levy general taxes.

Revenue bonds have been increasingly popular since World War II. Generally they are outside constitutional and statutory limitations, and in many cases need not be submitted to the electorate for approval. In some places, special authorities have been organized to finance the construction of school buildings with revenue bonds because limitations imposed on general obligation debt effectively preclude that form of borrowing. The buildings are leased to school districts, and their pledge of rental payments secure the bond issues.

The pace of revenue bond financing is likely to be accelerated further by continued urbanization and suburbanization, which generate demand for mass transportation and water supply and sewer systems. Although much of this kind of debt has been issued to avoid limitations on debt and bond elections, there is wide acceptance of the theory that the debt of a revenue-producing facility should be serviced from the fees paid by its users. Local officials often justify incurring the extra interest costs connected with the issuance of revenue bonds in order to conserve their tax base for servicing future issues of general obligation bonds.

Municipal bond specialists, however, are in general agreement that local agencies should avoid revenue bond issues except in rare circumstances, such as when a community is financing facilities to provide special services to only a limited portion of its area. They can be particularly useful in financing a regional project, such as a metropolitan area mass transit system. In these situations, a portion of the fare receipts can be reserved for servicing the revenue bonds. However, revenue bonds cost more than general obligation bonds because their marketability is more restricted. There are legal barriers to their purchase by certain important classes of investors. Yet they add to overall governmental costs and fixed charges just as surely as general obligation indebtedness. Indeed, they are even more of a drain on the income of a community because of the higher interest costs attached to them.

Furthermore, in jurisdictions where either revenue or general credit bonds require a referendum, voters may not examine spending proposals as carefully when the bonds are financed from the revenues of a project as when the issue requires additional taxes to meet debt service.

THE CREDIT RATING IS CRITICAL

Most bond obligations offered for sale by state and local governments are appraised as to their quality as a credit risk by one or more of the national rating services—Moody's Investors Services, Standard and Poor's, and one or two others. These credit ratings have an important influence on the investor not only as a reflection of what the expert analyst thinks of the issue, but also as an index of the resalability of the bonds should this become necessary. When New York City's rating was reduced one notch, from A to BBB, its finance administrator estimated the resulting increase in the rate of interest paid by the city between 1/4 and 1/5 of 1 percent.

The rating agencies guard their standards jealously, and resist both pressures and supporting evidence for an improved rating. A bond rating awarded a local government can be improved only on a showing that the borrower's situation has changed significantly for the better. This can be accomplished only over a period of time.

Currently, ratings are not being developed for governments that issue small amounts of debt. As a general rule, Moody's rates only the bonds of issuers with a debt of $600 thousand or more, and Standard and Poor's rates only governments with debt of at least $1 million. Moody's rates municipals only on request, and for a fee (a recent policy change).

The credit rating agencies' refusal to reveal the details of the criteria that guide them has generated considerable criticism. Some have charged these agencies with making quality rating decisions arbitrarily to the detriment of borrowing governments, particularly old central cities with greatest dependence on credit. A congressional committee has been moved to investigate these charges.

Whether the dissatisfaction with the rating system is well founded or not, borrowing jurisdictions are well advised to do all within their power to present their situations in the most favorable light to those who make the credit quality ratings, for there is no contesting the direct relationship between ratings and market reaction, i.e., the cost of borrowing.

Although the current ratings, particularly in the case of less frequent borrowers, may not reflect very exhaustive analyses of the strength of the local economy or of the borrowing jurisdiction's debt and budgetary situation, they are influenced by a variety of factors among which the following would be regarded as favorable to a good quality credit rating:

A long record of responsible and prudent financial management free of political machination.

An expanding local economy, backstopped by an affirmative public policy to encourage economic development.

The presence of a fair amount of trade and industry, preferably diversified, with a record of stable growth and the prospect of future growth.

A growing population with a good level of family income.

A low debt in relation to the size, wealth, and income of the population, and to a community's tax resources.

A good debt-service record, free of defaults.

A diversified tax system, including a well-administered property tax.

A minimum of state-imposed restrictions on the taxing and borrowing powers of the community.

Relatively limited future borrowing needs.

Enlightened political leadership supported by professionally competent staff and serving a citizenry interested in and proud of its community.

Perhaps the single most important factor is *management*. Good management can go a long way in compensating for weaknesses in capital structure and earning power; poor management can quickly dissipate the advantages afforded by a strong capital structure and good earning power.

CAPITAL PLANNING IS ESSENTIAL

An essential of good municipal credit is intelligent and realistic planning for the timely and orderly acquisition of capital plant needs, so that the investor will know that his investment is soundly based in relation to the complete capital program of the community. It could be argued that it would be better if he didn't know how much more borrowing is contemplated. However, the investor is "smarter than that." He knows that rapidly growing areas will have to finance expansion of facilities by borrowing. It is wiser for the borrower to inform the investor of his anticipated further borrowing needs than to oblige the borrower to estimate them on the basis of his worst expectations.

A capital outlay plan should cover a period of five to ten years, and should be reviewed annually and kept current. In a rapidly growing area, it is a sizable task for municipal management to recognize a community's full growth potential far enough in advance to provide for all contingencies and be prepared to alter them as changed conditions require. This is a responsibility, however, that management cannot safely escape.

Up-to-date planning is important not only with respect to newly-developing functions, but also for changes in old functions. Awareness of the development of new ideas is also of critical importance at this time with respect to changes contemplated in those municipal facilities which are included in plans for the alleviation of poverty and racial unrest.

A BALANCED DEBT STRUCTURE HELPS

Communities with the best credit ratings are those with a stable debt as well as a modest debt. Especially important is a well-balanced debt service structure. Such a structure consists of well-regulated debt service requirements over the years, with emphasis on maximum repayment in the early years, and a minimum of debt service commitment for the years far in the future. This permits a share of the cost of capital improvements to be borne by the present population and leaves room for additional debt-financed improvements as needs arise. The borrower should bear in mind the desirability of recapturing his ability to borrow as soon as possible.

It should be borne in mind that the longer a maturity schedule, the higher the interest cost—both because of the additional interest paid for each additional year of maturity, and because a longer average maturity can be expected to require a somewhat higher interest rate. For this reason maturity schedules should be as short as possible, and in no event extend beyond the longevity of the facility being financed. Other factors also enter into the determination of a maturity schedule. For example, possible obsolescence may dictate retirement of the debt much sooner than the expected life of the project. An examination of the maturity schedules of currently outstanding debt may indicate the need to arrange maturities for the proposed debt issue in such a way as not to unduly burden the budgets of years with already heavy debt maturities. The desires of the investors at the time bonds are offered will also affect the kind of maturity schedule indicated.

INVESTORS WANT TO BE INFORMED

Investors, underwriters, dealers, and credit analysts appraise management by how ably it tells the story of the community's economic and financial situation as well as by the facts themselves. The best of reporting tells a sorry tale if the facts are not good. But good facts alone are not enough; the investment world must be made aware of them.

It is universally felt that municipal financial management can do much to improve the appraisal of the credit of its jurisdiction by taking the responsibility for setting forth the facts about the jurisdiction both in writing and in person. City financial officials should not rely on credit-analyzing companies to furnish current and complete factual information to investors, underwriters, and dealers. Periodic publication of fully detailed financial and economic reports indicating all the salient factors in the community situation, prepared with appropriate care and attention to public relations, and distributed regularly and widely, serves greatly to enhance the marketability of a community's bonds. Such information is of critical importance when the volume of municipal security offerings is at record levels.

In a buyer's security market, it is good seller's strategy to make the buyer fully aware of the merits of his offering. In such a market, the buyer is inclined to pass over issues about which he lacks information in favor of those for which adequate information has been provided.

In view of the intimate personal character of the financial community, direct personal contact between the management personnel of municipalities and key personalities in the municipal market, including ultimate investors, is generally recognized to be a basic ingredient of successful borrowing management. Such personal contacts are best handled by individuals fully conversant with all aspects of their jurisdiction's economic, political, financial, and social situations. Good personal impressions made by an official of a city go a long way in reinforcing a strong financial statement.

These personal contacts should not be limited to credit analysts, underwriters, and dealers. They should include also the larger investors in the community's bonds. Alert municipal fiscal management not only keeps track of the ultimate investors in its securities, but also maintains personal contact with these investors and keeps them informed of favorable developments.

OTHER CONSTRUCTIVE PRACTICES

Most specialists believe that the finance officer himself should prepare the bond prospectus—the summary of the financial and economic situation of his community for the information of prospective bond buyers; that he himself should handle the details of the borrowing operation unless the financing is very complex. When this is the case, the employment of a financial adviser is desirable. It is management, in any event, which has to supply most of the relevant facts to the adviser. Since management is so important in establishing the credit rating of a community, the investment world in general is more favorably impressed in those cases in which management demonstrates its thorough knowledge of its community's situation.

In cases where it is necessary to have the voters decide on bond issues, it is desirable that the factors involved should be thoroughly aired through the medium of public forums and similar methods. Publicity will improve the prospects for a favorable vote, and will help reduce the likelihood of litigation proceedings by providing evidence that the majority of voters were conversant with the details of the project. It follows that the period of time allowed for public discussion should be long enough to assure complete public understanding of the need for borrowing.

It is also desirable that once a bond issue is decided upon it be announced, as early as possible, to the investment world through the media of financial journals. This is necessary because investors plan their investments in advance, and an issue offered on short notice may find all available investment funds already committed.

Credit can be improved by the adoption of appropriate financial controls. These include such operations as independent audit, performance budgets, centralized purchasing, and adequate attention to debt administration.

Finally, proper timing of an issue is most important to good debt management. The objective is to avoid a time when the offerings calendar is crowded, and when other issues are coming to the market from the same geographic area which are likely to be directly competitive. These are fully reported in the daily and weekly publications which specialize in news on municipals. In addition, certain times of the year—for example, federal corporation income tax due dates—are best avoided because they are generally characterized by money scarcity. The time to borrow is when everyone else wants to lend.

constitutional limits
on state and local debt

THEY TEND TO BE TOO RESTRICTIVE

Constitutions properly prescribe general guidelines to govern the use of public credit. In many parts of the country, however, state constitutions go beyond general guidelines and impose restrictive limitations on the borrowing powers of state and local governments. These limitations are expressed in various ways. The prevailing practice in the states is to limit the amount of local debt to a specified percentage of the assessed value of taxable real property. This is a kind of rubber yardstick, for it can be raised or lowered as the assessment ratio is increased or decreased, perhaps at the will of the assessing official, without regard to the actual trend in taxable property values—the determinant of revenue resources. Moreover, it is not a meaningful standard. Assessed valuation bears no predictable or stable relationship to the actual value of taxable property. Further, property tax is only one of the resources available to a community for meeting its debt obligations. For some, property tax is no longer even the most important revenue source.

These debt limitations, as already noted, had their genesis in the notorious failures to meet interest and repayment commitments on state and local debt. Some occurred during the past century in consequence of orgies of excessive borrowing to finance railroads and other developmental improvements; some during the depression of the 1930's, when property tax delinquencies and tax strikes emptied local and state treasuries and obliged many of these governments to default on various commitments including even employees' wages.

In principle, constitutional limitations on the amount of indebtedness have little to recommend them; those based on the assessed value of real property are particularly irrational, especially for prescribing the ceiling on state debt.

In the American governmental system the administration of public business, including debt management, is the proper concern of elected public officials, executives, and legislators, with such safeguards as are necessarily provided by a system of checks and balances. Public officials who are accountable for their conduct of public business should not be handicapped in discharging their obligations by constitutional restrictions which are likely to become obsolete even if soundly conceived at the time of their adoption.

This consideration notwithstanding, constitution framers appear to have a strong affinity for explicit debt limits. Restrictions of this kind cater to the public's disposition to keep tight financial reins on elected officials. This reflects an instinctive inclination to distrust them in the handling of the people's dollars.

SOME SENSIBLE GUIDELINES

In the final analysis, the principal safeguard that a state or municipality will not engage in excessive borrowing is the unwillingness of the market to buy its securities, except at prohibitively high interest rates. The market is quick to send up danger signals when a government departs from prudent financing. This suggests that if a meaningful debt limitation is deemed essential, it might be found in a prohibition against the payment of interest rates in excess of some multiple, say 125 percent, of the prevailing interest rate paid on prime obligations of a comparable maturity. No state has as yet used this kind of criterion in placing a ceiling on the amount of borrowing.

Another possibility is to express the limitation in terms of the aggregate annual personal income of the population represented by the borrowing entity. In the last analysis, the basic gauge of an area's debt-carrying capacity is its productivity: the value of the goods and services it produces and the income it earns. Since the purpose of a limitation on indebtedness is to keep debt within manageable levels, it has meaning only in terms of the resources available for covering debt obligations. This suggests that the limitation might be set in terms of the relationship between the volume of indebtedness or the amount of debt service (principal and interest requirements) and current tax and (net) nontax revenues available for general government purposes. This criterion was prescribed by Congress for the District of Columbia in 1967 on a three-year trial basis. It is also in effect in Connecticut.

It would not be illogical to prohibit a government from committing to the service of its debt more than 10 or 15 percent of its revenue receipts, keeping it on the low side of this range for jurisdictions with a stable or declining population and on the high side for those with population increases in prospect. In the interest of stability, a three- or five-year average may be desired. In that event, the percentage figure would need to be raised because in a growing community the average for past years will fall substantially below current levels. It follows that where a jurisdiction is dependent on a single revenue source, as in the case of local governments limited to the property tax, the same purpose can be achieved by a limitation expressed as a percentage of property tax revenues. By the same token, however, a limitation in terms of the property tax is wholly irrational in the case of a state that has stopped using the tax as a major source of revenue. A limitation in terms of the value of taxable property would be less meaningful than property tax collections because, as tax rates increased, it would result in a progressive lowering of the borrowing ceiling in relation to the size of the budget.

Of all forms of debt limits, the least rational are those expressed as a specified dollar amount for they belie economic growth. Such limitations are either excessive at the time of their adoption, or, if not excessive, quickly become unduly restrictive as the community grows and prospers. And of all safeguards against imprudent borrowing, none compares with those automatically derived from the judicious selection of the officials entrusted with the public's business and from a citizenry proud of its community and jealous of its reputation.

tax exemption of
municipal securities

A troublesome aspect of the reciprocal tax immunity institution in our federal system—the rule against one government burdening another with its taxes—is the tax exemption of government securities. Interest on state and local securities (commonly called municipals) is free from federal income tax, and interest on federal obligations is free from state and local income taxes. States generally also exempt their own and their subdivisions' securities, but tax those of other state and local governments. The federal government taxes the interest from its own securities. Before 1940, the policy of reciprocal tax immunity applied also to the salaries of government employees.

IT IS A LONG-STANDING ISSUE

The tax exempt security issue has been important since the advent of the federal income tax in 1913. At the time of the original federal income tax enactment spokesmen for the states were fearful that the language of the Thirteenth Amendment, authorizing the taxation of income "from whatever source derived," contemplated the taxation of interest paid on their securities. They were assured by the congressional leadership that it was not so intended, and since that time the Federal Revenue Code has specifically provided that interest on municipals may be excluded from income reported for tax purposes.

At the time of the Thirteenth Amendment it was generally believed that the Constitution mandated reciprocal exemption. A century earlier, Chief Justice Marshall had remarked that "the power to tax involves the power to destroy." The weight of legal opinion, particularly since the Supreme Court sanctioned nondiscriminatory federal taxation of the salaries of state employees in 1939, no longer holds with this constitutional theory. In the words of Justice Holmes, "The power to tax is not the power to destroy while this Court sits." The issue, however, has never been tested, and those who are watchful for the interests of state and local governments are vigorously on guard to prevent it. So long as the exclusion of municipal interest is explicitly provided by law (and before 1969, Congress had evidenced little interest in curbing it) the federal government has no opportunity to raise the issue with the Court.

IT IS A POOR BARGAIN

The income tax exemption of municipal bond interest is troublesome because it violates a fundamental principle of the income tax—that income "from whatever source derived" is taxable. The exemption from an ability-to-pay tax is particularly offensive in the case of municipal bonds because their ownership is typically associated with the upper-income groups. Wage earners do not own state or local bonds.

Tax exempt bonds are especially attractive, of course, to taxpayers in the high tax rate brackets. The middle-income taxpayer subject to a 20 percent federal tax rate derives as much income after taxes from a 4 percent municipal as if he held a 5 percent taxable bond. The 20 percent tax would take one-fifth of the taxable yield, leaving 4 percent net after tax. The taxpayer in the 50 percent bracket is as well off with the 4 percent municipal as he would be with a taxable investment yielding 8 percent. The investor who is in the top 70 percent bracket would have to obtain a 13⅓ percent yield from a taxable investment to match the after-tax equivalent of a 4 percent tax-exempt security.

High-bracket investors would be willing to pay relatively high prices for tax-exempt securities. Put another way, they would be willing to lend their funds to these governments at relatively low interest rates. However, they are not required to do so. They buy them on identical terms with other investors, at the market price set by the interplay of supply and demand. Because the supply of securities offered for sale by state and local governments is substantially larger than high-bracket taxpayers want to buy, the price drops to attract enough buyers in lower tax rate brackets and even nontaxable institutions to take the whole supply off the market. In the process, high-income taxpayers are afforded very attractive bargains— to the discomfort of the U.S. Treasury.

It should be quickly added that we have only fragmentary information on the ownership of bonds by individual investors. For many years taxpayers were asked to report on their federal tax returns the amount of tax exempt interest they received. The question was dropped from the income tax form some twenty years ago, however, to allow space for information more relevant to the determination of tax liability. Present information is restricted to that available from estate tax returns. As would be expected, it shows a particular concentration of municipals in the larger estates, particularly in those of older decedents. Men who withdraw from active business life, and their widows, are understandably attracted by the security and tax immunity afforded by municipals.

THE U.S. TREASURY IS THE PRINCIPAL LOSER

The U.S. Treasury has recently estimated that as a result of tax exemption of municipal bonds it is losing $1.8 billion of revenue a year.

This loss to the federal government can be viewed as a form of federal financial aid to state and local governments in that it is the price paid to enable them to borrow at reduced interest rates. The size of the interest rate reduction has been in controversy for some years and depends somewhat on market conditions. Most experts would probably agree that their exempt status enables municipal securities to enjoy an interest advantage somewhere between ½ and 1½ percentage points. They could further agree that the interest savings are greatest for fiscally strong and least for fiscally weak state and local governments.

Tax exemption of municipals is a very inefficient form of federal aid because only a relatively small part of its cost (in the form of lost federal tax revenue) accrues to the benefit of state and local governments. Much of it goes to high-bracket taxpayers, who save substantially more in taxes than they lose in reduced interest income. The exemption of municipals differs in this respect from the reciprocal exemption of government properties and enterprises. In those cases, one government's loss is another government's gain. Not so here. Third parties, the high-income investors, are the principal gainers. It has been estimated that the revenue lost by the federal government is twice the amount saved by states and local governments in reduced interest costs.

It will be appreciated, on the basis of the foregoing, that the U.S. Treasury regards the reciprocal tax immunity of government obligations as an unattractive bargain. Because some states have no income taxes, and others employ relatively low tax rates, the value of the exemption of federal interest payments and federal securities from state and local taxes in reduced interest costs on federal borrowing is hardly perceptible. Even this benefit has to be discounted because high quality tax-exempt state and local bonds compete for the investors' dollars with federally taxable federal bonds, tending to push federal interest rates upward.

From the viewpoint of overall public interest, the sum of federal, state, and local costs substantially exceeds the sum of the benefits. In addition to the estimated $1.8 billion lost by the federal government, states probably lose close to $250 million a year from the exemption of interest on federal bonds from their income taxes. The only net gainers are the high-income individuals and corporations who hold state and local bonds.

The tax exemption of municipal bonds is also objectionable for other reasons: it helps to undermine public confidence in the fairness of the income tax, and, by encouraging them to invest in municipals, diverts high-income investors from risky private ventures they alone can afford. A dynamic, innovative society needs risk-takers.

PROSPECTS FOR CHANGE ARE NOT VERY PROMISING

For several decades, federal officials and others concerned with tax fairness have been urging Congress to stop the exemption of municipal bonds. Before 1953, every national administration over a period of more than thirty years had recommended it; first through constitutional amendment, and after about 1940 by legislation. Nevertheless, Congress has on half a dozen occasions rejected legislation that would have rescinded the exemption, and on a substantially larger number of occasions did not even bother to bring the proposal to a vote. The three immediately preceding national administrations (1953–1968) were silent on the subject. This is all the more noteworthy because the size of the problem, and with it the inequity, has steadily continued to increase. Twenty years ago the total volume of all outstanding state and local securities was less than $20 billion. It is now about $130 billion, and each year $12 to $15 billion of new bonds are floated. Annual interest payments on these bonds now exceed $4 billion.

For many years tax reformers appeared to have lost interest in this "loophole" because the prospect for a remedy is not encouraging. Congress is troubled by the fiscal problems of state and local governments. It would be inconsistent, some members feel, to add to the costs of state and local governments at a time when, in order to help them, federal grants were being increased more and faster than ever before. At this writing, some favorable attention is being accorded to modest indirect approaches proposed by the U.S. Treasury Department, and others, including a "minimum" tax on those with a substantial income from various tax-favored sources, including municipal bonds.

In a sense, the time for a total remedy has passed us by. Because the volume of tax-exempt securities now outstanding is very large, the increase in federal revenues that would result from the taxation of municipal securities would fall substantially short of the increased cost of borrowing to state and local governments for a considerable number of years. This seeming paradox needs explanation.

There is no thought of taking away the exemption privilege of bonds now outstanding unless an equitable and acceptable way could be found to compensate their owners, who bought them on the basis of their exemption. It is usually proposed, therefore, to tax only future issues of municipals. The bonds already outstanding, now about $130 billion, would remain exempt until they matured and were repaid. In consequence, those in the high tax brackets who would want to buy tax-exempt bonds in the future would be able to buy them from those who hold the old tax-exempt issues and attach relatively less value to their tax exemption. Since some of the outstanding tax-exempt bonds will not mature for another twenty-five years, the process of their being shifted to high-bracket taxpayers could go on for many years.

During this transition period, while some outstanding tax exempts matured, the price of the longest maturities would gradually rise because they would progressively become more scarce, thus giving capital gains to those who were selling them, tax-exempt interest income to those who were buying them, and adding little to U.S. Treasury tax collections.

It will be appreciated that in the present widespread concern with the fiscal problems of state and local governments a proposal that would not add materially to federal revenues for some years (though it would immediately increase state and local interest costs on new issues) is not an attractive legislative proposition. This line of argument against the proposal, needless to say, is being made very effectively on behalf of state and local governments, municipal bond underwriters, and the bond dealers whose stock in trade is at stake.

STATE AND LOCAL GOVERNMENTS COULD BE PROTECTED

There is another, less disadvantageous solution to the problem of tax-exempt securities and one that would protect state and local governments against a financial loss and also protect other equities. Specifically, Congress could reimburse state and local governments for the increased cost on future borrowings resulting from removal of the tax exemption. Alternatively, a federal agency could stand ready to take up state and local governments' bond offerings on terms favorable to them. One variant of this approach would give state and local governments the option to continue selling tax-exempts, or to sell taxable securities with a federal subsidy to compensate for the higher interest cost. These governments are generally cool to ideas such as these, fearing that future Congresses may not continue to honor the arrangement, or may tamper with it.

It might be noted that, if it so desired, Congress could even repeal the exemption of outstanding municipal securities and compensate their owners for the price they paid for the tax-exemption feature when they acquired their municipals. However, Congress is not likely to move in this direction. It would be inclined to regard such an arrangement as an unwarranted violation of a past commitment. Nevertheless, if the owners of the securities were fairly compensated, the termination of the exemption of outstanding municipal bonds would keep faith with the old investors and measurably improve tax equities. Be that as it may, no recent national administration has evidenced any interest in undertaking the "selling" task that would be required to make any of the possible remedies acceptable to the people and to Congress. In the absence of an imaginative educational effort, it is unlikely that rationality will soon replace the emotionalism that now befogs this intergovernmental issue. In short, the prospect for anything more than token legislative reform is extremely dim. Meanwhile, each day's new municipal flotations add to the inequities of the tax exemption and raise the legislative hurdle in the path of a complete remedy.

chapter 16

the industrial development bond

Although the institution of the municipal bond exempt from federal income taxation appears to be here to stay for some time, an exception to this outlook is the tax-free municipal known as the industrial development bond.

IT GRANTS EXEMPTION FOR PRIVATE PROFIT TO ATTRACT INDUSTRY

Like other municipals, the industrial development bond is issued in the name of a state or a local government. However, instead of providing funds to acquire a school or some other structure for general public use, it finances the acquisition of an industrial or commercial facility for lease to private enterprise. Instead of being secured by the taxing resources of the issuing government, it is secured by a long-term lease with a business firm. It resembles a municipal revenue bond sold to finance an income-producing facility such as a toll road, where the toll proceeds are pledged for repayment of the bonds. But the toll road is a public enterprise, whereas the operation housed in an industrial or commercial plant is for private profit.

Basically the industrial development bond is a vehicle for making a government's tax exemption privilege available to a private firm as part of a deal to attract it to a particular community, or to keep it there. This is a powerful incentive, because tax-exempt municipal bonds command more favorable interest terms in the money market than comparable corporate bonds and enable a corporation to make substantial interest savings on funds borrowed to build a plant. A 1-percentage-point saving in the interest rate on a twenty-year $10 million bond issue amounts to $2 million. Use of the facility acquired with these bonds may, and often does, bestow other advantages on the leasing corporation. Although the community which is party to the transaction will want to make certain that the terms of the lease are adequate to repay the interest and principal on the bonds, it often adds to the attractiveness of the lease package by passing on to the leasing corporation the benefits of the exemption of its properties from its own and other overlapping governments' property taxes (including those of school districts) and the exemption of its rental income from state and federal income taxes. Most of the exemption it gives away, however, is not from its own but from other governments' taxes.

Arrangements of this kind are attractive to firms that require new plants. Although nominally the plant is financed, built, and managed by the municipality, in practice the operation is largely handled by the leasing corporation which generally makes all the arrangements, including the placement of the bonds with investors. This is especially the case when an unknown small community is used by a well-known national corporation to finance a multimillion-dollar plant. Little wonder that the practice has enjoyed popularity and increased press attention in the last few years.

IT, TOO, HAD SMALL BEGINNINGS

Like other loopholes, the industrial development bond began innocently enough in the 1930's. Mississippi invented the device to help supplement its faltering agriculture with industry and used it successfully to build a substantial number of relatively small plants, mostly in small places with little if any industry and no ready access to the money market for credit. The practice did not receive national notice until the 1950's, and did not become widespread until the 1960's. By that time it had spread to over half of the states. But the aggregate annual volume of industrial development bond financing remained small until the early 1960's. At the close of 1962, all industrial bonds issued since the beginning of the practice aggregated less than $500 million.

Subsequently, however, the movement gathered great momentum. Increasingly the practice attracted financially strong national corporations, and even foreign corporations. A Japanese steel firm and a Swiss aluminum firm reportedly acquired new plants in the United States in this manner. In 1967 alone, $1.4 billion of such bonds were issued; and in 1968, when Congress finally restricted the practice, the total for the year reached $1.6 billion. Although the worst of the abuses now appear to have been outlawed, their story is here detailed as illustrative of the potentials of tax exemptions for mischief.

IT HAD MANY CRITICS

As might be inferred from the fact that Congress was persuaded to curb industrial development bonds, their opponents were influential and vocal. The critics of the tax exemption privilege of all municipal securities cited industrial development bonds as a prime example of the inequity associated with it. They were vociferous in their criticism when this financing technique was used to build an industrial or commercial facility for a nationally prominent, financially strong corporation which had ready access to adequate financing through conventional channels. The abuse was particularly glaring when the benefited enterprise itself acquired some of the tax-exempt bonds issued to finance the structure it occupied and thus also became the beneficiary of tax-exempt income. The federal administration was aroused because, in addition to eroding revenues and damaging tax equities, this raised the level of municipal interest rates, hurt the regular municipal bond market, and indirectly increased the need for federal aid to these governments. The facts that these arrangements were usually negotiated in off-the-record sessions, and that the lessees of the new plants often enjoyed exemption from various taxes, were particularly objectionable.

In some instances, projects were undertaken far beyond the community's employment needs. A village with a population below 100 has been known to be the stooge for financing a multimillion-dollar operation. When this occurred, labor had to be imported, the local economy was disrupted, and community facilities were strained. In addition the community may have saddled itself with excessive contingent debt service liabilities, and also saddled nearby jurisdictions with the burden of providing schools and amenities for the families of imported workers.

Labor organizations were critical because tax-exempt industrial development bonds were a factor in looting industry from eastern and northern locations and relocating them in southern parts of the country, where labor is less organized and right-to-work laws prevail. Economists were critical because the tax-exempt financing interfered with normal business decisions on plant locations. The loudest critics of the practice, of course, were the political representatives of those areas that lost industrial plants to other locations, particularly if it appeared that the industrial development bond was an important consideration in the relocation decision.

Even the defenders of the tax exemption of regular municipal securities were troubled. They were fearful that public and political criticism of the financing of industrial facilities with tax-exempt bonds would build public support for terminating the exemption of all municipals. They were also concerned that the inflation of the supply of tax-exempt securities would reduce their scarcity value and depreciate their competitive advantage over taxable corporate obligations, thereby tending to raise state and local interest rates generally.

The financial community itself was split on the question. Firms that did not participate in this kind of underwriting were opposed. Specialists in industrial development bonds thought the practice sound, albeit small in volume.

BUT THE PRACTICE FLOURISHED

All the criticism notwithstanding, community after community felt obliged to join the parade in self-defense to hold its own against jurisdictions that used these bonds to attract business firms. Legislatures in more than forty states had authorized the practice before Congress stepped into the breach. The economic and political pressures to attract new plants and to hold old ones are extremely compelling, particularly where they hold promise of augmenting tax revenues without further increases in tax rates.

Tax officials of corporations, in pursuit of their professional objective of minimizing their firm's tax bills and of maximizing profits, felt under pressure to exploit the practice. They were encouraged, of course, by the legal and financial firms that make a specialty of this kind of business. In the meantime, as the practice spread and became more general, the advantage gained over other communities and corporations steadily diminished because practices of this nature are in the long run doomed to be self-defeating.

When the Advisory Commission on Intergovernmental Relations first looked at the problem in 1963, it concluded that local governments were not likely to desist from the practice because competition from those already using it would force others to follow suit. Therefore it urged state legislatures to step in and regulate the practice and proposed a variety of standards to keep it within reasonable bounds. However, very few states moved in this direction. In the meantime the practice spread from twenty-three to over forty states, obliging the commission to acknowledge (in 1968) that its efforts to promote state action had been largely unsuccessful and that "the states with a few notable exceptions have done nothing to heal this festering source of intergovernmental irritation." The commission concluded with regret that prospects for state initiative in this field appeared to be poorer in 1968 than they had been in 1963. The states were reluctant for fear of putting themselves at a disadvantage in competition with other states. As the list of states permitting industrial development bonds grew longer, the commission reluctantly admitted that asking the states to police themselves was like asking a fox to guard the chickens. The commission, therefore, rescinded its earlier recommendations and urged Congress to outlaw the practice.

Earlier in 1968, after numerous delays, the U.S. Treasury moved to curb the practice by regulation and proposed to rule that, in the future, industrial development bonds would not be accorded the tax exemption privilege of municipal bonds. The day following the Treasury's announcement, the Senate voted to direct the Treasury to continue indefinitely the tax-exempt treatment of these bonds. The critics, however, prevailed; and in the closing days of 1968, Congress limited the tax exemption of industrial development bonds to individual issues not exceeding $5 million. This appears to have limited the volume of new financing to relatively small amounts, and has encouraged tax reformers to think that not all of their efforts are necessarily condemned to failure.

part IV

BETTER GROUND RULES FOR OUR FAMILY OF GOVERNMENTS

chapter 17

our family
of governments

FEDERATIONS ARE TAILORED TO THEIR TIME
AND PLACE

Federations of states are the products of compromise. They represent the reconciliation of each affiliating state's desire for maximum sovereignty with its need for the security afforded by the collective strength of the affiliating group. The American federal system embodied the reconciliation of the colonial states' desire for local democracy to accommodate their respective political institutions, economic interests, and religious views with their need for the collective strength of all the states to deal with common problems at home and with the potentially hostile world around them.

The terms of the compromise vary from federation to federation because the balance between the emphasis on local democracy and on the need for pooled strength differs from place to place and from time to time. Because civilization's progress is marked by increased interdependence at home and more and more involvement abroad, the newer federations tend to reflect a greater emphasis on collective strength and a lesser emphasis on separateness than do the older systems.

Ours is the oldest federal system extant and its constitutional conceptions reflect its age. Old federations are not immune to the march of time. But the adjustment of their constitutional fabric to emerging needs is all the more painful, if only because the fabric must be stretched that much further.

American political history is in many respects the story of the adjustment of the 1787 conceptions to a relentless march toward interdependence, involving at every stage the reconciliation of competing and often conflicting social, economic, cultural, and political values. As the country's growth and development brought the several states closer together into one community the list of common problems grew longer, and each state's involvement in national concerns grew deeper.

The Founding Fathers could limit their concern to providing for the free flow of commerce, for a national monetary system, copyrights, patents, post offices, post roads, and federal courts of justice. They were able to leave responsibility for most functions of domestic government, and for the social and cultural services, to the states and their local governments. The Constitution reveals little concern, if any, with the adequacy of arrangements to care for the poor and the sick, to educate the children, and to nurture the environmental amenities. The founders were content to leave these matters to local discretion. Today, we do not have that option.

One objective of replacing the Articles of Confederation with the federal constitution was to improve and strengthen national finances. To this end, the states bestowed on Congress a monopoly of duties on imports and concurrent powers with their own over virtually all taxes. The states' estimate of their own future revenue needs matched their relatively modest concept of governmental responsibilities, which they confidently expected to be able to accommodate out of the taxing powers reserved for themselves. Their concern was with the adequacy of the federal government's revenue resources, not their own. They did not and could not have been expected to foresee that economic progress would increasingly enlarge their revenue needs while it restricted their freedom to tax, and that the terms of fiscal balance would move progressively in favor of the federal government.

On the whole, the fiscal provisions of the 1787 compact worked reasonably well up to the beginning of the 20th century. Until America's first involvement in a European war (1914–1918) the federal treasury lived primarily on customs and on liquor and tobacco taxes, and occasionally even suffered from an embarrassment of revenue riches. State and local governments relied chiefly on property taxes and appeared to be holding adequate untapped taxing powers in reserve. Thereafter, however, the changes were many and swift. It became progressively more difficult for state and local governments to accommodate the demand for domestic governmental services out of their own revenue resources.

GROWTH MULTIPLIES THEIR PROBLEMS

National growth and development increases the role of government and, under this federal system's division of governmental responsibility, impinges with particular weight on state and local government. Local governments must provide more police and fire protection, more streets and airports, more recreation facilities, more public schools, and a variety of services for increased numbers of people living in urban societies. State governments are faced with the need for more roads, better health and welfare programs, as well as the need to assist the localities in performing some of their critical functions such as, for example, public education.

In consequence of national growth and urbanization, state and local spending has been increasing considerably faster than the federal. Moreover, economic growth tends to curb the taxing freedom of state and local government. With increased economic interdependence, each state and community grows more sensitive to competition for business and taxpayers. This, too, contrasts with the situation at the national level. Although the federal government also labors against political restraints in practicing sound tax policy, it has jurisdiction over the whole country and can disregard state and local boundaries. There is also a third difference. Economic growth and prosperity work magic with the yield of the federal government's progressive income tax. Its yield, without changing tax rates, grows significantly faster than the economy. In contrast, state and local government largely depends on property and consumer taxes—and the yield of these taxes barely manages to keep pace with economic growth. In short, although national economic progress bestows fiscal bounties as well as fiscal burdens, it tends to concentrate its revenue bounties on the federal government and its cost burdens on state and local government.

This federal-state fiscal mismatch is not a new experience for Americans, but recent events cloak it with new urgency. So long as inadequate provision for educational or welfare programs were matters of local concern only, they could be left to local political decision. So long as local and state tax levels were not too far out of line with the public's notion of reasonableness, the financing of public programs could be left to local tax increases and new tax enactments. State and local taxes, however, have been increasing rather steadily for some years and, in an increasing number of places, are reaching levels to which the public has not as yet become adjusted— and the public has been expressing its displeasure in the voting booths with a consequent high rate of political mortality among state and local officeholders associated with the tax increases.

FEDERATIONS ARE LEFT WITH LIMITED ALTERNATIVES

A central-local government fiscal mismatch, it should be noted, is not critical for centralized governmental systems because these systems are free to rearrange the expenditure and revenue balance in their local governments through national decisions. They can use central government taxes to obtain revenues and deploy them wherever expenditure priorities require.

A federal-state fiscal mismatch does trouble federal democracies because they are less well equipped to cope with it. The obvious remedies, moreover, work at cross-purposes to the aspirations of their inherited political traditions.

Federal democracies aspire to decentralized decision-making in both taxing and spending. They want to leave maximum responsibility for domestic government in the hands of those close to the people—at the local level, if possible; at the state level, if necessary; but rarely at the federal level. With this goes a preference for each level of government to raise its own revenues so that the responsibility for taxing can go hand in hand with that for spending. We are reassured when those who have the pleasure of spending have to suffer the pain of imposing taxes.

So long as tax levels were moderate and considerable scope remained for tax increases, federal involvement in domestic government services logically concentrated on encouraging state and local effort by using federal grants. From time to time during the past one hundred years, and especially during recent decades, Congress became concerned with the inability or the unwillingness of states to give adequate support to this or that particular government function to the jeopardy of national policy objectives. When this occurred, Congress resorted to the traditional remedy: the incentive grant. The states were provided with funds for the particular activity on the condition that they satisfied prescribed program standards and matched federal funds in a prescribed ratio. The device typically stimulated an increased state effort in the aided function, and was particularly effective so long as the number and size of aided activities was small so that every state that wanted to do so was able to dredge up the sums needed to provide the matching funds.

Another approach to improving the federal-state fiscal balance is to shift responsibility for one or more of the costlier functions upward from the local to the state level, or from the state to the federal level. Although a few states have relieved their local governments of some of their responsibilities, notably those for welfare, the success with which proposals to shift functions have been resisted throughout the country's history and at all levels of government would seem to suggest that those impatient to reduce the federal-state imbalance might fruitfully add another string to their bow.

State and local governments' increasing difficulty in responding adequately to the clamor for more and better public programs may prove to be the most critical experience to confront this federal system in a century. Some of the short-fall doubtless reflects an unwillingness to make the effort and little else. Most of it, however, reflects a scarcity of fiscal resources at the local and state level as distinguished from the national level. This explains the widespread preoccupation with the federal-state fiscal imbalance and with ways to reduce it.

There are a number of possibilities for improving the ground rules governing the interrelationship within our family of governments in order to strengthen the fiscal capabilities of state and local governments. These range from the exchange of reciprocal courtesies and mutual help expected among closely affiliated governments to intergovernmental financial aids hitherto untried in this federal system. Local and state governments can be helped to make more effective use of their own resources, and their resources can be augmented by helping them to enact new taxes and increase the rates of old taxes; by restructuring the traditional grant-in-aid system; and by employing new forms of financial aid.

cooperation in tax administration

If federal, state, and local governments are viewed as an entity with a single mission, to serve the people's governmental needs, they probably are expected to work in concert and help one another at every turn. One would be hard pressed to find a public official who does not concur in principle; or one who would forego an opportunity to wax eloquent in the cause of intergovernmental cooperation, particularly on a suitable ceremonial occasion. But practice often departs from theory.

THERE ARE HURDLES TO CLEAR

Public officials are committed to their respective missions. Their loyalties are to their own jobs. They do their best to merit the approval of their superiors. Those exposed to public view crave the approval of their constituencies. But constituencies tend to rate their political representatives in terms of narrow personal interests; and the interests of one constituency, one community, or one state, as popularly interpreted, may conflict with interests of other communities or states, or with those of the nation. The tax exemption of the bonds of state and local governments reduces these governments' interest costs, but it also cuts into federal tax collections. The bootlegging of low-tax cigarettes increases trade in North Carolina, but it also cuts into New York's tax collections. One government's gain can often be had only at the cost of another government's loss, frequently at a substantially bigger loss.

Help extended to another tax administration generally absorbs manpower, and since public agencies generally are understaffed they are reluctant to "dissipate" their limited manpower in helping others unless they see an unequivocal quid pro quo. A town tax collector may be reluctant to spend a town dime to help the Internal Revenue Service to collect a dollar. The federal stamp tax on transfers of real property, in effect for several decades until 1968, went unenforced in many places because some local recorders of deeds felt no compulsion to assist federal tax enforcement to the inconvenience of their local citizens.

In some cases, helping another unit of government may require legislative authorization; either because confidentiality of taxpayer information is involved, or because the language of the agency's appropriation is construed to preclude the use of appropriated funds for helping another jurisdiction. State and local governments have been helping the federal government by withholding income taxes from their employees on the same basis as private employers. Federal agencies could not reciprocate by withholding state income taxes until Congress explicitly authorized it, because it had been ruled that existing legislative language did not cover using appropriated funds for this purpose. This is the reason federal agencies are still precluded from withholding city income taxes from federal employees, although cities withhold federal taxes due from their staffs. Interestingly, federal agencies are permitted to supply these governments with information on the compensation paid to federal employees.

In many states, special legislation would be required to permit the exchange of tax information with other states and with counties and cities. Even where the authority has been requested, legislatures have been known to refuse it. Why help other states to catch local constituents?

SOME COOPERATION IS GIVEN

Cooperation among tax administrations does occur despite the existence of barriers but typically takes place on the initiative of the higher level of government and, more particularly, its top-level leadership rather than its tax administrators.

Federal-state tax cooperation is most developed in the exchange of income tax information. It began over thirty years ago in response to one state tax commissioner's request for permission to inspect the federal income tax returns filed from his state so that he might check on state tax returns.

(The view prevails, with good reason, that taxpayers are more conscientious in complying with federal than with other jurisdictions' tax laws.) Ultimately the procedure was formalized by congressional legislation, which opened federal returns for inspection by state officials at the request of their respective governors. State employees were allowed to copy or photostat federal returns. In 1950, under cabinet level leadership, the federal government began exchanging the results of tax audits with states. These experiments proved profitable in terms of revenue recovered, particularly to states. Now nearly all states have agreements with the Internal Revenue Service that provide for the exchange of a wide array of data potentially useful in tax enforcement by both parties to the agreement.

The extent to which the opportunity for mutual benefit is utilized varies with the attitude and zeal of the state tax administrator and Internal Revenue District Directors. Those who espouse cooperation, however, have little difficulty in citing spectacular successes to match each dismal failure.

There is scope for cooperation among states and among local governments within states, and even in different states, but it is yet to be developed. Nevertheless, a more extended discussion of interstate tax cooperation could identify several illustrations of success such as, for example, joint tax audits and allocation of automotive tax revenues from multistate trucking operators. For some years the Advisory Commission on Intergovernmental Relations has been urging the states to enact one of its model laws that would authorize the exchange of tax information with one another and their political subdivisions. Some progress can be reported but it is not overwhelming and will not be so long as state and local officials undervalue its potential, and so long as it is politically unrewarding to extend a helping hand to the neighboring jurisdictions.

chapter 19

federal collection
of state taxes

PROSPECTS IN INCOME TAXATION

Increasingly, as more and more Americans are required
to file both federal and state income tax returns (and
even local income tax returns) people wonder why the two
cannot be handled together. Those subject to the income
tax laws of several states are particularly irritated by the
many differences of little tax consequence between federal
and state provisions, and among the provisions of the
several states. The idea of a common tax return form to
serve both federal and state needs was discussed in responsible tax circles as long as thirty-five years ago to
obviate the need for preparing separate tax returns for
each taxing jurisdiction; but the effort never progressed
beyond the idea stage.

Canada has more progress to report. When the Canadian government restored to the provinces the income tax
which was taken from them during World War II, it undertook to collect the provincial income taxes for any province
that desired it. Most provinces are availing themselves of
the opportunity. In the United States, we are familiar with
this joint tax-collection device in the sales-tax states that
collect also the sales taxes imposed by local governments,
and in one state (Maryland) with a corresponding tech-

159

nique employed for the collection of local income taxes. Federal collection of state income taxes, however, would encounter substantial resistance.

Internal Revenue Service operations are geared to uniformity across the country. This uniformity progressively grows more mandatory as federal income tax administration is automated. Federal tax returns from all over the country are now processed in specialized regional facilities. Such processing would be handicapped if it had to apply different tax rules to returns from fifty different states. Present state provisions vary from the federal, and, as already noted, variation among the states extends to numerous and even inconsequential details. Although considerable progress toward uniformity has followed from some states adopting federal provisions, substantially more progress toward uniformity is required before pooled administration on terms acceptable to the Internal Revenue Service becomes a realistic prospect.

The states, it should be stressed, are reluctant to contemplate joint tax administration. Federal collection would be least attractive to the states with well-established income taxes, especially those with well-developed statutes that reflect local political preferences, and with an effective tax enforcement apparatus. Some of these states believe that the quality of their enforcement, particularly at the lower income levels where most taxpayers fall, compares favorably with the federal government's. Federal collection of state taxes would probably be most attractive to a state enacting a new income tax. Such a state would not be confronted with the vexing need to abandon its own statutory design, to reassign its own personnel, and to appraise the quality of its own compared with the federal government's enforcement. There has been no opportunity to explore this technique with the income taxes enacted recently because, as of now, the Internal Revenue Service is without authority to collect a state's income tax.

In view of the understaffing of most state tax administrators' offices, none would have difficulty in making effective use of personnel made surplus by shifting income tax enforcement responsibility to the Internal Revenue Service. But rationality may not prevail. Political leadership takes pride in its administrative organization, and is predisposed to protect it.

State legislatures have a bias against allowing federal law to govern state income taxes. They value the option to exercise their independent sovereignty. They want to reserve their opportunity to bestow tax favors, inflict tax penalties, and to give legislative effect to their own policy judgments.

The case for federal collection of state income taxes improves as state laws move toward conformity with federal law. A couple of years ago, the U.S. Treasury expressed a willingness, if authorized by Congress, to undertake income tax collection for any state with which it could make a mutually satisfactory arrangement. Legislation authorizing it to do so is pending in Congress. It is sponsored by the Advisory Commission on Intergovernmental Relations so that the authority might be available when a state that is still without an income tax elects to enact one. When this occurs, the state may be interested in delegating the enforcement of the tax to the Internal Revenue Service since in this circumstance the opportunity for economy would not need to contend with the vested interests of an existing income tax enforcement bureaucracy.

PROSPECTS IN EXCISE TAXATION

A number of excises—notably those on cigarettes, liquor, and gasoline —which are used by the federal government are used also by all or nearly all states, and the question logically arises why these taxes cannot be collected together. The opportunities for economy to both government and industry from pooling the enforcement efforts of fifty-one separate tax administrations are obvious. Indeed, they are greater than this number suggests. The three federal excises mentioned are collected at the manufacturing stage and therefore involve only a few corporations; whereas the states' taxes are collected at the wholesaling and jobber level and involve dealings with thousands of business firms.

State and federal tax administration has not been combined for a variety of reasons. Perhaps the most important is the reluctance of state legislatures to surrender control over tax administration. Another is their desire to preserve their policy of freedom. The federal tax administration would be interested in joint administration only if all state taxes were substantially uniform and paralleled the substantive provisions of federal law. It could not operate under a multiple set of rules except at substantial additional expense.

Cigarette Tax. The problems inherent in joint federal-state tax collections are illustrated by the cigarette tax. This state tax is virtually universal. It is now levied by the federal government, the District of Columbia, fifty states, and some local governments. In recent years, governors and their legislatures have turned to it for additional revenue more frequently than to any other source.

The federal government collects its cigarette tax directly from the small number of manufacturers (six firms account for more than 99 percent of sales) and employs a simple tax return system. This obviates the need to affix a stamp to each package of cigarettes as evidence that a tax has been paid. In consequence, federal tax enforcement costs are minimal, less than 1/30 of 1 percent of collections.

The states' enforcement costs, on the other hand, approximate about 5 percent of collections. Their procedure requires the jobber or wholesaler to affix to each package a stamp or other evidence that tax has been paid. The stamps have to be produced and stockpiled, and the industry has to be compensated for the expense involved in opening each case and each carton of cigarettes to attach appropriate proof that the tax was paid.

This dramatic contrast between state and federal tax collection costs focuses periodic attention on possibilities for joint collection of cigarette taxes, to give the states the benefit of the low federal enforcement costs.

In the early days of state cigarette taxation it was often proposed that the states abstain from this tax area; that in return for exclusive federal taxation, the states be given a share of the collections. After the tax had spread to many states, and wide variations developed in state tax rates, federal taxation with state revenue sharing lost its attractiveness. In mid-1969, state tax rates ranged from 2 cents to 16 cents. The most common rates were 8 cents used by nine states, and 12 cents used by eight states. A sharing formula generous enough to compensate the states with relatively high tax rates would be costly in federal revenue and would bestow windfalls on states with low rates.

The states, of course, could not be mandated to vacate the cigarette tax field. Their withdrawal would need to be voluntary and, therefore, would have to be induced by terms acceptable to them. It is difficult to visualize circumstances when these conditions could be satisfied. In stipulating the terms under which they would be willing to give up their own tax, the states would be inclined to look not only to their present tax rates and collections but also to such further tax rate increases as they might have in prospect for the future. Moreover, federal collection with state sharing or joint collection would be practicable only if all states joined in it—and there is little precedent, if any, for fifty states to subscribe to a common tax policy where large revenue amounts are at stake.

Exchange of tax information between federal and state tax administrators, the practice that helps to mitigate the wastefulness of duplicate income tax administration, is not promising in cigarette taxation. Since federal and state tax administrations function at different levels of distribution—one at the manufacturing and the other at the wholesaling level—they have little information potentially useful to one another.

Tax supplements and tax credits also appear unsuitable. They are incompatible with wide tax-rate differentials among states. Some states choose to tax cigarettes relatively lightly; others tax them very heavily. Such tax differentials reflect interstate differences in tax philosophies; and though troublesome to those concerned with administrative efficiency, they are cherished attributes of federal-state separation.

There remains the possibility of the states continuing to enforce their own cigarette taxes, but shifting the process to the manufacturing level.

An investigation of the feasibility of this procedure led the Advisory Commission on Intergovernmental Relations to conclude that it has now become practicable. There are problems, to be sure; but with interstate cooperation and the good will of the manufacturers they are surmountable.

Manufacturers have been reluctant to consider assuming responsibility for collecting state cigarette taxes, particularly if they must bear uncompensated compliance costs and the financial burden associated with the prepayment of state taxes. Wholesalers can also be expected to resist it. The present arrangement (the states compensate them for affixing stamps) yields them a sizable profit. In any case, changes in established business practices are rarely embraced readily.

On the other hand, the speed with which tax rates can be raised has caught the industry by surprise. Manufacturers might come to consider it a good bargain to collect the states' taxes for them if the arrangement would help to stabilize state tax rates, if not restrain further increases. State officials charged with policymaking responsibilities would need to be assured that the cooperation of the manufacturers and of the officials of other states would be forthcoming before consenting to the liquidation of an ongoing enforcement organization, however costly. Those charged with the administration of state cigarette taxes, sensitive to the problems involved in changing from one system to another, would need to be assured that their superiors appreciate the need for patience during the period of transition.

Enough has been said to make clear that changes in intergovernmental tax arrangements are more easily formulated than implemented.

Three years have already elapsed since the Advisory Commission recommended to the states that they explore the collectibility of their cigarette tax at the manufacturing level and asked the Internal Revenue Service to assist the states in the undertaking. The suggestion is only beginning to receive attention. Not much progress can as yet be reported. This suggests either that the potential savings in administrative costs, however substantial, are of little interest to state policymakers, or, alternatively, that these opportunities interest them less than the convenience of continuing in familiar albeit costlier paths.

Liquor Tax. At the time of the repeal of prohibition, several proposals looking to the combined administration of federal and state beverage taxes were considered. It was an ideal time to plan a coordinated enforcement effort. The administrative machinery had been disbanded during prohibition, and there was no tax collection bureaucracy with vested interest in an existing arrangement. It would have been practicable to provide for federal collection of alcoholic beverage taxes at the manufacturing level and to share the revenues with the states. That system was rejected. Instead the federal and state governments developed independent alcohol tax and control systems.

Separate state and federal administration was rationalized on the ground that the taxation of liquor is closely tied to the regulation of liquor consumption. Accordingly, both the repeal amendment and the implementing federal legislation left regulation to the states. That system is now established, and there appears to be general agreement that the federal and state governments are best left free to continue their separate ways in liquor taxation.

Gasoline Tax. An excise for which joint collection shows more promise is the tax on gasoline. However, the variation in state tax rates is a substantive barrier to joint federal-state tax administration. Although all states have used gasoline taxes since 1929, their rates have always varied. Rates in mid-1969 ranged from 5 cents per gallon in three states to 9 cents in two states.

Joint federal-state tax enforcement would mean collection at the refinery level. That is, the place of federal collection. Petroleum companies distribute their products from regional storage farms that serve areas which do not necessarily coincide with state boundaries. If these companies were required to collect state taxes at different rates, they would need to keep current records on the place of final sale of their products in order to reflect each state's tax rate in the sale of their products within its borders. Because the record-keeping problem would be substantial, petroleum companies are understandably reluctant to undertake it.

It has always been assumed that variations in gasoline-tax rates are inevitable because of differences in the states' need for highway funds. In recent years, however, the states have tended to move toward more uniform rates. Today the rates of forty-one states are within the 7-8-cent range. If this trend continues, the collection of both federal and state gasoline taxes at the refinery level may well be a realizable objective.

chapter 20

relinquishing
tax sources

It is fashionable among champions of state and local government to blame their chronic revenue shortage on federal monopoly of the principal tax resources. Many states blame their ineffective use of the income tax, for example, on high federal tax rates. They are critical of the dominant federal role in the inheritance-estate taxes. Some were particularly critical of the increased federal use of excises on commodities and services during the Depression, and again during World War II. Many of these "temporary" taxes proved to be quite permanent and for many years those who spoke for the states conducted a veritable crusade to persuade Congress to relinquish them, particularly those suitable for local use. At one point, in 1949, the U.S. Treasury Department publicly endorsed this objective for implementation at the first budgetary opportunity.

HAS NOT HELPED THE STATES

Over the years, Congress has reduced or repealed several excises. While in the course of the legislative consideration of these reductions, mention was usually made of the state and local interest in these taxes, the primary objective in nearly every instance was something else. Helping state and local governments was incidental. A case in point is the tax on admissions to places of amusement.

Local governments have long been interested in admissions taxes on the theory that the neighborhood movie theater is substantially free of competition from theaters in other communities and therefore could be taxed by the municipality without driving business away.

In the last several years, Congress has gradually repealed the federal tax on admissions. Nothing remains of it now. Despite repeal of the federal tax, local governments have not picked it up and for good reason: they are sensitive to the financial condition of local businesses. They are not likely to increase their taxes at a time when competition from the television screen prompts Congress to reduce the federal tax in the hope of improving business. An industry with enough political influence to persuade Congress to give it tax relief is likely to have the capability to restrain states or cities from increasing their taxes on it.

The experience with other excises is similar. In 1950, for example, Congress repealed its 10 percent tax on electrical energy—again, not to relinquish it to local governments but to end the tax discrimination in favor of publicly produced power. Local governments have not moved into the field.

A different story may be evolving in the case of the tax on transfer of titles to real property. On the recommendation of the Advisory Commission on Intergovernmental Relations, Congress in 1965 repealed this federal tax, which had been in continuous use, albeit poorly enforced, since 1932 and at various earlier times for over a century. That commission had been urging the states to use this tax as a vehicle for obtaining information on current real property values to assist in improving the quality of the assessment of real property for tax purposes. Congress made the repeal effective on January 1, 1968, to allow the states time to enact a tax of their own.

The objective has the support of the International Association of Assessing Officers as well as several other professional groups. It would give a strong assist to the widespread effort in many states to improve property assessment administration.

Most states now have real estate transfer taxes, but a number do not. The most powerful opposition to state enactment has come from real estate interests. For the time being, real estate interests in the laggard states have won the day. However, efforts on behalf of state enactments continue.

These experiences with excises relinquished by the federal government suggest that the barriers to state and local tax enactments are more deep-seated than the existence of a federal tax. Lawmakers are vulnerable to the argument that a tax increase will affect local business adversely. The experience with the gasoline tax is revealing.

In the middle 1950's, favorable consideration was being given by Congress to repeal of the federal tax on motor fuel so that the states might increase their gasoline taxes for financing accelerated highway construction. The plan, strongly urged by the governors, won White House approval, and near-term implementation appeared to be in prospect. On reflection, however, the governors formally changed their position and requested instead that the federal government retain the tax and either dedicate it for highway construction purposes or allow a tax credit for state gasoline taxes.

A tax credit for state taxes would have enabled the states to increase their rates, secure in the knowledge that existing tax rate differentials among states would not be disturbed. The credit would have provided a floor below which a state could gain no advantage by tax reduction, since the tax would have to be paid in either event, if not to the state, then to the federal government. Congress ultimately retained and increased the gasoline tax and earmarked its yield, together with that of other automotive taxes, for a trust fund that finances grants to the states to pay for the construction of the interstate highway network and other federally aided highways. The governors, understandably apprehensive about their ability to replace a repealed federal gasoline tax with a corresponding addition to the state tax, were more than satisfied to leave the imposition of the tax to Congress so long as gasoline tax collections were reserved for them to spend on one of "their" functions.

THE SPECIAL CASE OF THE INCOME TAX

Even the most ardent exponents of the view that Congress should relinquish tax sources to the states recognize that by now there can be no thought of the federal government giving up the income tax. They would be content with federal tax rate reductions.

In view of the crucial role of the income tax in national economic and budgetary policy, not much weight can be given to state and local desires in setting federal tax rate levels. Nevertheless, the level of federal income tax rates has a substantial effect on state and local governments and operates principally in two ways.

About half the states with income taxes allow their taxpayers to deduct the federal tax in computing the amount of income subject to state tax. As a result, a federal tax reduction automatically increases state income tax revenues by reducing deductions and correspondingly increasing the amount of income subject to state tax.

The deductibility of state taxes in arriving at taxable federal income is helpful to the states, particularly with respect to high-income taxpayers.

It shifts part of the burden of the state tax to the federal government, and to that extent reduces its net cost to the state's taxpayers. The net cost of a state tax dollar to a taxpayer in the 60 percent federal tax bracket is 40 cents, since the deduction of the dollar reduces his federal tax by 60 cents. States might be expected to exploit this opportunity by sharply graduating their taxes on high-income taxpayers, but no attempt in this direction is discernible—perhaps out of compassion for the taxpayers subject to these high federal rates.

A more important and widespread effect of a federal tax reduction comes through the stimulation to economic activity that results from it. The increase in business activity from 1964–1965 tax reductions was so pronounced that, despite lowered rates, federal tax collections continued to rise.

Since some state income tax rates are changed every year, it is difficult to isolate the influence of increased economic activity from that of tax changes in accounting for increases in state income tax collections. Between 1962 and 1968, state personal income tax collections more than doubled: from $2.7 billion to $6.2 billion. There is not much doubt that the larger part of this growth was the result of increased personal incomes. The evidence is quite conclusive that, apart from sharing its revenue with them, the most important contribution the national government can make to help states realize more income tax revenues is to maintain a high level of national economic activity.

Increased economic activity reflects itself also in increased collections from other kinds of state and local taxes. In 1964, the then national administration made much of this result in justifying its tax reduction program when the federal budget was showing a sizable deficit.

It cannot be gainsaid, nevertheless, that the prevalence of a strong federal income tax system influences public acceptability of state income taxes. Certainly those opposed to state taxes use the existence of a high federal tax as a telling point for their side of the argument, although they find it increasingly more difficult to do so as the federal government succeeds in making the public appreciate the advantages of income taxes over consumer taxes.

Realistic consideration of prospects in income taxation must conclude that the federal government's use of the income tax will continue to dominate, and that state and local governments can utilize their own income taxes most successfully by accepting the leading role of the federal tax. With state fiscal needs continuing to expand rapidly, no state can afford to remain without this growth-responsive tax.

chapter 21

categorical grants-in-aid

THE GRANT IS AN OLD INSTITUTION

The time-honored instrument for federal financial aid to state and local governments—almost as old as the Union itself—is the grant-in-aid. As territories were granted statehood, part of the proceeds from the sale of public lands was distributed to the states—first (after 1802) for road construction, later to encourage learning. Millions of acres were distributed to endow public schools and to establish land grant colleges.

Scholars are not agreed as to which of these early measures marks the beginning of the modern federal grant. By 1887, when the Hatch Act grants of cash for agricultural experiment stations began, the practice of requiring each state to submit annual reports on the use of federal funds was definitely established; and when the Weeks Act of 1911 provided grants for forest fire protection, these were made conditional on federal approval of state plans for the use of the funds and federal supervision to ensure compliance with the approved plans.

These conditions to ensure that the funds were used for the purpose intended are the hallmarks of the categorical grant-in-aid. The point to note is that the practice of attaching strings to the states' use of federal aid funds—a practice now in controversy in connection with proposals for federal revenue sharing—was well established by the turn of this century.

The use of federal grants (apart from those for highways and special education programs) did not become widespread until the depression of the 1930's, when a dozen or more programs were enacted—chiefly for social welfare, health, unemployment, and agricultural relief. After World War II, and especially in the 1960's, came the big surge in federal grant enactments with programs for school lunches, airports, hospitals, civil defense, elementary, secondary, and higher education, the economic development of depressed areas, health services and medical care of the indigent, relief of poverty, and the alleviation of slums and blight-ridden cities.

By 1967, 95 separate program categories were on the statute books, 10 of which were established before 1930, 17 during 1931–1945, 29 during 1946–1960, and 39 during 1961–1966. Some of these represent more than one piece of legislation, some several, and most of them are represented by several authorizations. By the beginning of 1967 the number of grant authorizations reached 379, and by the end of the decade the count was around 400.

ITS DOLLAR AMOUNTS HAVE RISEN

The annual level of federal grants approached $3 billion during the 1930's, but dropped to $1 billion during World War II. It did not reach the $3-billion level again until 1954–1955 when it accounted for about 14 percent of federal domestic expenditures, excluding defense and foreign affairs. It has increased rapidly since then, and is now approaching $25 billion. Its share of federal domestic outlays is now about 22 percent. In other words, more than a fifth of federal expenditures for domestic programs now take the form of grants and are actually spent by state and local government.

The share of state and local revenue supplied by federal grants has risen from about one-eighth to about a sixth. The increase in the share would be greater except for the fact that these governments have increased their own financing efforts very sharply in recent years. They continue to finance nearly 85 percent of their expenditures from their own revenue sources, and this percentage is very slowly declining.

ITS CHARACTERISTICS HAVE CHANGED SLOWLY

Although the federal grant has been evolving for over a century, its principal characteristics emerged quite early. Its purpose from the begin-

ning was to encourage states and local governments to devote more resources to a particular activity for which they were historically responsible,
but which they were not supporting adequately to satisfy objectives of
national policy. The use of the grant in this way, as a federal-state partnership instrument to encourage (but not mandate) at least a minimum level
of program operation in a particular function in every state, is to be distinguished from the use of an all-purpose grant to generally assist state and
local governments' finances.

Federal grants have certain well-defined characteristics. The legislative
authorization for each grant specifies the purpose for which it is to be used.
Each is the culmination of a congressional finding that the national interest
requires a minimum level of service in a particular function, which the
state with its local governments may be unable or unwilling to provide of
its own initiative.

A relatively recent development is the emergence of project grants, as
distinguished from the formula grants. The latter are distributed to *all* aided
governments on the basis of a statutory formula. The recipients are entitled
to these grants as a matter of "right," subject to a ceiling imposed by the
amount of money authorized and then actually appropriated. Grants to
meet specific problems—project grants—on the other hand, are not necessarily spread uniformly. Eligible jurisdictions are specified (frequently
with a limitation on the amount available in any one state) but each jurisdiction must take the initiative in applying for the grant, generally by
submitting plans for the activity it wishes to have financed. Subject to
legislative guidelines and within funding limitations, federal administrators
use their judgment in making project grants, e.g., urban renewal grants or
neighborhood youth corps contracts. The funds appropriated for each pro-
ject-grant program are usually small; this places a further premium on state
and local initiative in requesting the funds and following up on applications,
and on administrative selection at the federal level.

The apportionment rules for formula grants vary considerably, but
generally include one or more criteria to take account of the relative size
of the problem by apportioning funds on the basis of the need for the
program in each eligible jurisdiction and its financial ability. Program need
is usually based on total population or the relevant population group, such
as school-age children or blind persons in public institutions. Financial
ability is generally measured by average per capita income in the state
compared with the national average.

The matching provisions specify the proportion which the grant recipients
are required to share in the cost of the program. In some cases the requirement is uniform for all recipients. Increasingly, however, variable matching is prescribed to allow for differences in the relative fiscal capacities of
the states by raising the matching requirements for prosperous states and

lowering it for poor ones. In the hospital construction program, for example, the high-income states are required to put up $2 for every federal dollar received; whereas those with a low average income have to put up only $1 for every two federal dollars.

The apportionment and matching rules work together, at least in congressional intent, to make the terms of some federal aid programs more generous for jurisdictions with relatively large needs and small resources, and vice versa. In their absence, the needed matching funds would require a greater tax effort in the poorer than in the richer states.

In structuring grant programs no overt effort is made to ascertain whether inadequate state-local performance has been the result of indifference or fiscal inability, although the more generous matching provisions of recent enactments may reflect a growing concern with both. It merits underscoring that, apart from rare exceptions (such as, for example, an emergency measure for the relief of flood damage, and the new elementary and secondary education funds geared to poverty) federal grants, unlike those in some other federal systems, are not intended to help some states or cities because they are relatively poor but rather to persuade all of them to devote more resources to the activity of interest to Congress. It matters not that, in the process, another governmental activity may be shortchanged because funds are diverted to take up an available federal grant.

A conspicuous case in point is the welfare program. Because federal public assistance grants are available to assist the needy aged, blind, physically handicapped, and families with dependent children, in many states expenditures for these services are far more generous than those for the poor who cannot qualify for one of the aided categories. The fact that federal aid is always conditioned on its use for a specified purpose is the focus of the current debate surrounding proposals for the introduction of general purpose aid through revenue sharing or other means.

Another characteristic of the federal grant system is that Congress holds itself accountable to its constituents for the use made of their federal tax dollars by insisting on an "adequate" expenditure standard. This is another characteristic of federal grants that has been criticized with increasing frequency and unanimity.

THE NUMBER OF GRANTS HAS MULTIPLIED

The grant system is under fire, and among its most vociferous critics are the grant recipients themselves—the state and local governments. They would like more freedom in their use of federal funds, with fewer federal controls and less exacting reporting requirements. Spokesmen for federal executive agencies and some members of Congress support them in this.

Some of the criticism centers on the mere increase in the number of different grants—their proliferation in numbers. Much is made of the fact that the number of separate authorizations is around 400, including several for identical or very similar purposes, each with its separate ground rules, and some administered by competing agencies. The Advisory Commission on Intergovernmental Relations was recently prompted to find that "in terms of manageability, at least, the law of diminishing returns applies to the steady proliferation of federal categorical grants." It is alleged that the typical local or state official is confused and uncertain as to what grants are available, who administers them, what are the requirements of each, how closely related grants differ, and ways to make effective applications. The larger, better staffed states and cities are said to have the upper hand in winning grants because they have acquired the skills of "grantsmanship." The smaller ones are dependent on a newly spawned breed of consultants who, for a fee, help the grant applicant through the maze of bureaucratic procedures which must be mastered by those who would see a grant application to a successful conclusion.

The problems posed by the multiplicity of grants have brought forth proposals to consolidate groups of related programs. This would leave the recipient states and cities more latitude in deciding how they can use the federal funds to best advantage. The idea has begun to gain congressional acceptance. A striking illustration of its application is the Partnership in Health program legislation enacted in 1966 and in 1967. It consolidated some twenty separate health grants (TB, cancer, heart, venereal disease, and so on) and established a single set of requirements, a single authorization, and a single appropriation for the group. This leaves governors with more freedom to apportion the funds among the several health programs on the basis of their respective priorities.

Grant consolidation is not welcomed by the patrons of the individual programs that lose some of their identity. Those who have worked to persuade Congress to appropriate funds for one or another vocational educational program prefer not to surrender the identity of "their" funds and to leave their cause to the judgments of fifty different state administrations.

In view of the opposition of politically important groups, the prospect for extensive consolidation of grants *by legislation* is not promising. This is the reason the Advisory Commission on Intergovernmental Relations has proposed (and a committee of Congress has concurred) that the President should be authorized to submit grant consolidation proposals to Congress in a procedure similar to that used for administrative reorganization plans. It envisages the development of plans for the consolidation of grants by the Administration. Each plan would be submitted to Congress for its information, to become effective at the end of 90 calendar days, unless either House passed a resolution objecting to it. The commission proposes to cut the number of grant authorizations at least by half. It believes that consolidation of grants relating to vocational education and those for water and sewer line construction deserve priority attention.

EQUALIZATION HAS MADE SLOW PROGRESS

The term equalization has a specialized connotation for the grant-in-aid. It refers to those of its features, and there may be several, which are intended to recognize that some states or some communities need or ought to have more help than others in providing a desirable level of service in the function for which the federal or state grant is being made.

Some governments require more help than others because their needs may be above average or their financial resources below average. The two conditions are likely to exist side by side. Financially weak states generally have relatively many needy residents, and vice versa. Without some recognition of these conditions, the poorer states would be unable to provide the desired minimum standard of service except with an unusually high tax effort. They cannot be expected to do that, particularly in providing services that benefit not only their own citizens but those of the nation as a whole.

There are different degrees of equalization. The most important equalizer in our system is the graduated income tax. It collects the larger part of the federal government's revenues in high income states. Delaware's per capita personal income tax payments to the U. S. Treasury are four times as large as Mississippi's. Furthermore, when these revenues are spent on federal programs they tend to be weighted in favor of the low-income states, because a Mississippi or an Arkansas is likely to have relatively more people who are helped by such programs.

It should be pointed out that where a grant provides for allotments to states on the basis of need, a measure of equalization automatically results since the states with the greatest number of needy cases receive relatively the largest grants. This form of equalization has been used for a long time. Thus the grant enacted in 1879 to stimulate the manufacture and distribution of instructional materials to the blind was and continues to be allocated to the states according to the number of persons in public institutions for the education of the blind.

We are familar with a special version of equalization in the concept of the needs test in some relief programs. A calculation is made of the family's need for subsistence and of its own resources available for meeting that need. The deficiency, if any, serves as a limit on the amount supplied from relief funds. Some federal governments, notably Australia and Canada, follow this approach in providing general financial aid to their poorer states. Any suggestions that it be used here for general aid would probably arouse a storm, perhaps even from the poorest states.

American federalism has traditionally rejected the notion that the national government has a residual obligation for the support of state and local government. It uses federal aid to encourage the state to spend more on a particular activity; but the state is always free to reject the funds, as some have.

American federalism rejects also the notion of a uniform level of service in every state. It lays great store by each state's right to set its own expenditure levels for particular programs. These inequalities among the states, even when occasioned by unequal fiscal resources and not a result of free choice alone, are treasured as the hallmark of local self-determination—provided only that they are not incompatible in an important way with essential national objectives. The difference between this system and a centralized system, where the national government determines the level of government service in all parts of the country and finances it from the proceeds of nationwide taxes, is a difference Americans lay great store by.

Some go so far as to entirely reject the concept of equalization. In their view, the provision of governmental services is the responsibility of the state. It has the obligation to provide services at the level the citizens want and are willing to finance without regard to what Congress believes to be desirable.

Critics of equalization argue that federal grants tend to perpetuate uneconomic use and location of resources; for example, that a grant for the relief of an economically depressed area tends to dissuade the needy from picking up roots in search of a livelihood elsewhere. It is also argued that equalization raises the share of federal funds so high in some states that it undermines interest in efficiency and economy. They maintain that the gap between low- and high-income states is narrowing, and the need for fiscal equalization is disappearing. It is said, too, that high-income states contribute relatively more to the support of the federal government through the income tax than the others, and that equalization in federal grants only compounds an inequity.

This line of argument probably explains the relatively small amount of equalization in the federal grant system in past years. Indeed, it wasn't until the middle 1930's, when the Social Security program was enacted, that an explicit move was made toward equalization. It provided for the distribution of some funds for general public health grants, and grants for maternal and child-health services, on the basis of financial need. Up to that time—except for emergency relief programs—grants were apportioned either as a flat sum to each state or on the basis of relative state population (except for highways). All states were required to match the federal grants on a dollar-for-dollar basis.

BUT EQUALIZATION IS DIFFICULT

Increasingly recent Congresses have been disposed to prescribe some measure of explicit equalization. An equalizing grant typically provides that the appropriated funds be allotted among the eligible jurisdictions in proportion to program need as measured by total population or the relevant population group, such as children of school age or people over 65. It may provide, further, that the allotment be modified to reflect differences in the states' fiscal capabilities. The matching requirements may also vary with financial ability. In a sense, the larger the state's relative allotment in recognition of its above-average need, the greater the case for varying the matching requirement in its favor, because the relative tax effort required to take up the allotment is greater.

It should be emphasized that even in equalizing grants, the scope of equalization is quite limited; only a partial allowance is made for differences among states. Since the level of personal income in the poorest state is less than half the average in the richest state, thoroughgoing equalization would almost imply that the entire cost of the governmental service in the poorest state be covered from grant funds. If the poor state did not tax itself at all, the average income of its population would still be strikingly lower than the after-tax income in the rich state.

Because the scope of equalization in the grant system has been limited, it has not been urgent to develop meaningful measures of state and local needs, financial resources, or tax efforts. Congress generally uses average personal income as a proxy for financial ability. This is not a wholly satisfactory measure. A dollar of personal income in the heart of a large city is significantly less real income than in a rural area or in an out-of-the-way small town. Moreover, personal income ignores significant differences in the cost of providing governmental services and does not directly measure the ability to raise revenues through property and consumer taxes on which most local and state governments depend.

The states also use equalization in some of their grant programs, particularly those for education. Conceptually, equalization raises less difficult problems for them than for the federal government. Since the states create local governments, determine their taxing powers, and charge them with certain responsibilities, they are obliged to make certain that local governments are capable of discharging these responsibilities. It is not illogical, for example, for states to relate their education aid to variations in the amount of taxable property available per child in each school district.

In addition to the federal grants to states, substantial federal aid is distributed directly to local jurisdictions. Presumably, some recognition should be given in these programs to differences in relative local needs and resources. This, however, raises a formidable measurement problem. Local jurisdictions function under 50 different state systems, comparable statistical data are very limited, and dealing evenhandedly with thousands of dissimilar communities will test the objectivity of even the most analytically inclined federal administrator.

chapter 22

federal credit
for income taxes
paid to states

The tax credit is the most effective instrument available to the federal government for helping states, and available to states for helping local governments to levy new taxes. In effect, it is a device by which a national or a state government invites lower-level governments to divert part of its tax revenue to their own treasuries.

THE TAX CREDIT HAS PROVED ITSELF

The original tax credit was the invention of necessity to meet the problems of people who receive income from other countries. When it enacted its income tax in 1913, the federal government undertook to tax people on all their income from whatever source. Those with income from abroad are generally taxed also by the foreign government. In these situations, double taxation of the same income would result if special provision were not made to prevent it. The tax credit was invented to do just that. Double taxation is prevented by allowing the American taxpayer to take a credit for the taxes paid to the foreign government against tax otherwise payable to the United States. He pays all or part of his U. S. tax with receipts for taxes he paid abroad.

The tax credit used in this way is a device for recognizing that the foreign country in which the income originates has the prior tax claim to it. It leaves the foreign government free to tax that income even when the recipient is an American, secure in the knowledge that so long as the foreign tax is not heavier than the American tax it is not adding to the American's total tax burden, since he can use his foreign tax receipts to pay his U. S. tax.

The states use the income tax credit in much the same way. They generally tax their residents on their income from home and out-of-state sources and credit them for taxes preempted by other states. In some situations, the other state gives a credit for taxes paid by the income recipient to his home state. The intention in either case is to minimize the likelihood of double taxation.

In 1935, when the unemployment insurance system was devised and it was decided to operate through separate state programs rather than one national program, the technique of the credit was used again; this time on a state-federal basis to induce the states to join the system. This was accomplished by levying a 3 percent federal payroll tax, and by allowing 2.7 percent of that tax liability to be discharged with receipts for state unemployment taxes. The states, in other words, were left with no alternative but to join the insurance system, for employers within their borders would have had to pay the tax in any event—if not to the state, then to the federal government.

This is comparable to the way the credit is used in the inheritance-estate tax field. There the credit is employed to make it unprofitable for states that try to attract wealthy people to reduce their death taxes below a certain point.

State use of the credit in state-local relations is well illustrated by the Florida cigarette tax. When that state had a 5-cent per package cigarette tax (now 15 cents) it allowed a credit for local cigarette taxes up to 5 cents. The objective was to enable local governments to levy cigarette taxes without danger of tax competition among them. As might have been expected, every county in Florida levied the 5-cent cigarette tax.

IT HOLDS PROMISE IN STATE INCOME TAXATION

Our present interest in the tax credit centers on its usefulness in encouraging the enactment of state income taxes. A substantial body of informed opinion favors this objective for a variety of reasons. It would provide the states with additional revenue they urgently need; and, what is perhaps even more important, it would provide them with a tax source that responds well to economic growth. Income tax collections generally increase faster than the economy, and therefore keep at least partial pace with growth in state expenditures.

Those troubled with the widening fiscal disparity between the old city centers and the new industrial and residential suburbs, and among rich and poor suburbs, see an urgent need for deploying some of the suburban fiscal capability to help finance central city and area-wide needs. Revenues generated by state income taxes, if channeled into social programs, would facilitate this objective because the large health and welfare expenditures are in the old cities.

Effective income taxes would provide the states with an efficient vehicle for relieving the adverse impact of retail sales and real property taxes on low-income families. In the absence of income taxes, the states that want to help these groups are obliged to employ such costly relief measures as exempting all food from sales taxes and the homes of older citizens and other hardship residents from real property taxes. The states could realize these objectives more economically and effectively through tax credits and refunds under broadly based income taxes, as demonstrated by states such as Indiana and Wisconsin.

The nation's tax burden distribution would be improved if effective state income taxation obviated the need for some further increases in sales and property taxes. In many areas, both property and sales tax rates have been raised to a point where there is strong public resistance to further increases even for the purpose of financing critical needs.

More effective and widespread state income taxation would improve also the states' case for a share of federal revenue, as proposed by various revenue-sharing plans. The failure of so many high-income industrial states to make effective use of their own resources, notably by foregoing the revenue potential of the income tax, is a telling argument against the federal government sharing its income tax collections with them.

IS STATE INCOME TAXATION DESIRABLE?

Before examining the income tax credit in greater detail it should be made clear that the desirability of encouraging income taxation at the state level is not an open-and-shut question. Indeed, if we had the privilege of drawing a new blueprint for a federal system in the light of present day conditions, the case would be strong for a grand design that would enable the states to finance their obligations without the income tax and leave this source for exclusive national government use.

The fairest and most productive of revenue producers is also an effective and essential instrument of national social and economic policy. In view of vast revenue demands for national defense, foreign aid, and domestic programs, and the potency of the income tax on behalf of economic and social policies, it would be well if the federal government were free to use the income tax unhindered. It is today hampered in doing so because two-thirds of the states also impose income taxes.

Although some of these states have only token taxes, a few employ substantial tax rates, and the national government must necessarily proceed as if the situation in the states with the heaviest tax rates prevailed also in all the other states. This is so, because federal tax rates must be uniform across the land and there is always a political limit to the combined federal-state tax burden. A comparable situation in Canada, it will be recalled, obliged the national government to lease the states' income tax rights in order to permit effective national use of the income tax for financing World War II needs.

The case for limiting income taxation to the national government is supported also by the limited taxing jurisdiction of the states and by the desire to minimize duplicate tax enforcement. It goes without saying, of course, that if the states had to function without income taxes, they would have to be relieved of an appropriate share of their financing obligations.

In point of fact, a few states already derive a large part of their tax revenue from this source and probably will continue to do so. The practicable course of action, therefore, is to encourage the other states to make more effective use of income taxes. It is obvious that the more uniform the fifty state taxes, the greater the national government's opportunity to build its own tax on top of the states' taxes—with a minimum loss of efficiency and productivity.

HOW A TAX CREDIT COULD WORK

A federal income tax credit for income taxes paid to states could be constructed in various ways. The Advisory Commission on Intergovernmental Relations has suggested that the credit be offered as an alternative to the deductibility of state income taxes from federally taxed income. The federal taxpayer could either deduct state income taxes in arriving at taxable income, as at present, or deduct a part of his state payment from his federal income tax bill.

In this form it would be of no interest to taxpayers in the higher brackets, who would obviously prefer deductibility so long as the maximum federal tax rate applicable to them exceeded the rate of the credit. A tax credit for 40 percent of taxes paid to states would have no appeal for a taxpayer in the 60-percent tax bracket, for whom a deduction of the state tax from income is equivalent to a 60-percent credit. The credit would be attractive, however, to the vast majority of taxpayers who employ the standard deduction, or itemize their deductions, but are subject to the lower ranges of the tax rate schedules.

Under a plan advanced by the Committee for Economic Development, the credit would supplement deductibility. It would be calculated at a uniform 25 percent of the net cost (after the tax value of the federal deduction) of the state income tax. The net cost of the state income tax to a federal taxpayer in the 28-percent bracket, for example, is 72 percent, because the deduction reduces each dollar of federal tax by 28 cents. Consequently his tax credit under the CED plan would be one-fourth of 72 percent, or 18 percent of his state income tax payment.

HOW IT WOULD HELP THE STATES

Either of these forms of the credit would help states only to the extent that they were willing to claim for themselves, through increased state taxes, the benefits provided for their taxpayers by the federal credit. This is so because the credit goes to the taxpayer and not to the state. If the state itself did nothing, the credit would only serve to reduce the tax liability of people in states that already had income taxes. It would, however, help states without income taxes to enact them, and would help those with relatively low rates to increase them. It would be of no help to states with relatively heavy income taxes.

To help states with relatively high income taxes, the credit would have to be made conditional on those states increasing their taxes above present levels. This would be subject to a twofold criticism: that Congress is coercing the states, and that it would preserve existing differentials between low and high tax rate states. These interstate differences are now very substantial among some states and are a disruptive influence in economic and business decision-making. In the $10,000 bracket, for example, the Missouri rate is 4 percent and the Minnesota rate 10 percent.

It would be possible to design a tax credit to avoid these consequences by routing its revenue yield directly to state governments and not to taxpayers, as both the ACIR and CED proposals contemplate. Such a credit could vary in accordance with a state's own income tax effort. One possible criterion is tax collections as a percentage of the personal income of the residents of the state. Another is the ratio of state to federal income tax collections. The federal government, for example, might credit the state with $5 per capita for each 1 percent of the people's personal income the state itself takes in personal income taxes. When state collections average 2 percent of personal income, the state would receive $10 per capita. Thus a state with a population of 10 million and with income tax collections equivalent to 2 percent of personal income would be entitled to a grant of

$100 million ($10,000,000 \times \$5 \times 2$). In this kind of formulation, poor states would have to raise relatively fewer dollars through their own taxes than those where incomes are high. They would fare better than under a dollar-for-dollar matching arrangement. Moreover, a per capita basis related to total population would introduce a significant equalization factor on behalf of states with a relatively small proportion of taxable individuals.

If this kind of credit resulted in fifty state income taxes, the federal cost of a $5 credit per capita would approximate $1 billion for each 1 percent of effective state rate. If such a credit persuaded the states in the aggregate to double their present income tax collections, the cost to the U. S. Treasury would be about $2 billion.

Under this plan, states with relatively high income tax rates would immediately qualify for relatively large credits. The other states would be encouraged to raise their rates; and if the device included a maximum limitation, above which the states would not receive additional credits, the long-term tendency would be for state tax rates to stabilize at approximately the ceiling level with corresponding elimination of present-day interstate tax rate differentials.

In any of its forms, the federal credit for state income taxes would involve a loss of federal revenue. Its acceptability, therefore, hinges on a balancing of the states' case for more federal aid and the federal government's case for conserving its dollars.

chapter 23

state sharing
in federal revenues

There is widespread concern with the proliferation of federal grants reserved for specifically defined purposes in the face of the state and local governments' need for general-purpose, unrestricted revenue. This has directed attention to the case for general-purpose federal financial aids. These would be distributed to state and local governments to be used and handled much as the funds they themselves raise, subject only to some generally applicable safeguards. A version of this idea that attracts wide attention is the suggestion that the federal government share some of its income tax collections. Conference programs and periodicals provide space for it, governors and mayors daydream about it, candidates for public office endorse it, economists debate it, Congress has had dozens of bills on it, and its committees have taken testimony on it. Rarely has a government finance idea generated so much dialogue so quickly.

The state-local revenue dilemma is perplexing to many, and the thought that federal revenue sharing might provide even the beginnings of an answer understandably intrigues them.

THE IDEA HAD AN INTERESTING BEGINNING

The suggestion that the federal government divide some of its income tax collections among the state and local governments on a continuing basis first attracted wide public notice when it was advanced in 1964 by Walter Heller, the then Chairman of the President's Council of Economic Advisers. It was subsequently examined in depth by a Presidential task force chaired by Joseph Pechman of the Brookings Institution. This is the reason why it is frequently cited as the Heller-Pechman plan.

In its original formulation, revenue sharing was advanced as a partial alternative to future federal tax reduction. Earlier in 1964, it will be recalled, federal income taxes were cut by about 20 percent, even though the budget was still unbalanced, because the Administration was fearful that the fiscal drag would threaten continued economic growth. The economy at that time had enjoyed several years of uninterrupted expansion, and economists were apprehensive that the strong revenue response of the highly graduated federal income tax would siphon tax dollars out of the income stream faster than the government was likely to spend them and this would be a drag on the economy. The stimulation to economic activity resulting from the tax cut, it was believed, would quickly produce new revenue to compensate for the reduction in tax rates—a prediction subsequently proved right.

It was then confidently expected that, in the absence of a defense emergency or massive new federal responsibilities, further tax reduction would be in order in another couple of years. Heller offered his revenue sharing proposal as a possible alternative for part of future tax reductions. Although concern with future federal tax reduction lost its urgency as a result of Vietnam-generated defense costs and the backlog of urgent social program requirements, the revenue sharing proposal need not be considered in that context alone.

The practice of a central government sharing its tax collections with its political subdivisions is widely used and accepted. In this country, states often share the proceeds of specific taxes with their local governments. It would be a departure, however, in established federal-state arrangements. The division of an embarrassingly large federal surplus among the states under the Andrew Jackson administration one hundred and fifty years ago did not have happy results. The use some states made of funds left much to be desired, and the sharing was never repeated. The federal government now distributes among Western states a share of mineral royalties and grazing rights collected on public lands within their borders; but these, among others, are special arrangements that compensate these particular governments for restrictions placed on their taxing rights within federal enclaves. Other federal systems, notably Canada and Australia, share national taxes with their states, a practice explained by their respective fiscal histories.

HOW REVENUE SHARING MIGHT WORK

The detailed mechanics of the revenue sharing proposal, as developed in 1964 by the Presidential task force, have never officially been made public. The essentials of the plan, however, are known to be as follows:

1. A special trust fund would be created for the states much like the existing highway, unemployment, and social security trust funds.
2. A share of the federal income tax collections would be deposited regularly in the trust fund. Its amount would be calculated as a specified percentage, say 2 percent of total taxable personal income. Taxable income for the nation now exceeds $300 billion and is increasing about 8 to 10 percent a year. This is the amount, after all deductions and exemptions, on which income taxes are actually paid. The purpose of basing the amount to be shared on taxable income and not tax collections is to make it independent of future federal tax rate changes.
3. The trust fund would make annual or quarterly distributions to the states. These distributions would presumably be somewhat less than annual receipts, to permit the accumulation of a working balance to allow for possible declines in federal tax collections and for other contingencies.
4. The states would share in the fund in proportion to their population, although a small share of the fund could be reserved for supplemental payments to the poorer states. Most of the fund would be distributed in proportion to population, in recognition of the fact that the populous industrial states contain the large concentrations of disadvantaged peoples and social program needs.
5. Each state would share its federal distribution with its local governments, presumably on the basis of some acceptable measure of state-local needs.
6. The state and local governments would be free to use their shares for general government purposes and with fewer constraints than generally apply to present federal grants, which are always reserved for specified functions.

SEVERAL POINTS ARE IN CONTROVERSY

Although the revenue sharing proposal was advanced as recently as 1964, it has attracted an unusually large number of supporters as well as detractors—larger than can be attributed to an exceptionally articulate and persuasive sponsor and a seeming Presidential endorsement during the 1964 campaign.

The basic case for revenue sharing, advanced by Heller and articulated by the governors, is that the states need it and would make good use of it. Although state and local expenditures have been increasing about twice as fast as federal expenditures for domestic programs, and have already entailed sizable tax increases and new tax enactments, the level of service provided in many places is inadequate and some needs are totally unmet. The backlog of unsatisfied state-local needs is growing year by year, but public resistance to further tax increases is becoming progressively more compelling politically.

Friends of revenue sharing also argue that it is to the self-interest of the national government to help resolve the fiscal crisis of the states. Since most civilian government activity is a state-local responsibility, the federal government cannot hope to realize its national policy objectives unless state and local governments are able to finance adequate government programs. The realization of national government policy objectives in public education, antipoverty, equal opportunity, economic growth, and even foreign policy, are contingent on adequate local and state financing. Economic growth, for example, depends on the availability of municipal facilities to satisfy businesses' expanding needs, and foreign policy objectives can be furthered only if the image of Americans at home is more appealing to the uncommitted peoples in Asia and Africa than the face of communism.

National policy objectives would be advanced also by the substitution of federal income tax dollars for more state-local dollars raised through consumer and property taxes. The combination of state and local consumer and property tax rate increases and the federal income tax decreases from 1963 to 1965 has shifted the pattern of tax burden distribution in favor of the upper-income groups and to the disadvantage of the lower- and middle-income groups. This conflicts with America's concept of tax fairness and with the nation's antipoverty policy objectives.

Supporters of revenue sharing argue further that the federal government can afford it. Continuing economic growth inevitably will increase federal tax collections faster than expenditures, except during a war emergency.

The critics, including some federal administrators, disagree. They contend that the federal government's unfulfilled commitments in its social and economic programs will require all the monies generated by economic prosperity, and more. Some contend that states have the revenue resources and lack only the will to use them. They point particularly to the ineffective use of income taxes in most states and to the nationwide maladministration of property taxes. Those who lobbied for existing federal grant programs and those who have not as yet succeeded are fearful that the distribution of federal general purpose funds to the states would inevitably reduce the richness of their own programs.

As the number of functional grants has multiplied and matching requirements were made progressively more favorable for the states, they have had a tendency to preempt available state funds, reducing state legislative and administrative budgetary latitude and flexibility. For this reason, advocates of revenue sharing argue, states should be given some federal aid with few restrictions. They will inevitably deploy these funds where the needs are greatest, because state legislators are subject to the same political pressures as those that converge on Congress.

In order to distinguish between the categorical grants available only for specific functions and revenue sharing for governmental purposes in general, Heller suggested that no strings be attached to the functional use made of these funds. Much of the criticism of the plan centers on this feature.

Some critics read the "no strings attached" designation as an invitation to substitute federal money for state and local tax increases; possibly even to invite tax reduction. They underestimate the size of the revenue gaps. Others see it as potential license for governors and state legislatures to play fast and loose with federal dollars. They argue that federal dollars would be used less effectively than the dollars raised by state-local governments themselves. This is the "easy come, easy go" argument. But if it has any validity, it applies more to special purpose grants than to general purpose grants. The opportunity to obtain 70 percent or even 90 percent federal matching money doubtless encourages states or local governments to dig up the remaining 30 or 10 percent for a program they would not undertake on their own initiative alone. In this case, federal dollars passed up are dollars lost. In contrast, general purpose grants are promptly commingled with locally raised dollars; and neither governing board members nor line administrators have any way of knowing whether they are spending federal or local dollars. In any event, the compelling consideration in the minds of political leaders is to avoid tax increases. Therefore, so long as federal grants are insufficient to remove the need for tax increases altogether, public officials will try to conserve every dollar, whatever its genesis, to keep tax increases to a minimum.

THE CITIES WANT A SAY

Some spokesmen for the cities have been negative toward revenue sharing proposals—largely out of concern for the treatment they might receive from state legislatures. Cities generally are critical of the antiurban bias of the legislatures, and with good reason. They have reacted adversely to the earmarking of federal funds for the states. Subsequent discussion has recognized the validity of the concern that cities have to be assured of their share in any revenue sharing. Congress can be expected to insist on it. Having established their point, the city spokesmen are turning their attention to ways that would best assure this result.

Granting that the states would be required to share their general purpose grants with their political subdivisions, we face the question: On what basis? It is a difficult question, because the division of responsibility for spending programs between the state and its local governments varies widely among the states.

The fund could be shared in proportion to state-local tax collections or expenditures for general government purposes, excluding trust fund and utility-type operations. Since local governments have unequal needs and resources, and these are reflected in tax and expenditure levels, sharing on these bases may tend to freeze existing differentials.

Variations in needs and resources would be difficult to take into account because there is no agreement on how these should be measured; and, in any event, the necessary data are unavailable on a jurisdiction-by-jurisdiction basis. The report of the National Commission on Urban Problems contained suggestions for dealing with this problem.

Population as a criterion would not satisfy the cities because governmental costs tend to increase with density of population. The number of families with substandard incomes is another possibility, but only if it can be adjusted for variations in the cost of living and the cost of providing governmental services—items that vary importantly between urban and rural communities and between urban communities of different size.

Enough has been said to illustrate that proposals for state-local sharing in the federal revenues pose complex procedural problems.

DIVIDING UP THE LOCAL SHARE

In allocating the local share among the political subdivisions of each, the need for equalization is perhaps even greater than in the interstate allocation, for variations in needs and resources are extremely wide. The old industrial centers have the heavy needs, while their resources, at least on a relative basis, are diminishing. Therefore, to make the most effective use of the funds, a high proportion should be reserved for the older cities.

As between the cities and the suburbs, public school expenditures are higher in the suburbs, and the reverse is true with regard to noneducational expenditures. Either friends of schools are politically less influential in the city centers, or the noneducational needs are so costly and compelling that they preempt a larger share of the available revenues. A distribution on the basis of noneducational expenditures, therefore, would favor the cities. If noneducational expenditures were chosen, an index related to the welfare load such as public assistance expenditures or aid to dependent children could be used.

LEGISLATIVE PROSPECTS ARE IMPROVING

Whatever the merits of revenue sharing, its advocates made little legislative progress before 1969. However, a new national administration has taken over in Washington, and the President is on record as favoring revenue sharing. But important hurdles remain to be overcome.

Congressmen react to appropriation proposals on the basis of the merits of each spending program. Each congressman has pet expenditure projects that remain unrealized. He also is reluctant to dissipate an opportunity to vote tax rate reduction. Few would view with enthusiasm a plan to turn federal funds over to governors and state legislators so that these officials might choose the object of expenditure or divert the funds into politically appealing state and local tax reductions.

In any event, the Congressional interpretation of "no strings attached" is not easily reconciled with the interpretation of the governors and mayors. The issue of "federal control" will have to be confronted and compromised. At a time when the electorate has exhibited a conspicuous tendency to judge governors on the basis of their position on tax issues, it may be looking for too much altruism from senators to expect them to be enthusiastic about a program that would help build governors into potential competitors for their seats. However, the revenue sharing idea has popular appeal, and it would not come as a surprise if a strong Presidential recommendation, embodying a formula for state-local sharing acceptable to spokesmen for the cities, sufficed to carry the day. Neither will it be surprising if enactment of revenue sharing is followed by some disappointments, at least in the early years, because such sums as the national administration would be willing to allocate to it, irrespective of budgetary conditions, will not give financially hard-pressed state and local governments the relief they hope for.

part V

COMING TO TERMS

chapter **24**

coming to terms

The preceding chapters focused on ways of increasing state and local governments' revenue resources. These governments' need for increased revenues was taken for granted, if only because during most of our lifetime the story of state and local finances has been one of trying to make do with too few dollars: cities and towns contending with under-manned police forces, infrequent trash collections, broken curbs and sidewalks, understaffed institutions, schools and colleges making do with too few teachers, inadequate pay scales, and overcrowded, obsolete, poorly maintained class-rooms.

In rich and poor places, in small and large communities, and in new towns and old towns, performance has typically lagged behind needs and goals, short-run expediency has prevailed over long-term objectives, and principles have had to yield to political realities. Diligent search, no doubt, would uncover exceptions to this generalization as to every other. However, fiscal ease has been rare in state and local experience except in the midst of a total war, when labor and material shortages have enforced abstinence.

The past, moreover, is but a foretaste of what lies ahead. Public service needs are likely to become progressively more demanding as the nation continues to grow and pros-per. The reasons have been identified over and over again.

195

The monthly increase in population is approaching 200,000; Americans live longer and retire earlier, thus adding to the dependent age groups; people concentrate more and more in and around cities where government must do more things for them, and each public operation is costlier; continuing prosperity is whetting the public's appetite for more and better public services; business firms need improved community services to grow and to hold their own against ever keener competition; political leaders, regardless of party or government affiliation, promise social reforms and stimulate the expectations of the less privileged; and organized demands for larger shares in national prosperity have reached a militancy new in the American experience.

The impact of these influences on the revenue requirements of state and local government is reflected in about a 10 percent average yearly increase in their expenditures, not to mention the needs that are left wanting. It is reflected in the more than fourfold increase in their annual spending level from less than $18 billion to $100 billion in the last twenty years.

NEEDS GROW FASTER THAN REVENUES

Some increase in public spending can be taken in stride with the aid of a growing economy, because economic growth generates revenues at existing tax rates. Unhappily, it does not generate enough directly to state and local governments.

In recent years, each 5 percent increase in the production of goods and services has tended to be accompanied by nearly a 10 percent increase in state and local expenditures. Tax collections, excluding new taxes and rate increases, grew only at about half this rate. The other half of expenditure increases, except for the part covered by increased federal aid, required new tax measures, and each such increase made the next one even more elusive.

The revenue responsiveness of tax systems to economic growth depends on the kind of taxes on which these systems rely. Over three-quarters of all state and local tax revenues come from consumer and property taxes, and the response of these taxes to increased economic activity is sluggish. As people's incomes rise, they tend to devote a declining share to taxable consumer expenditures. In consequence, consumer tax receipts do not increase proportionately. The response of the property tax to economic growth also tends to be less than proportional, although in recent years new construction and rising property values have helped property taxes to put in a fair performance.

Only the personal income tax, as federal experience has made clear for some years, has a growth potential even approaching that of public spending. Its revenue yield grows more than half again as fast as the economy. As income levels rise, people with very low incomes move into taxable brackets, and those in the lower tax-rate brackets into the adjoining higher brackets. Rate differences in state income taxes between adjoining brackets typically represent a substantial increase in percentage terms. A shift from a 2 percent to a 4 percent bracket, for example, doubles the tax payable on the portion of income subject to the higher rate. This is the main reason that state income tax collections have increased dramatically in recent years, at a rate even faster than federal collections. However, even after more than doubling their yield since 1963, personal income taxes still provide just over one-tenth of state and local tax revenues; and because these governments use them sparingly, the influence of income taxes on their total financial condition is quite diluted, except for a few states.

This combination—expenditures that grow at nearly double the rate of the economy and taxes that do well to keep pace with it—produces the persistent gap between requirements and resources and the periodic revenue crises that haunt state and local officials. It explains their recurring need for major tax increase measures.

THE PEOPLE COULD AFFORD MORE—IF THEY WOULD

On the face of it, state and local governments' rising revenue needs ought not to cause undue anguish against the backdrop of record prosperity. A nation with a median household income of over $8,000 can afford a fair complement of government services. As employment, production, incomes, and profits increase, people are able to devote a larger share of their resources to the services they want their state and local governments to supply; particularly when the national government's percentage tax-take is not becoming more demanding. It is well to remember that the $82 billion increase in annual state and local spending during the last twenty years was backstopped by a $600-billion growth in the production of goods and services.

The people can afford higher taxes if only they would agree to the need. Instead they have an instinctive aversion to taxes for reasons none of us can be sure about. Public officials interested in political longevity, in electoral support, feel obliged to heed the people's voice and echo their complaints. Thus these essays end as they began, concerned with the people's attitude toward the government of their choice, with their disposition to force shortsighted self-interest policies on their elected officials.

Governors, state legislators, and local governing boards shun tax increases lest they offend the voters and for fear that business will stay away from their jurisdiction and take its installations and jobs elsewhere. When

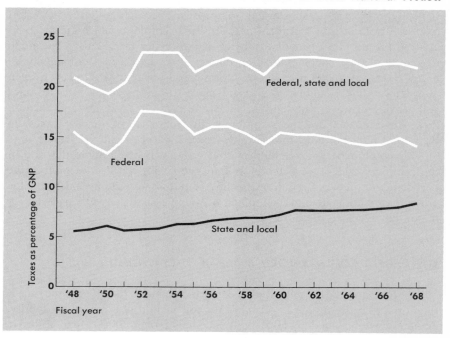

figure 12

Federal and State-Local Taxes, 1948-1968: as Percent of Gross National Product

pressures for additional spending and more revenue can no longer be ignored, these officials resort to revenue measures calculated to minimize political hazards. Moreover, this compulsion, felt by state and local officials, to heed the people's aversion to tax increases grows progressively more controlling with the passing years. As the nation's economy becomes more and more interdependent and competition for business more widespread, as the ratio of public spending to national output rises, and as the voters become more and more sophisticated in carrying their tax views into the voting booths, state and local governments' elbow room in taxation shrinks. Their revenue options become fewer and fewer.

The national government is immune from at least some of the restraints that immobilize state and local governments. Its tax laws operate across the country regardless of state and municipal boundaries and, as the 1964 and 1965 income tax reductions have so well publicized, its budget largely depends on a tax that responds well to economic growth and prosperity. The national government, moreover, is at liberty to finance part of its

figure 13

**Federal Income Tax and State-Local
Sales and Gross Receipts Taxes
as Percent of Personal Income
1948-1968**

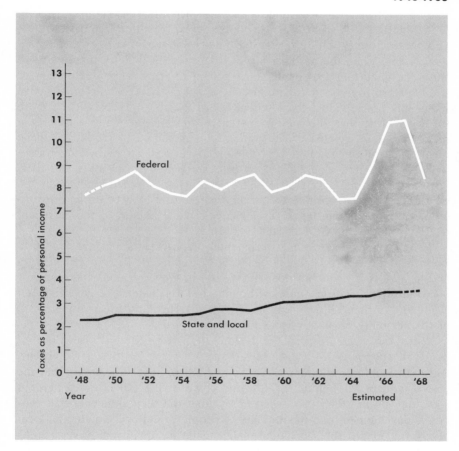

operating costs by credit—an escape from immediate tax increases largely denied state and local governments. The aphorism that national prosperity bestows its cost burdens on state and local government and its revenue dividends on the federal government is close to the mark. It is an elegant way of saying that this federal system's division of spending responsibilities and its division of revenue resources among governments is out of step with the times.

THE SYSTEM NEEDS UPDATING

One surmises that if the Founding Fathers had anticipated the extent of the country's future economic development and its implications for the role of government, they would have designed differently.

A Jefferson who argued for providing each child with a free basic education because the nation's progress depended on it, would not now be content —at a time when the nation's survival depends on it more than ever—to leave the quality of that educational system to the chance distribution of taxable real property among minuscule school districts, or to the subjective judgments of individual local school board members. He would be more likely to insist that the nation guarantee all children ready access to a school program capable of developing their maximum potential to enable them to make an optimum contribution to national strength and productivity. A Hamilton would insist on safeguards to restrain state and local governments from engaging in self-defeating tax competition and in the distribution of tax subsidies to attract business and industry in an effort to influence the location decisions of business undertakings, to the detriment of the productivity of the nation's resources.

The obsolescence of our governmental arrangements and our failure to keep them abreast of changing conditions explains the fiscal plight of state and local governments but does not excuse it. Governmental arrangements —constitutions, statutes, political boundaries, assignments of governmental rights and responsibilities—can be changed, particularly by a people proud of the flexibility of its governmental system.

When the states formed the Union, they retained most functions of domestic government for themselves and for their political subdivisions. They felt secure in retaining these responsibilities, not anticipating that the cost of education, welfare, health, and some of the other services would some day swamp their fiscal systems. Neither did they anticipate that economic development and the mobility of people would bridle state and local taxing freedom at the same time that it made the quality of government's performance critical to the people's continued prosperity. In short, they did not foresee that unrestrained decentralization of governmental responsibility would some day jeopardize the very ends of the Union they were in the process of creating.

We see clearly, with the benefit of all that has gone before, that in this economic and social environment the financing of an adequate complement of public services cannot be left largely to the kind of financial resources within the command of local and state governments, buffeted by the mandates of political expediency and competition for jobs and industry. The fiscal imbalance in the federal system urgently cries out for rectification. The question is: How?

THE FISCAL BALANCE CAN BE ALTERED

Over the years a variety of suggestions have been made to improve the fiscal viability of state and local governments, ranging from relieving their expenditure pressures to fortifying their resources, with special emphasis in recent years on coupling increased financial aid with more local freedom in the deployment of federal aid funds.

If state and local governments' fiscal problems stem from an imbalance between their revenue requirements and their revenue resources, a readjustment in intergovernmental fiscal responsibilities could correct it. These governments, for example, could be relieved of some of their responsibility for public schools, public welfare, or other costly functions.

Over the years some shifts have occurred from local to state government, principally in the welfare functions, and the federal government has assumed some new responsibilities, such as in Social Security, to fill a vacuum that existed because the states had not stepped forward to meet a need that had developed. In general, Americans prefer to leave the responsibility for spending where it is; and when the revenue gap is no longer tolerable, they try to bridge it by shifting financial resources. Even this, however, is accepted only reluctantly, ostensibly out of fear that financial aid will be accompanied by centralizing controls and inefficiency.

Nevertheless, recent years have witnessed significant increases in state financial aid to local governments and in federal aid to state and local governments—and without demonstrable damage to the vitality of the states or their local governments. On the contrary, after a most dramatic growth in federal aid (from 10 to 17 percent of all state-local general revenue in the last ten years) state governments are more aggressive in their independence than at any time in memory. Indeed, on federal initiative, federal aids are being restructured explicitly for the purpose of invigorating state and local leadership and self-reliance. It can be demonstrated, and it has been, that far from undermining the states, federal aid is strengthening them and fortifying their keystone position in the federal system. No longer is it commonplace—as it was forty years ago—to describe state governments as historic vestiges of a simpler era.

If local and state governments could be relieved of the primary responsibility for financing such costly functions as welfare or education, in which the national interest so clearly overshadows the local interest, enough state and local revenue resources would be liberated to enable these governments to cope adequately with the remaining and more clearly local functions. In the process the prospect for decentralized decision making, at least in the local functions, would be improved.

INCREASED FEDERAL SUPPORT OF SCHOOLS IS A POSSIBILITY

A case can be made for materially increasing the federal government's share of the financial responsibility for public education, and, more particularly, for increasing both the state and federal share so that local government is largely freed of this drain on its limited financial resources. Public schools typically preempt half of the local governments' dollars, even though this still leaves vital school needs unsatisfied.

None can quarrel with the political leadership of the early 19th century for its belief that the function of education was ideally suited for local handling. The Americans of that day inhabited relatively isolated communities. Only the venturesome—the pioneers—wandered far afield. The great majority lived out their days and were buried not far from where they were born. In these circumstances the rewards of an exceptional local school effort were enjoyed locally, and the penalties of an indifferent school effort were suffered locally. In those days, moreover, the only important tax source was property. When the states granted local school districts the power to tax property, they in fact provided all children with an approximately equal educational opportunity because property value consisted largely of agricultural land and tended to be distributed in proportion to population. Property was then a good proxy for people's taxpaying ability, and a tax on property could be levied and collected locally without much difficulty.

Conditions have changed drastically since this school finance pattern first emerged. Americans in increasing proportions are continually on the move. Increasingly, the rewards of rich education programs and the penalties of poor ones are visited on communities other than those responsible for them. Weaknesses in school systems anywhere now concern communities everywhere.

The Elementary and Secondary Education Act is an effective vehicle already at hand for increasing material support. Although its present purpose is to supplement and not supplant available school revenues, it is a potential vehicle for federal sharing of a substantial part of the cost of public schools. Congress need only raise the family income and associated criteria on which the count of "disadvantaged" children is based. This is especially true for the older cities where the problem of the disadvantaged child and the inadequacy of municipal resources are particularly acute.

CONGRESS HAS OTHER OPTIONS

The federal government could also assume an increasing share of financial responsibility for education in other ways. It could prescribe, for example, a nationwide foundation program for public education to ensure that, with state participation, every child has equal access to at least a basic educational program and to the services of a qualified and adequately paid classroom teacher. The heart of the school financing problem is the compensation of the instructional staff, for it typically accounts for two-thirds of school budgets.

States could be required to share in the cost of such a foundation program by contributing to it, say, an amount equal to 1 percent of the personal incomes of their residents. Ability to support government is best gauged by the population's income. If, for example, the measure of a national foundation program were fixed at $10,000 a year per teacher for each group of twenty children, approximately 2¼ million teachers would be required at 1969 enrollment levels. It might be desirable to reflect variations in living costs in the salary base and to vary the teacher-pupil ratio to provide children from deprived homes, both rural and urban, with relatively more teacher time.

A program of these dimensions would cost about $22.5 billion. The states' share of the cost of teachers at 1 percent of personal income would approximate $7 billion. The federal cost would be the difference or $15 billion, less the $2.5 billion already provided for public elementary and secondary education.

There would be logic in the federal government accepting the basic responsibility above a uniform state effort for the support of a foundation education program. The national interest in education is paramount. The national government has the superior financial resources and could manage a financial obligation of this scale—an obligation now equal to about one-fourth of one year's increase in the American people's personal income.

The new federal money, phased-in gradually over several years, would support a dramatic improvement in school programs and relieve the pressure on the property tax sufficiently to enable local governments to concentrate more of this tax on governmental functions in which the national interest is less pervasive.

FEDERAL INVOLVEMENT IN LOCAL SCHOOLS
IS RESISTED

Federal involvement in the financing of public education automatically invokes the image of federal control, even though Congress has repeatedly demonstrated both the ability and the determination to design federal aid programs in ways to ensure that local control of the aided function is unimpaired. It has developed techniques for safeguarding the careful handling of federal funds without infringing on local prerogatives. Many school systems have been receiving significant shares of their revenues through federal aid to impacted areas without perceptible diminution of local control over the education program.

Some will allege with emotion that if local governments were relieved of the primary responsibility for financing public schools, they would become less careful with the school dollars. One need not share this concern. Each local governing board would continue to be subjected to pressure from its constituency to improve the quality of its program above the foundation level and to provide adequately for the school system's other needs, including capital plant. This means that school boards would remain dependent on local taxes, and that the political motivation to minimize local tax increases would preserve the incentive to make the most effective use of state and federal dollars. Those receptive to evidence on this point need look only at the experience with existing programs of federal aid for education.

Although federal participation in the financing of public schools is certain to increase in the approaching years, the likelihood is that it will take place indirectly, possibly as a feature of the war on poverty, rather than directly through the forthright adoption of some such approach as a school foundation program.

FEDERAL FINANCING OF WELFARE IS MORE LIKELY

Another possibility is to relieve local and state governments of most of their remaining financing responsibility for the costly welfare functions. (About a $5 billion increase in federal costs is involved.) Here, too, the state and national interest clearly overshadows the local responsibility. Again, revenue resources would be liberated to enable these governments to better cope with the remaining, more clearly local functions. There would then be less need for federal involvement in the less costly local chores, and the cause of true and effective decentralization would be served.

Complete federal financing of the welfare function is being suggested with increasing frequency, most recently by the Advisory Commission on Intergovernmental Relations. Some would abandon the traditional social-service approach to welfare and replace it with a form of income maintenance at federal expense. Its cost has been placed at $10 to $15 billion. Those who would supplement the incomes of the poor through family allowances, negative income taxes, guaranteed minimum incomes, or with some combination of these techniques are motivated by a desire to reduce poverty and simplify welfare administration. Whatever its form, a significant increase in the federal share of the financing of welfare programs would materially ease the expenditure pressures on state and local governments; particularly in the older industrialized sections of the country with relatively large numbers of disadvantaged residents.

REVENUE SHARING IS ANOTHER POSSIBILITY

Increased federal financial aid could be deployed also in other ways. The suggestion that the federal government share its income tax revenues with state and local governments, for example, enjoys strong support. The case for revenue sharing has been put persuasively, and it probably will come; but how quickly is difficult to predict with confidence.

The more ambitious of the revenue sharing plans look forward to an ultimate distribution of an amount equal to 2 percent of the taxable income of federal taxpayers. If this level were reached, say, in four years, it would then add about $7 billion to state and local revenues. In the meanwhile, however, the general expenditures of these governments will have jumped another $30 billion.

The juxtaposition of these two numbers should make clear that revenue sharing on the scale contemplated will help state and local governments but will not eliminate their fiscal problems. A $7-billion share in federal revenues would barely equal even one year's growth in state and local spending. During the four years 1963 to 1967, federal aid also increased by about $7 billion, from $8.6 to $15.5 billion, but it did not eliminate the fiscal squeeze on state and local governments because during these same four years their expenditures had increased by $30 billion.

THERE IS NO SUBSTITUTE FOR STATE AND
LOCAL EFFORT

The implications of these figures should not be ignored. Whatever comes of proposals to increase federal aid—and, hopefully, much will come of them soon—the need for better, more effective local and state financing effort will remain. In 1967, after a most dramatic increase in both state and federal aid, America's cities were still financing three-fourths of their expenditures from locally raised revenues, and state and local governments were still financing over 80 percent of their expenditures by their own fiscal efforts.

It follows that any state and federal help that can be mobilized to improve the effective use of local taxes, and any help the federal government can give the states to improve their tax effectiveness, is as critical to the future fiscal capability of cities as revenue sharing and the other forms of federal financial aid in prospect.

It has been noted at several points in this book that a majority of the states, particularly some of the older industrial states, could materially strengthen both their revenue-raising capability and the quality of their tax structure by effective income taxation. Other states could make more effective use of consumer taxes, but are deterred from doing so by a fear of handicapping their relative competitive position.

THE FEDERAL GOVERNMENT COULD HELP TO CONTAIN TAX COMPETITION

Interlocal and interstate competition for business and for residents is not a new phenomenon. Ways to overcome it are well known.

Over forty years ago, Congress helped the states to halt their potentially destructive inheritance tax competition for wealthy residents by providing a federal estate tax credit to place a floor under the states' inheritance taxes below which competitive tax cutting availed a state nothing.

Ten years later, Congress imposed an unemployment insurance tax with a federal credit for corresponding state taxes to remove tax competition as a deterrent to the financing of a state unemployment insurance system.

In 1956, at the request of state governors, Congress abandoned its plan to vacate the gasoline tax field for state use, and increased the federal tax instead. It was feared that the states would be unable to replace the federal tax with additions to their own taxes. By retaining the federal tax and earmarking for the states the revenue it produced, the states were assured that they would have the funds required to build an improved network of highways.

The tax credit remains a powerful tool for helping state and local governments to overcome their fear of competitive tax disadvantage. Its potential usefulness in helping the states toward more effective income taxation has been urged by the Advisory Commission on Intergovernmental Relations and the Committee for Economic Development. The tax credit has not received the public attention lavished on revenue sharing proposals; but it remains a powerful contender for some of the federal dollars that will become available for increased aid to state and local governments, if it is desired to help these governments to increase their own tax effort.

MORE FEDERAL MONEY IS NOT ENOUGH

The nation's preoccupation with the social problems in both the urban and rural sections of the country and the growing appreciation of local governments' difficulties in financing the continuing pressures for more and better local services are likely to be reflected in further increases in federal financial support, particularly if defense needs taper off or decelerate their rate of increase. Congress has various options in structuring additional federal aid programs. Current discussion appears to be preoccupied with the pros and cons of these alternatives, and a consensus is developing that state and local governments must be afforded more freedom in the use of federal funds: that the present federal grant system does them some disservice by making their management problems more difficult.

State and local governments complain that the sheer number, variety, and complexity of grants make it all but impossible for eligible recipients to be fully aware of what is available, which federal agency administers what program, and what program is best adapted to particular local needs. Officials who lack the "grantsmanship" skills resent that expertise in securing federal grants has become a prerequisite to success in public office. Those preoccupied with national policy objectives in Congress, national commissions, and professional organizations, echo these complaints and support state and local officials' pleas for broader and more general grant categories and for more freedom in the use of federal funds.

The debate surrounding the federal grant delivery system comes at a time when increasing attention is being focused on the urban crisis and on the need for a dynamic national policy to cope with it. The urban crisis, it should be remembered, has developed and continues to fester (among other reasons) because local and state institutions and practices feed the divisiveness and tensions in the country's urban areas and block the mobilization of the local resources required to heal the social and economic ills within them. If increased federal aid relieves the pressure on local political leadership to reconsider their established political ways, it may be helping to perpetuate these divisive practices by subsidizing them. By the same token, it may relieve the pressure on state legislatures to face up to the need for restructuring the arrangements for financing social programs.

This possibility is posed frankly, because no purpose would be served by blinking away the fact that political leadership at both the local and state level is obliged to cater to the pocketbook interests of its constituencies; that it is handicapped in adapting governmental institutions to changing times.

Man's nostalgia for the past, for the comfortable feeling he associates with familiar surrounding, has a dampening influence on public officials with innovative ideas. They are constrained to say the things voters like to hear. And voters' affinities are for the old ways, including the timeworn political clichés.

At a time when the nation is preparing to deploy additional billions of federal taxpayers' dollars to the support of state and local governments, it is auspicious to inquire whether these dollars should be allowed to continue to underwrite practices that nourish and perpetuate weaknesses of the federal system and aggravate the urban crisis and other problems associated with it.

FEDERAL STRINGS COULD BE HELPFUL

To put the proposition affirmatively, the time may be right to consider using the occasion of further increases in federal and state financial aids to help curb state grant-in-aid discrimination against central city schools, fragmentation of local jurisdictions, intercommunity tax competition, anti-social tax practices, and all the other destructive policies practiced in the name of local autonomy to the detriment of national well-being.

Some versions of congressional proposals for state-local sharing in federal income tax revenues would move in this direction. One proposal would condition eligibility to a share in federal revenues on the adoption of an approved state plan for modernizing state and local government. The use of federal grants to nudge state and local governments toward desired goals would not be a departure from established practice.

Most federal grants now on the statute books came into being explicitly for the purpose of encouraging, inducing, and even obliging state and local governments to move in directions which Congress determined to be in the national interest. Interlocal comity to defuse urban crises and to increase the effectiveness of public policies, and affirmative state policies to foster this objective, are very much in the national interest; and Congress has declared them to be so on numerous occasions.

The grant-in-aid, as was demonstrated over and over, is one of the effective instruments for moving state governments in desired directions by providing them with incentives to strive for desired goals. We should not hesitate to exploit its potential, for example, for helping local and state governments to fiscal strength and independence by repairing their own revenue systems and improving their local government structures.

The conditioning of financial aids on such requirements is easier in state-local than in federal-state or in federal-local relations. Local governments are creatures of the state, and state involvement in their administrative and economic practices does not generate the emotionalism that so often bars the application of effective lubricants to federal-state friction points. The strategy indicated for Congress is to operate on local governments through the states to an extent that is practicable.

The nation's stake in improving the effectiveness of state and local government cannot continue to be forfeited in order to indulge those who see in every piece of new legislation a conspiracy to undermine state independence and to nourish centralization. There is no escaping state and local governments' inability, if left to their own resources, to alter their established ways. There is no escaping the fact that this political system tends to reward those leaders who practice divisiveness and to banish those who eschew it.

Local leadership will not appreciate being told that it cannot be expected to improve its ways, unless forced to do so as the condition of state financial aid. State leadership will not welcome comparable "coercion" by the federal government. The conventional wisdom runs precisely in the opposite direction: that the strings of state aid and federal grants should be cut. It is incontrovertible, however, that the unprecedented recent increases in federal aid and in state aid have produced no appreciable improvement in the viability of our governmental arrangements and cannot be expected to do so automatically.

It avails little to lecture central cities and their suburbs that they must pool resources and make common cause in providing uniformly good quality service to all area residents out of their collective resources. The political leaders of middle-income white suburbs cannot take the lead and espouse sharing the burdens of central cities overcrowded with underprivileged minorities.

It avails little to exhort state legislators representing urban, suburban, and rural constituents to make common cause in strengthening the finances of a state so that it might be more responsive to the needs of its less affluent communities. The political process obliges each legislator to espouse the best terms of trade for his own voters.

It avails little to lecture the states that they make common cause with one another to curb interstate tax competition and to speed congressional responsiveness to their revenue needs. A popularly elected governor, constantly in fear of losing ground to his competitor, is not free to forego short-run local advantage in the cause of the long-run national advantage.

There is overwhelming evidence that local leadership cannot and will not abandon the conventional pursuit of local self-interest—the attitude of voters being what it is—unless sheltered by the protective umbrella of the state, and that state leadership cannot break with the past without the protective umbrella of the national government.

It is no compliment to popular democracies to end with the conclusion that the people's prospects for sound public policies improve with the distance between voters and their elected representatives. Neither would it serve the cause of democracy to pretend that middle-income suburbanites, whose numerical majorities grow increasingly larger, will soon be shamed into compassion for their less prosperous neighbors. It avails little to shun the reality of the political constraints which voters impose on their elected leaders.

State and local governments need and no doubt will receive increased federal financial aid; but federal funding must always remain a secondary source of financing for them, compared with the revenues they themselves raise locally. Federal financial aid can continue to relieve some of the revenue pressures on state and local governments. However, it could—and should—make an even more important contribution to the strength and vitality of these governments. It could and should guide and encourage them into constructive practices and reforms.

I write this prescription with awareness that it will be resisted alike by state and local and by federal leadership, and further, that it fails to come to terms with the political barriers to fiscal strength and health at the local and state levels.

Governors, mayors, legislators, and council members will not appreciate the helplessness attributed to them, especially in the wake of 1969 when their new tax enactments and tax increases reached an all time high. Members of Congress will see little pay dirt in assuming a larger share of the local financing burden, possibly obliging them to forego tax reduction opportunities that might otherwise become available to them; nor will they willingly assume the onus of foisting their will in behalf of structural and fiscal reform on a reluctant state and local officialdom. Brickbats can be expected also from traditional political theologians, for the image of the voter obsessed with his pocketbook interests will not please them. It tarnishes the halo on popular democracy's brow. Even the economist will balk for he is not quite ready to abdicate his post at the bedside of fiscally ailing state and local government to the political strategist.

There is no escaping, nonetheless, that despite the financing of successively larger spending levels year after year, important municipal needs remain unmet and breed social unrest; that the persistence of financial crises in the cities is driving some of the most able political leaders out of government service; that voters in increasing numbers are saying "no" to tax and debt increases and raising their voices to condemn tax collectors' insatiable appetites for their dollars.

It was asserted above that the prospect for adequate financing of social programs appears to improve with distance between voters and their elected representatives. This is a warranted inference from the many programs pushed through Congress, at times over the objections of the national administration, in such areas as education, environmental health, conservation, welfare, and poverty. Members of Congress appear to profit from being associated in voters' minds with one or another of these spending programs and apparently are not called upon to account for the implications of their new program enactments for people's tax bills. The members of Congress we associate with this or that desirable social legislation far outnumber those we associate with high federal taxes. The contrast with the image of local politicians is striking. Voters' appreciation of the Congressional friends of the poor, the minorities, the school children, the retired, etc. is often reflected in election night tallies. The disdainful characterization of Washington as a place where ". . . you discover a problem, throw money at it, and hope that somehow it will go away" does not appear to be widespread.

The record number of new social programs enacted in the last several years speaks for the political effectiveness of the partnership of the Congressional patrons of these programs with city political organizations, civic groups, organized labor, and concerned private enterprise and professional groups, among others. If this be true, its implication for local fiscal and political strategy is clear. Those wanting to fortify the financial resources of local government, particularly in the large urban centers, can ill afford to indulge in indifference toward the electoral fortunes of "desirably biased" legislators, including the like-minded representatives of the increasingly more populous suburbs.

bibliographical note

Readers wanting to delve further into topics discussed here will find plentiful material, especially if they focus on the particular subject of interest to them, rather than on the more general books on state-local finance. The number of items on specific fiscal issues is increasing rapidly. A comprehensive listing of new books, reports, and periodical articles on state-local finance can be found in the *Bookshelf,* issued twice a year by the Tax Institute of America, Princeton, New Jersey.

The Advisory Commission on Intergovernmental Relations (Washington, D.C.) established by Congress in 1959, publishes two or more reports each year. The Commission supplies a list of its publications and single copies of its reports on request. These cover such fiscal subjects, among others, as income taxes, property taxes, cigarette taxes, documentary taxes, estate and gift taxes, local non-property taxes, and federal grants-in-aid.

The Studies of Government Finance series of the Brookings Institution (Washington, D.C.) already contains some thirty items, including: James A. Maxwell, *Financing State and Local Governments;* Dick Netzer, *Economics of the Property Tax;* and George F. Break, *Intergovernmental Fiscal Relations in the United States.*

The literature on intergovernmental relations in the

United States is vast, reaching back to the beginnings of the Republic. All the reports of the Advisory Commission on Intergovernmental Relations treat with it. A concise introduction to the theory of this federal system is Senator Edmund S. Muskie's foreword to Henry N. Schreiber's *The Condition of American Federalism: A Historian's View,* published as a committee print by the Subcommittee on Intergovernmental Relations of the Senate Committee on Government Operations. A particularly stimulating (and, as it has developed, controversial) essay on federalism is Morton Grodzin's "The Federal System" in the report of the President's Commission on *National Goals,* published as a Prentice-Hall Spectrum Book.

As to the politics of financing state-local government, nothing published can take the place of some personal involvement with one's own state or community. An undertaking to work on behalf of a significant revenue or expenditure program is in educational value second only to personal involvement in a campaign for a local or state office. A general book on the subject is still to be written. However, Duane Lockard's *The Politics of State and Local Government* (Macmillan, 1963) contains an extensive bibliography of writings on politics, the items grouped by the states and cities with which they deal.

Many organizations are active in the field of state-local finances and publish periodicals, reports, and special publications: Committee for Economic Development, National Bureau of Economic Research, Tax Institute of America, Tax Foundation, National Tax Association, and, more recently, the U.S. Chamber of Commerce. Specialized areas of state-local finance are covered by publications of professional organizations and associations such as the Council of State Governments, International Association of Assessing Officers, International City Management Association, National Education Association, National League of Cities—U.S. Conference of Mayors, National Association of Counties, and National Association of Tax Administrators. Increasingly also, studies of state-local and intergovernmental problems are issued under the auspices of congressional committees, particularly the House Committee on Ways and Means, the Joint Economic Committee, and the Subcommittees on Intergovernmental Relations of the House and Senate Committees on Government Operations.

Tax Systems. A primary source for the details of state and local tax laws is the Prentice-Hall tax service *State and Local Taxes,* which reports on legislation in process and codifies tax laws in force as well as administrative rulings and court decisions. Tabulations of the major provisions of state tax laws also are provided. The Commerce Clearing House (Chicago) provides a comparable service.

The major current provisions of the more important state and local taxes, together with a summary of legislative tax developments are summarized in a convenient report of the Advisory Commission on Intergovernmental Relations, *State and Local Taxes—Significant Features.* This information report is periodically updated a few months after state legislatures have adjourned.

Readers interested in the tax problems of their own state or in local government would do well to begin at home. The finances of most states and of an increasing number of cities (and metropolitan areas) have been the subject of special studies in recent years. Some of these, frequently prepared by prominent scholars, provide fiscal details on the particular jurisdiction together with comparable information for other and particularly nearby governments. State and local Leagues of Women Voters often cover finances in their series "Know Your Local Government," "Know Your County Government," and "Know Your State Government." Other sources are the publications of state leagues of municipalities, state associations of counties, local bureaus of governmental research, research bureaus of local universities, and, on occasions, feature articles in the local press. In metropolitan areas, the councils of area local governments organized in recent years are becoming increasingly involved in municipal finances and may have published reports available to the public.

Financial Statistics. I have not burdened this volume with the usual tables because the rapid pace of state-local fiscal activity quickly renders them obsolete. The more basic data, moreover, are generally available in widely circulated publications.

For individual states and local governments, the primary source is the financial report of the audited accounts published regularly by the particular government. Because reporting terminology varies, the reports of any two government entities often are not comparable. However, some states publish standardized data for some or all of their political subdivisions.

The primary source for comparative financial statistics for all state and local governments is the U.S. Bureau of the Census Governments Division. It publishes separate annual reports (on) *State Tax Collections, State Government Finances, City Government Finances,* and *Finances in Selected Metropolitan Areas.* Its annual report, *Governmental Finances,* includes national totals covering all governments—federal, state, and local—with comparative summary data for selected previous years and state-by-state financial statistics for both state and local governments. These annual publications, typically available about a year after the period they cover, report on most aspects of the financial operations of the states and the larger local governments on an individual basis, and for all local governments on a state-by-state basis.

At five-year intervals, the Governments Division also publishes the results of its comprehensive *Census of Governments*. The most recent of these (1967) provides information on the number and characteristics of state and local governments, the value of taxable property, public employees and payrolls, and governmental revenues, expenditures, debts, and financial assets. The *1967 Census of Governments,* published in 1969, consists of seven volumes, some with several parts. Volume IV, for example, includes separate reports devoted to the finances of school districts, special districts, county governments, municipalities and townships, and a summary—*Compendium of Government Finances.* It provides national totals by type of government and state-by-state detail for state and local finances, including a breakdown by type of government and local government totals for counties.

The *1967 Census of Governments* also includes a number of "Topical Studies" of particular value for specialized purposes. The report *State Payments to Local Governments,* for example, describes (state-by-state) each grant program to local governments, arranged by function. A separate report (on) *Historical Statistics* provides key financial and employment data for selected years from 1902 to 1967. A bibliographical volume contains a listing, by states, of periodic state government publications that report on state and local government finances. Readers concerned with a particular state will find especially useful the separate reports for individual states which bring together in one place the Census information on governmental organization and structure, public employment, and government finances.

State and local financial data originate also in other federal agencies, particularly the Department of Commerce. The *Budget of the United States Government* contains a yearly special analysis feature, "Federal Aid to State and Local Governments."

Much of the basic data on state-local finances assembled by the U.S. Bureau of the Census and other agencies or organizations are reprinted in the *Statistical Abstract of the United States,* published also commercially as the *U.S. Book of Facts, Statistics, and Information* (available on newsstands). These annual editions contain a description of the U.S. government publications which present historical data, county and city data, and inventory federal statistics available on state and local area bases.

A convenient reference volume for personal use is the yearly edition of *Pocket Data Book, U.S.A.* This compact paperbound volume presents summary statistics on fiscal and other subjects in graphic and tabular form. Another useful secondary source for state financial data is *The Book of the States* (Council of State Governments, Chicago); for city data, *The Municipal Yearbook* (International City Management Association, Washington, D.C.); for state-local data, *Facts and Figures* (Tax Foundation).

Mailing Addresses of Organizations:

Advisory Commission on Intergovernmental Relations, Washington, D.C. 20575

Brookings Institution, 1775 Massachusetts Avenue, N.W., Washington, D.C. 20036

Committee for Economic Development, 477 Madison Avenue, New York, New York 10022

Council of State Governments, 1735 DeSales Street, N.W., Washington, D.C. 20036

International Association of Assessing Officers, 1313 East 60th Street, Chicago, Illinois 60637

International City Management Association, 1140 Connecticut Avenue, N.W., Washington, D.C. 20036

League of Women Voters of the United States, 1200 17th Street, N.W., Washington, D.C. 20036

National Association of Counties, 1001 Connecticut Avenue, N.W., Washington, D.C. 20036

National Association of Tax Administrators, 1313 East 60th Street, Chicago, Illinois 60637

National Bureau of Economic Research, Inc., 261 Madison Avenue, New York, New York 10016

National Education Association, 1201 16th Street, N.W., Washington, D.C. 20036

National League of Cities—U.S. Conference of Mayors, 1612 K Street, N.W., Washington, D.C. 20006

National Tax Association, 100 East Broad Street, Columbus, Ohio 43215

Tax Foundation, Inc., 50 Rockefeller Plaza, New York, New York 10020

Tax Institute of America, 457 Nassau Street, Princeton, New Jersey 08540

U.S. Chamber of Commerce, 1615 H Street, N.W., Washington, D.C. 20006

U.S. Bureau of the Census, Governments Division, Washington, D.C. 20233

U.S. Senate Committee on Government Operations, Subcommittee on Intergovernmental Relations, 357 Old Senate Office Building, Washington, D.C. 20510

U.S. Superintendent of Documents, Government Printing Office, Washington, D.C. 20402

TAX CHARTS

Selected charts from Vol. I of the 39-volume *State and Local Taxes Service* published by Prentice-Hall, Inc., Englewood Cliffs, New Jersey.

10-28-69   All States—**103**

ALL STATES TAX CHART

[¶ 101] Introduction.—On the following pages appears a chart showing the principal taxes imposed in each of the states and the District of Columbia. The bullet (●) indicates that the tax is imposed.

Under "Franchise" are included taxes based on anything but income, for the privilege of being or operating as a general business corporation within the state. Franchise taxes based on income are covered under "Income".

Under "Property" taxation of realty is not indicated since every state permits the taxation of real estate locally. Under "Intangibles" where footnote does not indicate that a special low intangibles tax rate or a special low valuation is permitted, intangibles theoretically are taxed at the general property tax rate and valuations. Actually, however, because of difficulty of enforcement, it is doubtful if much tax is collected on intangibles in those states.

Under "Admissions and Amusements" are included not only taxes on admissions price but taxes or fees determined by gross receipts or seating capacity. In some instances the tax is imposed under the state sales tax.

[Footnote ¶ 101] (1) N.H.—Meals and rooms tax. (2) N.Y.—Mortgage tax. Realty transfer tax. (3) Vt.—Sales-use (eff. 6-1-69); meal and rooms tax. (4) Del.—Tax based on gross receipts or purchases (retailing and wholesaling). Use tax on leasing tangible personalty (eff. 7-1-69). (5) Ariz. & S.C.—Law on books apparently unenforced. Gross income tax imposed only on corporations. (6) Ill.—Tax is on retailers; based on gross receipts. (5) Conn. & R.I.—Gross income tax on unincorporated businesses also imposed. *Repealed in Conn. (for tax years starting after 12-31-68).* (8) D.C. & N.Y.—Net income tax imposed on unincorporated business also. (9) N.H. & Tenn.— Tax is on income from intangibles only. (10) Alaska—License tax on business; based on gross receipts. (11) Wis.—Low grade iron ore property. (12) Intangibles taxable at lower value or lower rate than other property. (13) N.C.—Tax on cigarettes (eff. 10-1-69). (14) S.C.—Chain store tax part of sales and use tax law. (15) Amusements are taxable under gross income, gross receipts or sales tax laws. (16) Tax applies only to commuters in the "critical" transportation area (N.Y.-N.J.). Gross receipts on unincorporated business also imposed. (17) Kan.—Mortgages and instruments creating liens. (18) Mich.—Repealed as of 3-31-69. (19) R.I.—Only cities and towns can levy tax. (20) Nev.—Nearly all intangibles exempt by law. (21) Ill.—Corporation and individual income tax (eff. for tax years ending after 7-31-69). (22) Me.—Corporation income (eff. for tax years starting after 12-31-68) and individual income (eff. 7-1-69) taxes. (23) R.I.—Tax is on interest, dividends, capital gains (eff. for tax years starting after 12-31-68). (24) Ark.—Eff. 7-1-69. Wis.—Eff. 9-1-69. (25) Okla.—Mortgage tax. Realty transfer tax. (26) Conn.—Tax on capital gains (transactions after 7-1-69). (27) N.J.—Gross receipts tax on retail business also imposed. (28) S.C.—Eff. 1-1-69. (29) Okla.—Repealed 1-1-69. (30) Conn.—Effective 9-1-69. (31) R.I.—Repealed as of 5-15-69. (32) Wash.—Corporation and individual income tax enacted subject to voter OK. Tax effective 1-1-71, if OKd in 11-69; eff. 1-1-72, if OKd 11-70. (33) Md.—State realty transfer tax (eff. 7-1-69) is additional to document recording tax (rates vary locally).

[See chart on following pages]

104—All States   Charts and Tables

All States Tax Chart

State ⟫Taxes→	Cap. Values Franchise	Corp. Income	Individ. Income	Sales	Use	Tangible Personalty	Intangibles	Stock Transfer	Recording Documents
Alabama	●	●	●	●	●	●	●		●
Alaska		●	●	(10)	●	●	●		
Arizona		●	●	●	●	●	●(5)		
Arkansas	●	●	●	●	●	●	●		●(24)
California		●	●	●	●	●			
Colorado	●	●	●	●	●	●			●
Connecticut	●	●	●(7,26)	●(7)	●	●			●
Delaware	●	●	●	(4)	(4)				●
Dist. of Columbia		●	●(8)	●	●	●			●
Florida	●			●	●	●	●(12)	●	●
Georgia	●	●	●	●	●	●	●(12)		●
Hawaii		●	●	●	●	●			●
Idaho	●	●	●	●	●	●			
Illinois	●	●(21)	●(21)	●(6)	●	●		●	●
Indiana		●	●	●	●	●	●		
Iowa		●	●	●	●	●	●(12)		●
Kansas	●	●	●	●	●	●	●(12)		●(17)
Kentucky	●	●	●	●	●	●	●(12)		●
Louisiana	●	●	●	●	●	●	●		
Maine	●	●(22)	●(22)	●	●	●			
Maryland	●	●	●	●	●	●	●(12)		●(33)
Massachusetts	●	●	●	●	●	●			●
Michigan	●	●	●	●	●	●	●(12)		●
Minnesota		●	●	●	●	●			●
Mississippi	●	●	●	●	●	●	●		
Missouri	●	●	●	●	●	●	●(12)		
Montana		●	●			●	●(12)		
Nebraska	●	●		●	●	●			●
Nevada				●	●	●	●(20)		●
New Hampshire	●		●(9)	(1)		●			●
New Jersey	●	●(27)	●(16)	●	●	●			●
New Mexico	●	●	●	●	●	●	●		
New York	●	●	●(8)	●	●	●		●	●(2)
North Carolina	●	●	●	●	●	●	●(12)		●
North Dakota		●	●	●	●	●	●		
Ohio	●			●	●	●	●(12)		●
Oklahoma	●	●	●	●	●	●	●(12, 29)		●(25)
Oregon	●	●	●		●				
Pennsylvania	●	●		●		●	●(12)		●
Rhode Island	●	●	●(7,23)	●(7)	●	●(19)	(31)		●
South Carolina	●	●	●	●	●	●	●(5)	●	●
South Dakota				●	●	●	●(12)		●
Tennessee	●	●	●(9)	●	●	●	●		●
Texas	●			●	●	●	●		
Utah		●	●	●	●	●			
Vermont		●	●	●(3)	●(3)	●			●
Virginia	●	●	●	●	●	●	●(12)		●
Washington	●	(32)	(32)	●	●	●			●
West Virginia	●	●	●	●	●	●	●(12)		●
Wisconsin		●	●	●	●	●			●(24)
Wyoming	●			●	●	●	●		

(Notes to chart appear on page 103)

¶ 101   PRENTICE-HALL, Inc., Englewood Cliffs, N. J.

All States Tax Chart

State →Taxes→	Estate	Gift	Inherit-ance	Motor Fuel	Admissions & Amusement	Chain Store	Tobacco	Minerals	Timber
Alabama	•			•	• (15)	•	•	•	
Alaska	•		•	•			•	•	•
Arizona	•			•	• (15)		•	•	
Arkansas	•			•	• (15)		•	•	
California	•	•	•	•			•	•	•
Colorado	•	•	•	•			•	•	
Connecticut	•		•	•	• (30)	•	•		
Delaware	•		•	•			•		•
Dist. of Columbia	•		•	•			•		
Florida	•			•	• (15)	•	•	•	
Georgia	•			•	• (15)		•	•	
Hawaii	•		•	•	• (15)		•		
Idaho	•		•	•	• (15)	•	•		
Illinois	•		•	•			•		•
Indiana	•		•	•	• (15)		•	•	
Iowa	•		•	•	• (15)	•	•		
Kansas	•		•	•	• (15)		•	•	
Kentucky	•		•	•	• (15)		•	•	
Louisiana	•	•	•	•	• (15)	•	•	•	
Maine	•		•	•			•	•	•
Maryland	•		•	•	•	•	•		
Massachusetts	•		•	•			•		•
Michigan	•		•	•		• (18)	•		•
Minnesota	•	•	•	•	• (15)		•	•	•
Mississippi	•		•	•	•		•	•	•
Missouri	•		•	•	• (15)		•		•
Montana	•		•	•		•	•	•	
Nebraska	•		•	•	• (15)		•	•	
Nevada	•			•			•	•	
New Hampshire	•		•	•			•		
New Jersey	•		•	•	• (15)		•		
New Mexico	•	•		•	• (15)		•	•	
New York	•		•	•	• (15)		•	•	•
North Carolina	•	•	•	•	•	•	• (13)	•	
North Dakota	•			•	• (15)		•	•	
Ohio	•			•			•		
Oklahoma	•	•		•	• (15)		•	•	
Oregon	•	•	•	•			•		•
Pennsylvania	•	•	•	•			•		•
Rhode Island	•	•	•	•	• (15)		•		
South Carolina	•	• (28)		•	•	• (14)	•		
South Dakota			•	•	• (15)		•		
Tennessee	•	•	•	•	•	•	•	•	
Texas	•			•	•	•	•	•	
Utah	•			•	• (15)		•	•	
Vermont	•		•	•	• (15)		•		
Virginia	•	•	•	•	• (15)		•		•
Washington	•	•	•	•	• (15)		•		•
West Virginia	•		•	•	• (15)	•	•		•
Wisconsin	•	•	•	•	• (15)		•	• (11)	•
Wyoming	•		•	•	• (15)		•	•	

(Notes to chart appear on page 103)

PRENTICE-HALL, Inc., Englewood Cliffs, N. J.

¶ 101

STATE—FEDERAL INCOME TAX CONFORMITY

[¶ 1002] Over half the states taxing income now use federal income in one form or another as the basic starting point for figuring state income taxes. More and more the states are following the federal rules to avoid the complexities that accompany an income tax not tied into the federal income tax rules. The chart on the next page shows the extent to which the states rely on the federal law and rules.

Explanation of chart information: Column I, computational starting point, shows the states that use a specific federal figure to begin figuring the state tax. (If a state adopts federal law as of a specific date, the date is given, otherwise current federal law is used.) Column II gives the official policy that the states use in interpreting their laws: "A" are those states that follow the IRC when not in conflict; "B" shows states that use federal law as a source and IRC as a guide; "L" are states that use the IRC precedents to a limited extent. Columns III and IV are states with independent laws that resemble the federal law a little or a lot. ("C" indicates the entry is limited to corporations; "I" indicates other taxpayers.)

➤**USE THE CHART**→ as a take-off point in (1) projecting estimated overall and comparative liabilities in any area, (2) noting probabilities of policy concurrence on points having no precedent, and (3) participating in private or public movements for tax reform.

[Footnotes to chart on page 1004]
[Footnote ¶ 1002] **(1)** Eff. for tax years starting after 12-31-68. Was limited use of IRC. **(2)** Corporate income follows federal income but deductions vary. **(3)** Individual income tax applies only to New Yorkers working in N.J. **(4)** State adopts a great many IRC amendments as of 1-1-67. **(5)** Tax on net capital gains only (transactions after 7-1-69 through 6-30-71). **(6)** Corporation tax effective for tax years ending after 7-31-69; individuals, as of 8-1-69. **(7)** Means current IRC unless taxpayer elects (statement) IRC 12-31-68 (for tax years 1968 and after). Was 12-31-66. **(8)** Based on percentage of Fed. tax. **(9)** Eff. 1-1-69. **(10)** Effective for tax years starting after 12-31-68 for corporations; as of 7-1-69, for individuals. **(11)** For tax years starting after 12-31-68; only on interest, dividends and net capital gains. **(12)** May elect IRC 12-31-68 plus subsequent amendments. If constitutional amendment (HJR) gets OK at 1970 general election, option will be repealed. Basis will be IRC for taxable year of return. **(13)** Effective for tax years starting after 12-31-69. **(14)** For 1969 calendar year and fiscal years ending after 1-30-69. Was 7-20-67.

1004—All States   **All States Tax Lists**

State—Federal Income Tax Conformity

P-H CHART OF STATE-FEDERAL INCOME TAX CONFORMITY

State	Computational Starting Point Col. I	Official Policy Col. II	Major Resemblance Col. III	Minor Resemblance Col. IV
Ala.		A		X
Alaska	X(8)	A		
Ariz.		B	X	
Ark.		A		X
Calif.		A	X	
Colo.	X	A		
Conn.	X(C)	A		
	X(I)(5)	A		
Del.	X(C)	A(C)		X(I)
D.C.		A		X
Ga.(1)	X(C-1-1-69)	L(I)		X(I)
Haw.(4)	X(6-7-57)	A		
Idaho(9)	X(1-1-69)	A		
Ill.(6)	X(7-1-69)	A		
Ind.	X(1-1-69)	A		
Iowa	X(6-30-67)	A		
Kan.	X(1-1-69)	A		
Ky.	X(12-31-66)	A		
La.		L	X	
Me.(10)	X(6-1-69)	A		
Md.	X	A		
Mass.	X(C)	L(I)		X(I)
Mich.(14)	X	A		
Minn.	X(I)	A	X(C)	
Miss.				X
Mo.	X(13)	A		
Mont.(2)	X(1)	A	X(C)	
Neb.	X(8)	A		
N.J.(3)	X	A		
N.M.	X	A		
N.Y.	X	B(C); A(I)		
N.C.	X(C)(1-1-67)	A(C)	X(1)	
N.D.	X(12-31-68)	L		
Okla.		L(C)		X
Ore.(12)	X(I—12-31-68)	A(C)		X(C)
Pa.	X(C)	A		
R.I.(11)	X(C)	A		
	X(I—1-1-69)	A		
S.C.		L		X
Tenn.		A(C)		X
Utah		A		X
Vt.	X(8)	A		
Va.		A		X
W.Va.	X(I—1-1-69)	A		
	X(C—12-31-66)	A		
Wis.(7)	X(I)	A(I)		X(C)

[Footnotes appear on page 1003]

PRENTICE-HALL, Inc., Englewood Cliffs, N. J.

PERSONAL INCOME TAX RATES

[¶ 1007] All-States rate chart.—Following shows tax on individuals applicable, if not otherwise shown, to net income less personal exemptions.

STATE	RATES	EXEMPTIONS(1)
Ala. (54)	1.5% on 1st $1,000 3% on next $2,000 4.5% on next $2,000 **5% on balance**	S—$1,500 M—$3,000 H—$3,000 D—$300
Alaska	16% of federal income (35) (28, 46)	
Ariz. (5)	2% on 1st $1,000 3% on 2nd $1,000 4% on 3rd $1,000 5% on 4th $1,000 6% on 5th $1,000 7% on 6th $1,000 **8% on balance**	S—$1,000 M—$2,000 H—$2,000 D—$600 B—$500 A—$1,000
Ark. (5)	1% on 1st $3,000 2% on 2nd $3,000 3% on next $5,000 4% on next $14,000 5% on balance	S—$17.50(2) M—$35(2) H—$35(2) D—$6(2, 14) B—$17.50(2, 14)
Calif. (5, 28)	1% on 1st $2,000(21) 2% on next $1500 3% on 2nd $1500 4% on 3rd $1500 5% on 4th $1500 6% on 5th $1500 7% on 6th $1500 8% on 7th $1500 9% on 8th $1500 10% on balance	S—$25(2) M—$50(2) H—$50(2) D—$8(2) B—$8(2) E—$8(2)
Colo. (4, 5, 33)	3% on 1st $1,000 3.5% on next $1,000 4% on next $1,000 4.5% on next $1,000 5% on next $1,000 5.5% on next $1,000 6% on next $1,000 6.5% on next $1,000 7% on next $1,000 7.5% on next $1,000 8% on balance	S—$750 M—$1,500 D—$750 B—$750 A—$750
Conn.	6% Min. $5 (49)	NONE
Del.	1.5% on 1st $1,000 2% on 2nd $1,000 3% on 3rd $1,000 4% on 4th $1,000 5% on 5th $1,000 6% on 6th $1,000 7% on next $2,000 8% on next $22,000 9% on next $20,000 10% on next $50,000 11% on balance	S—$600 M—$1,200 D—$600 B—$600 A—$600 H—$300
D.C. (5)	2% on 1st $1000 3% on next $2000 4% on next $2000 5% on next $5000 6% on balance	S—$1,000 M—$2,000 H—$2,000 D—$500 B—$500 A—$500
Ga. (5)	1% on 1st $1,000 2% on next $2,000 3% on next $2,000 4% on next $2,000 5% on next $3,000 6% on balance	S—$1,500 M—$3,000 H—$3,000 D—$600(37) B—$600(23) A—$600 E—$1200(37)
Haw. (5, 17, 28, 45)	2.25% on 1st $500 3.25% on 2nd $500 4.5% on 3d $500 5% on 4th $500 6.5% on next $1,000 7.5% on next $2,000 8.5% on next $5,000 9.5% on next $4,000	S—$600 M—$1,200 D—$600 A—$600 B—$5,000(34) E—$600

STATE	RATES	EXEMPTIONS(1)
	10% on next $6,000 10.5% on next $10,000 11% on balance	
Ida. (5, 28, 32)	2.5% on 1st $1,000 5% on next $1,000 6% on next $1,000 7% on next $1,000 8% on next $1,000 9% on balance	S—$600 ; $10(2) M—$1,200 ; $20 (2) D—$600; $10(2) B—$600; $10(2) A—$600; $10(2)
Ill. (52)	2½%	S—$1000 M—$2000 D—$1000 A—$1000 B—$1000 E—$1000
Ind. (43)	2%	S—$1,000 M—$2,000 D—$500(3) B—$500(3) E—$500 A—$500
Iowa (31)	0.75% on 1st $1,000 1.5% on 2nd 1,000 2.25% on 3rd $1,000 3% on 4th $1,000 3.75% on next $3,000 4.5% next $2,000 5.25% over $9,000	S—$15(2) M—$30(2) H—$30(2) D—$10(2) A—$15(2) B—$15(2)
Kan. (5,28)	2% up to $2,000 $40 + 3½% next $1000; $75 + 4% next $2000; (6) $155 + 5% next $2000; $255 + 6½% bal.	
Ky.(5)	2% on 1st $3,000 3% on next $1,000 4% on next $1,000 5% on next $3,000 6% on balance	S—$20(2) M—$40(2) D—$20(2) B—$20(2) A—$20(2)
La. (28)	2% on 1st $10,000 4% on next $40,000 6% on balance	S—$2,500(9) M—$5,000(9) H—$5,000(9) D—$400 E—$400 B—$1,000(29)
Me. (28, 50)	1% 1st $2000; $20 + 2% next $3000; $80 + 3% next $5000; $230 + 4% next $15000; $830 + 5% next $25000; $2080 + 6% bal.	S—$1000; M—$2000; D—$1000; A—$1000; B—$1000; E—$1000
Md. (5, 20, 48)	2% on 1st $1,000 3% on 2nd $1,000 4% on 3rd $1,000 **5% on balance**	S—$800 M—$1,600 D—$800(41) B—$800 A—$800 E—$800
Mass.(5)	Int. & Divs. 8% Annuity 2% Intangible gain 8% Income from business or employment. 4%	(10, 42) (10) (10) S—$2,000 M—$4,000(26) D—$600 C—$2,000 A—$600 L(25) B—$2,000
Mich. (47)	2.6% income	(38)

Footnotes to chart appear on page 1009

1008—All States   All States Tax Lists

Personal Income Tax Rates

STATE	RATES	EXEMPTIONS(1)	STATE	RATES	EXEMPTIONS(1)
Minn. (5, 8)	1.5% on 1st $500 2% on 2nd $500 3% on next $1,000 5% on next $1,000 6% on next $1,000 7% on next $1,000 8% on next $2,000 9% on next $2,000 10% on next $3,500 11% on next $7,500 12% on balance (22)	S—$19(2) M—$38(2) H—$38(2) D—$19 B—$20(7) A—$20(7)	N.C. (5)	3% on 1st $2,000 4% on next $2,000 5% on next $2,000 6% on next $4,000 **7% balance**	S—$1,000 M—$2,000 H—$2,000 D—$600 E—$600 B—$1,000 A—$1,000
Miss.	3% on 1st $5,000 4% over $5,000	S—$4,000 M—$6,000 H—$6,000	N.D. (13)	1% on 1st $3,000 2% on next $1,000 3% on next $1,000 5% on next $1,000 7.5% on next $2,000 10% on next $7,000 11% on balance	S—$600 M—$1,500 H—$1,500 D—$600 B—$600 A—$600
Mo.(5)	1% $0-1000(12) 1.5% $1,000.01-2,000(12) 2% $2,000.01-3,000(12) 2.5% $3,000.01-5,000(12) 3% $5,000.01-7,000(12) 3.5% $7,000.01-9,000(12) 4% $9,000.01 and up(12)	S—$1,200 M—$2,400 H—$2,400 D—$400	Okla. (5, 28)	1% on 1st $1,500 2% on 2nd $1,500 3% on 3rd $1,500 4% on 4th $1,500 5% on 5th $1,500 6% on balance	S—$1,000 M—$2,000 H—$2,000 D—$500
Mont.(3)	2% on 1st $1,000 3% on next $1,000 4% on next $2,000 5% on next $2,000 6% on next $2,000 7% on next $2,000 8% on next $4000 9% on next $6000 10% on next $15,000 11% on balance	S—$600 M—$1,200 D—$600 B—$600 A—$600 E—$600	Ore. (5, 28, 51)	4% 1st $500; $20 + 5% next $500; $45 + 6% next $1000; $105 + 7% next $1000; $175 + 8% next $1000; $255 + 9% next $1000; $345 + 10% bal.	S—$600 M—$1,200 D—$600 B—$600 and A—$600 E—$600
Neb. (28, 44)	10% of federal tax liability	(35)	R.I.	10%(30)	(53)
N.H.	4¼ on Int. and Divs.	$600	S.C. (5)	2% on 1st $2,000 3% on next $2,000 4% on next $2,000 5% on next $2,000 6% on next $2,000 7% on balance	S—$800 M—$1,600 H—$1,600 D—$800 B—$800 A—$800
N.J. (19)	2% on 1st $1,000 3% on next $2,000 4% on next $2,000 5% on next $2,000 6% on next $2,000 7% on next $2,000 8% on next $2,000 9% on next $2,000 10% on next $2,000 11% on next $2,000 12% on next $2,000 13% on next $2,000 14% on balance	S—$600(18) M—$1,200(18) D—$600 B—$600 A—$600 E—$600	Tenn.	6% (16)	B—(24)
			Utah	2% on 1st $1,000 3% on next $1,000 4% on next $1,000 5% on next $1,000 6% on next $1,000 6.5% on balance	S—$600 M—$1,200 D—$600 B—$600 A—$400(27)
			Vt. (5, 28, 40)	25% of federal tax (15) (35)	
N.M.	1% 1st $500 $5 + 1.5% 2nd $500 $12.50 + 1.5% 3d $500 $20 + 2% next $500 $30 + 2.5% next $1,000 $55 + 3% next $1,000 $85 + 3.5% next $1,000 $120 + 4% next 1,000 $160 + 4.5% next $1,000 $205 + 5% next $1,000 (5, 28,36)	(6)	Va.	2% on 1st $3,000 3% on next $2,000 5% on balance	S—$1,000 M—$2,000 D—$300(11) B—$600 A—$600
N.Y.	2% on 1st $1,000 3% on next $2,000 4% on next $2,000 5% on next $2,000 6% on next $2,000 7% on next $2,000 8% on next $2,000 9% on next $2,000 10% on next $2,000 11% on next $2,000 12% on next $2,000 13% on next $2,000 14% on balance	S—$600(18) M—$1,200(18) H(18) D—$600(18) B—$600(18) A—$600(18)	W.Va. (5, 28)	1.2% on 1st $2,000 **1.3% on next $2,000** 1.6% on next $2,000 1.8% on next $2,000 2% on next $2,000 2.3% on next $2,000 2.6% on next $2,000 2.8% on next $2,000 3% on next $2,000 3.1% on next $2,000 3.4% on next $2,000 3.5% on next $4,000 3.7% on next $6,000 3.9% on next $6,000 4.1% on next $6,000 4.3% on next $6,000 4.5% on next $10,000 4.7% on next $10,000 4.9% on next $10,000	(6)

Footnotes to chart appear on page 1009

¶ 1007

Personal Income Tax Rates

STATE	RATES	EXEMPTIONS(1)	STATE	RATES	EXEMPTIONS(1)
	5% on next $10,000 5.2% on next $10,000 5.3% on next $50,000 5.4% on next $50,000 5.5% on balance			1.7% on next $1,000 5.2% on next $1,000 5.7% on next $1,000 6.7% on next $1,000 7.2% on next $1,000 7.7% on next $1,000 8.2% on next $1,000 8.7% on next $1,000 9.2% on next $1,000 9.7% on next $1,000 10% on balance	E—$10(2)
Wis. (5, 39)	2.7% on $1,000 2.95% on next $1,000 3.2% on next $1,000 4.2% on next $1,000	S—$10(2) M—$20(2) H—$20(2) D—$10(2)			

NOTES to chart ¶ 1007 (corresponding to parenthetical numbers in chart):

(1) S-Single; M-Married; H-Head of household or family; T-Taxpayer; D-Dependents (each); B-Blind (additional); A-Over 65 (additional); E-Educational; C-Member of U.S. armed forces in combat zone; L-Low income.

(2) Credit against tax.

(3) Mont.—For tax years starting after 12-30-68: 5% tax credit repealed; 10% surtax added. Was 8% next $15,000; 10% balance.

(4) Colo.—Also add 2% surtax on interest and dividends in excess of $5,000.

(5) Optional tax table may be used.

(6) $600 for each federally allowed exemption.

(7) Minn.—Added to other credits. If married, spouse's credit for B is $25; A, $20.

(8) Minn.—Lower rates and credits against tax scheduled to start 1-1-70.

(9) La.—Applied against 1st bracket.

(10) Mass.—On income from all sources to $2,000 ($2,500 if married; $2,600, for tax years ending after 12-30-69), $2,000 exemption allowed.

(11) Va.—For unmarried taxpayer with dependent parent, child, brother or sister. $1,000 for 1st and $300 per dependent thereafter.

(12) Mo.—Rate is for total net income. Credits: 2d bracket, $5; 3d, $15; 4th, $30; 5th, $55; 6th, $90; 7th, $135. For tax years starting after 12-31-69, following rates (subject to possible referendum) apply: 1% + $0-$1,000; $10 + 2%, 2nd $1,000; $30 + 2½%, 3rd $1,000; $55 + 3%, 4th $1,000; $85 + 3½%, 5th $1,000; $120 + 4%, 6th $1,000; $160 + 4½%, 7th $1,000; $205 + 5%, 8th $1,000; $255 + 5½%, 9th $1,000; $310 + 6% over $9,000.

(13) N.D.—Additional 1% tax (min. $20) on privilege of doing business in ND (for tax years starting after 12-31-69).

(14) Ark.—Credit only for dependent with gross under $1,750 and, return not jointly with spouse. Addtl. $17.50 for blind spouse.

(15) Vt.—Plus 15% surcharge on Vt. taxes due (for tax years starting after 12-31-68).

(16) Tenn.—On income from stocks and bonds; 4% on income from corporations assessed on 75% or more of property.

(17) Haw.—Special rates apply for head of household.

(18) N.J., N.Y.—Credit against tax also allowed: S-$10; M-$12.50 on each separate return or $25 jointly; H-$25.

(19) N.J.—Tax applies only to New Yorkers working in N.J.

(20) Md.—Also, 23 counties and Baltimore City tax from 20% or "5%" multiple, if less, of state income tax liability.

(21) Calif.—Head of household, 1% of 1st $3000.

(22) Minn.—"Senior citizens" get $600 tax credit for property tax and/or rent paid.

(23) Ga.—Exemption allowed to blind taxpayer by departmental ruling.

(24) Tenn.—No return unless taxable income exceeds $25. Blind are exempt.

(25) Mass.—L = credit against tax; $4 for qualified taxpayer with taxable income not over $5,000, $4 for spouse, $8 for dependent.

(26) Mass.—Limited to $2,000 plus income of spouse having smaller income; add $600 if spouse has $2,000 income or less.

(27) Utah—Exemptions: 1970 and after, $600; same for spouse over 65.

(28) On joint returns, income splitting allowed. Kan., Me., Ore., W. Va., Ariz., Calif., La., Ida., N.M., Haw., Okla. Automatically allowed in Alaska, Neb., Vt.

(29) La.—$1,000 additional exemption allowed to handicapped person or dependent.

(30) R.I.—Base: Interest, dividends, capital gains (IRC) for tax years starting after 12-31-68.

(31) Iowa—Each resident and dependent gets annual sales tax credit: $12 for under $1000 income to $9 under $3000 income (for 1968 tax years; eliminated thereafter).

(32) Idaho—Additional flat tax of $10 except blind persons; those getting public assistance payments. Also, credit against tax: $10 per personal exemption claimed.

PRENTICE-HALL, Inc., Englewood Cliffs, N. J.

¶ 1007

1010—All States   **All States Tax Lists**

Personal Income Tax Rates

(33) Colo.—For credit, divide taxable income by 200. But none given for income over $9,000. Also, credit against tax: $7 times personal exemptions (not B or A). Also, added $750 for dependent mentally retarded (eff. after 1969).

(34) Haw.—Single or separate return, $5,000; joint return (both blind) $10,000; $5,000 if one spouse blind plus $600 for other if under 65 or $1200 if over 65.

(35) Alaska, Neb., Vt.—Federal personal exemptions automatically allowed.

(36) N.M.—$255 + 6% next $2,000; $375 + 7% next $2,000; $515 + 7.5% next $8,000; $1,155 + 8% next $30,000; $3,515 + 8.5% next $50,000; $7,765 + 9% bal.; separate rates for head of household (for tax years ending after 12-31-68). .

(37) Ga.—$600 additional if taxpayer or student-dependent (not if qualification for head of household); "disabled" dependent addtl., $600.

(38) Mich.—$1,200 times personal or dependency exemptions on Fed. return.

(39) Wis.—Credit for property tax or rent paid.

(40) Vt.—Sales tax credit or refund given based on income and exemptions (not blind or age) (eff. 6-1-69). Also, "senior citizens" get up to $300 "credit" for property taxes or rent on residence.

(41) Md.—Additional exemption for each dependent 65 or over at close of tax year. Added $800 for blind spouse.

(42) Mass.—Exemption against interest and dividends is excess of annuity exemption over amount of income from annuities.

(43) Ind.—Annual "food and drug" credit against tax: $8 per 6-month resident. Also, credit for contributions to "educational" institutions.

(44) Neb.—For tax years starting 1970 rate goes to 13%. Residents' tax credit: $7 times allowable exemptions (not blind or aged).

(45) Haw.—Credits against tax: $21-$1 per 9-month resident; dependent's education, before college, $20 to $2; in college, $50-$5.

(46) Alaska—Based on Fed rates as of 12-31-63.

(47) Mich.—Credit against tax allowed for Mich. city income tax, property tax and/or rent and contributions to "educational" institutions.

(48) Md.—Credit for state personalty taxes (payable after 6-30-68).

(49) Conn.—Base: Capital gains (after 7-1-69) on sale or exchange as reported for Fed tax, over $100; $200, filing jointly.

(50) Me.—Tax effective 7-1-69; prorate for 1969.

(51) Ore.—For tax years begun after 12-31-68. Was 3% on 1st $500 to 9.5% over $8000.

(52) Ill.—Tax effective for tax years ending after 7-31-69; prorate for years spanning 8-1-69.

(53) R.I.—$2000 exemption prorated in ratio of interest and dividends (IRC) to Fed adjusted gross (less specified amounts). Exemption double for those 65 or over, widowed or blind.

(54) Ala.—Max. rate would go to 7% (from 5%) for 1970 calendar or fiscal starting in 1970, if proposed amendment OKd at 11-70 election.

PRENTICE-HALL, Inc., Englewood Cliffs, N. J.

11-24-69   **251**

SALES-USE TAX RATES, BASES, REPORTS, PAYMENTS

¶ 250   **A comprehensive picture** of the sales and use tax rates, and bases on which they are imposed, for all states with general sales or use taxes is presented below. The return and payment dates, and the official to whom the return or payment is made, are also listed. Notes supplementing entries in the chart start on page 255.

⋙**MEANING OF A STAR**(*)→ In the first column, under the state name, is a starred (*) entry showing whether the primary tax (sales or gross receipts) is a "seller" or "consumer" tax. See ¶ 3010 for a complete discussion of the implications of such designations. Although many taxes are designated as "seller" taxes, the tax is, or may be, passed on to the buyer in all the states mentioned except Alaska and Haw. However, in any state you can adjust your selling price to take the tax into account.

STATE (1)	RATE OF TAX	BASIS OR MEASURE OF TAX (2)	RETURNS & PAYMENT	
			Last Day Without Penalty	To Whom
Alabama *Seller (40)	4% (10); MVs, house trailers, mining. manufacturing, machinery, 1½%.	*Sales:* Gross proceeds. *Use:* Sale price of tangible personalty bought at retail.	*Sales:* 20th of month. *Use:* 20th of month **after** quarter.	St. Dept. of Rev., Montgomery
Alaska *Seller	*Business License:* ¼-½% (10, 12).	Gross receipts.	Annually, last day of Feb.	Comr. of Rev., Juneau
Arizona *Seller	*Sales:* Retailers, 3%; other businesses, ⅜-3%. *Use:* 3% (10)	*Sales:* Gross proceeds or gross income. *Use:* Sale price of tangible personalty bought at retail.	*Sales:* 20th monthly. *Use:* 15th monthly.	St. Tax Comn., Phoenix
Arkansas *Consumer	3%	*Gross Receipts:* Gross receipts from sales. *Use:* Sale price of tangible personalty.	*Gross receipts:* 20th of month (4). *Use:* 15th of month.	Comr. of Rev., Little Rock
California *Seller	4% (10).	*Sales:* Gross receipts. *Use:* Sale price of tangibles.	Last day of month after quarter (37).	St. Bd. of Eq., Sacramento
Colorado *Consumer	3% (10)	*Sales:* Price to consumer. *Use:* Purchase price of tangibles.	20th of month (4, 5).	Dir. of Rev., Denver
Connecticut *Consumer	5% (3½% before 7-1-69) 2½ (1¾% pre 7-1-69) on sales under 11¢ (15¢), if records kept.	*Sales:* Gross receipts. *Use:* Price of tangibles purchased.	Last day of month after quarter (6).	Tax Comr., Hartford
Dist. of Columbia *Seller	4% (35).	*Sales:* Gross receipts. *Use:* Sales price.	20th of month; annual sales return 30 days after end of tax year.	*Return:* Dept. Fin. & Rev. Wash., D.C.

© 1970 by Prentice-Hall, Inc.—State Tax Guide   ¶ 250

252   Charts — Sales-Use Tax Rates, Bases, Reports, Payments

STATE (1)	RATE OF TAX	BASIS OR MEASURE OF TAX (2)	RETURNS & PAYMENT	
			Last Day Without Penalty	To Whom
Florida *Consumer	4% (24).	*Sales:* Sales price. *Use:* Cost of property used.	20th of each month.	Dept. Rev. Tallahassee.
Georgia *Consumer	3% (10).	*Sales:* Gross proceeds. *Use:* Cost price or fair market value of property, if less.	20th of month for preceding month. (4).	St. Rev. Comr. Atlanta
Hawaii *Seller	*Gross Income:* 4% (15). *Use:* 4% (Imports for resale, ½%.)	*Gross Income:* Gross receipts of sale or value of product. *Use:* Value of property	End of month Annual return. Apr. 20.	Div. Tax Assr. or Dir. of Rev. Honolulu.
Idaho *Consumer	3%.	*Sales:* Total sales price. *Use:* Value.	*Rept.:* 25th after quarter close. *Payt.:* Estimate by 25th monthly; adjusted with quarterly return.	Tax Comr. Boise
Illinois *Seller	*Retailers' Occupation (or Use):* 4% (4½% before 10-1-69) *Service Occupation (or Use):* 4% (4½% before 10-1-69) (10).	*Retailers Occupation:* Gross receipts. *Use:* Selling price of tangibles purchased at retail. *Service occupation (or use):* Cost price of property to serviceman.	End of month (32).	Dept. of Rev., Springfield (or Chicago)
Indiana (16) *Consumer	*Gross retail (sales) or Use:* 2%.	*Gross retail (sales):* Gross proceeds. *Use:* Sale price.	30th of each month (29).	Dept. of St. Rev., Indianapolis
Iowa *Consumer	3%	*Sales:* Gross receipts. *Use:* Sale price of tangibles.	End of Jan., Apr., July, Oct. (38).	St. Tax Comn., Des Moines
Kansas *Consumer	3%	*Sales:* Gross receipts. *Use:* Purchase price of tangibles.	*Sales:* Last day of month. *Use:* Last day of month (4, 30).	Dir. of Rev., Topeka
Kentucky *Seller	5%	*Sales:* Gross Receipts. *Use:* Sale price of tangibles.	20th of month (4). Annual return, 30 days after Fed return.	Dept. Rev., Frankfort
Louisiana *Consumer	2% (10).	*Sales:* Gross retail sales, rentals, service charges. *Use:* Cost price (39).	20th of month (39).	Coll. of Rev., Baton Rouge

STATE (1)	RATE OF TAX	BASIS OR MEASURE OF TAX (2)	RETURNS & PAYMENT — Last Day Without Penalty	To Whom
Maine *Seller	5% (4½% before 6-1-69).	*Sales:* Gross sales, rentals. *Use:* Sales price.	15th of month (9).	St. Tax Assr., Augusta
Maryland *Consumer	4% (34) (3% before 6-1-69).	*Sales:* Sales price. *Use:* Same.	20th of month.	St. Compt., Baltimore
Massachusetts *Seller (31)	3%.	*Sales:* Gross receipts. *Use:* Sale price of tangibles.	20th of month (41).	Comr. of Corps. & Tax., Boston
Michigan *Seller	4%.	*Sales:* Gross proceeds. *Use:* Price of tangible personalty.	15th of month; annual sales return 30 days after federal return.	Dept. of Rev., Lansing
Minnesota *Consumer	3%.	*Sales:* Gross receipts. *Use:* Sales price.	25th of month.	Comr. of Taxation, St. Paul
Mississippi *Seller	*Sales:* 5% (19). *Use:* 5% (19). Wholesale Compensating: (19). Salesmen's: 3% retail; ⅛% wholesale.(10).	*Sales:* Gross proceeds or income. *Use:* Cost of property or services. *Wholesale Compensating:* Purchase price. *Salesmen's:* Gross proceeds.	20th of month (27).	St. Tax Comn., Jackson
Missouri *Seller	3%.	*Sales:* Gross proceeds. *Use:* Sale price.	Quarterly (11), 30th of Jan., Apr., July, Oct.	Dir. of Rev., Jefferson City
Nebraska *Consumer	2½% (2% before 1-1-70) (10).	*Sales:* Gross receipts. *Use:* Sales or rental price.	Last day of month (4, 5).	Tax Comr. Lincoln
Nevada *Consumer	2% (1% state-wide county tax (10)).	*Sales:* Gross receipts. *Use:* Sale price of tangibles.	Last day of month after quarter (28)	Tax Comn., Carson City
New Jersey *Consumer	3%.	*Sales:* Gross receipts or service charge. *Use:* Price of tangibles or service charge.	Quarterly (20), 28th of Jan., Apr., July, Oct.	Director, Div. of Taxation, Trenton
New Mexico *Seller	4% (3% before 7-1-69) (10).	*Sales:* Gross receipts. *Use:* Value of property and service.	*Sales:* 25th (20th before 7-1-69) of month (26)	Bur. of Rev., Santa Fe
New York *Consumer	3% (2% before 4-1-69) plus up to 3% in some localities. NYC-State 6% (5% pre-4-1-69).	*Sales:* Gross selling price or service charge. *Use:* Purchase price or service charge.	20th of Mar. (42) June, Sept., Dec.	St. Tax Comn. Albany.

© 1970 by Prentice-Hall, Inc.—State Tax Guide

¶ 250

254   Charts — Sales-Use Tax Rates, Bases, Reports, Payments

STATE (1)	RATE OF TAX	BASIS OR MEASURE OF TAX (2)	RETURNS & PAYMENT: To Whom	
North Carolina *Seller	3%. Selected items, 1%; vehicles (10). boats, aircraft 2% (1½% pre-7-1-69) (21).	*Retail:* Gross sales. *Compensating use:* Sale price of tangibles.	Last Day Without Penalty 15th of month (4).	Comr. of Rev., Raleigh
North Dakota *Consumer	4% (3% before 1-1-70) (36).	*Sales:* Gross receipts. *Use:* Sale price of tangible personalty (36).	Last day of Jan., Apr., July, Oct.	Tax Comr., Bismarck
Ohio *Consumer	4% (10).	*Sales:* Gross selling price. *Use:* Price of tangible personalty.	*Seller:* Last day of month (17). *Purchaser (Use)* 15th of Jan., Apr., July, Oct. (if not paid to seller).	St. Treas., Columbus
Oklahoma *Consumer	2% (10).	*Sales:* Gross proceeds. *Use:* Purchase price.	*Sales:* 15th of month (4). *Use:* 20th of month.	Okla. Tax Comn., Okla. City
Pennsylvania *Consumer	6%.	*Sales:* Gross selling price. *Use:* Purchase price (3).	Licensee, 15th of month (13); nonlicensee, end of month.	Dept. Rev., Harrisburg
Rhode Island *Consumer	5%.	*Sales:* Gross receipts. *Use:* Sale price of tangible personalty.	20th of month (4).	Tax Admr., Providence
South Carolina *Seller	4% (3%, before 6-1-69)	*Sales:* Gross proceeds. *Use:* Sale price of tangible personalty.	*Sales:* 20th of month (4). *Use:* 20th of Jan., Apr., July, Oct.	St. Tax Comn., Columbia
South Dakota *Seller	4% (3% before 7-1-69); farm machinery 2% (10,18).	*Sales:* Gross receipts. *Use:* Purchase price of tangible personalty.	15th of Jan., Apr., July, Oct. (5).	Dir. of Tax., Pierre
Tennessee *Seller	3% (10, 33).	*Sales:* Gross sales. *Use:* Cost of tangibles.	20th of month.	Comr. of Rev., Nashville
Texas *Consumer	3¼%. (3% before 10-1-69). (10, 24).	*Sales:* Retail sales price and rentals. *Use:* Same.	Quarterly by last of Apr., July, Oct., Jan.	Comptr. Austin
Utah *Consumer	4% (3% before 4-1-69) (10).	*Sales:* Price paid. *Use:* Same.	30th of Jan., Apr., July, Oct.	St. Tax Comn., Salt Lake City
Vermont *Consumer	3% (eff. 6-1-69)	*Sales:* Sale price. *Use:* Purchase price	15th monthly	St. Tax Comr. Montpelier
Virginia *Seller	3% (10, 24).	*Sales:* Gross sales (also lease, rental, storage). *Use:* Cost of tangibles Gross proceeds of leasing, storage.	20th of month.	Tax Comr., Richmond

¶ 250

Always consult the CROSS REFERENCE TABLE for latest developments

STATE (1)	RATE OF TAX	BASIS OR MEASURE OF TAX (2)	RETURNS & PAYMENT	
			Last Day Without Penalty	To Whom
Washington *Consumer	4.5%.	*Sales:* Selling price. *Use:* Same.	15th of month (4)	Dept. Rev. Olympia
West Virginia *Consumer (23)	*Gross Sales: Retail,* ½%; *Wholesale,* ¼% (22). *Consumers' Retail Sales:* 3%. *Use:* 3%.	*Gross Sales:* Gross proceeds or income. *Consumers' Retail Sales:* Monetary consideration of sale. *Use:* Purchase price of tangibles.	*Gross Sales:* End of Apr., July, Oct.; annually Jan. 31. *Consumers' Retail Sales:* 15th of month (4). *Use:* 15th Jan., Apr., July, Oct.	St. Tax Dept. Charleston
Wisconsin *Seller	4%. (3% before 9-1-69) (10, 43)	*Sales:* Gross receipts from sale, lease or rental of tangible personalty and services. *Use:* Sales price.	Quarterly, last day of Jan., Apr., July, Oct. (25)	Dept. of Taxn., Madison
Wyoming *Consumer	3%.	*Sales:* Price charged. *Use:* Price of tangibles.	15th of month (4)	St. Tax Comn. Cheyenne

NOTES to chart ¶ 250 (corresponding to parenthetical numbers in chart):

(1)   Covers sales and use taxes having statewide applicability.

(2)   Use tax is usually imposed on property purchased for storage, use or consumption in the state. For taxability of rentals, see ¶ 1340.

(3)   Special optional basis for instate use for 6 months or less.

(4)   Quarterly returns in Jan., Apr., July and Oct. if monthly tax is: $5 or less in Ark. and Okla. (sales tax only); $10 or less in S.C., W.Va. and Wyo.; $15 or less in Neb., in Ky. with Comr's OK; under $60 in Colo.; under $10 average for 6 months, with Comr's. OK, in Ga. and R.I.; $100 or less in Kan.; under $5 in N.C.

(5)   Permission may be granted to file on some other basis.

(6)   Annual returns allowed for seasonal sellers grossing $500 or less.

(7)   Consolidated returns required if taxpayer is in 2 or more like businesses.

(8)   Quarterly returns by end of Apr., July, Oct., Jan. permitted if annual liability not over $500.

(9)   With Assr's OK: Annually (by 1-15) if liability not over $50 annually; semiannually (before 7-15, next 1-15) if not over $100 annually; quarterly (before 4-15, 7-15, 10-15, next 1-15) if not over $200 annually.

(10)   Additional local (county, city, town, etc.) taxes ranging from ⅛% to 4% are imposed in many states including: Ala., Alaska, Ariz., Ark., Calif., Colo., Ill., La., Mo., Minn. (eff. 1-1-70), Neb., Nev., N.M. (repealed for municipalities after 6-30-68), N.Y., N.C., Ohio, Okla., S.D., Tenn., Tex., Utah, Va. and Wis. (after 12-31-69).

(11)   Starting 1-1-70, if (1) quarterly tax under $45, pay annually by 1-31; (2) tax over $250 for 1st or 2d calendar quarter month, pay by 15th of next month.

(12) $20,000-$100,000, ⅛%; over $100,000, ¼%; initial fee, $25.

(13)   If tax for previous 3d calendar quarter over $600, file, pay monthly on 15th of 2nd month, except that tax for May is due 6-20. Quarterly taxpayers file, pay by end of Jan., Apr., July (for June only; Apr.-May is due June 15), and Oct.

© 1970 by Prentice-Hall, Inc.—State Tax Guide

256 Charts — Sales-Use Tax Rates, Bases, Reports, Payments

(14) Commission may allow monthly estimated payments (for 90% of true liability, but at least ⅓ of previous quarter's tax, but whichever is greater for use tax) with reconciliations quarterly, semi-annually or annually.

(15) Wholesalers, ½%; manufacturers, producers or blind persons, ½%; pineapple canners, sugar processors, ½%; insurance solicitors, 2%.

(16) Imposes gross income tax; ½% on wholesale sales, etc., all others 2%.

(17) Under "advance payment authority" vendor pays monthly but files semi-annually 7-31 and 1-31. Regs allow semi-annual returns based on county residences.

(18) Tax on MV, 3%.

(19) Retailing generally and leasing, 5%; automobiles, aircraft, trucks and truck-tractors, 3%; farm tractors sold to farmers, 1%; wholesaling ⅛%-5%; machinery and parts, 1%; contracting, 2½%; other businesses 1-5%. Wholesale compensating rates same as wholesale sales.

(20) Monthly by 28th if monthly tax exceeds $100.

(21) Rate is 1% on selected items ($80 top tax on some) of machinery, equipment, supplies purchased by certain commercial and industrial businesses and farmers; wholesale tax repealed. MVs, airplanes, 2% (1½% before 7-1-69), $120 max.

(22) Rates on other businesses range from 4/10% to 7 85/100%.

(23) Gross sales tax is "seller" tax.

(24) Tax on MVs 3% in Tex., Fla.; 2%, Va.

(25) Annual return, 90 days after year-end. Monthly by last day if quarterly tax over $500, on Dept. notification.

(26) Report, pay (combined gross receipts, use, county sales and withholding taxes) monthly by next 25th (20th before 7-1-69).

(27) If monthly tax is under $10, quarterly return and payment permitted on application and filing of bond.

(28) Monthly, by last day, if quarterly tax exceeds $15,000.

(29) Annually on 1-31 if liability under $10 monthly; on 7-31 and 1-31, if under $25 monthly; 4-30, 7-31, 10-31, 1-31, under $50 monthly.

(30) Annually by 9-30, if monthly tax not over $5 or annually over $60.

(31) National banks exempt under Fed law (1st Agricultural Bank, US Sup. Ct. 6-17-68).

(32) Annually by Jan. 31, if monthly average tax $20 or less; all others, monthly by last day. If previous calendar year tax averaged $5000 (min.) monthly, prepay monthly by last day: 100% of previous month's tax or 90% (min.) of current month.

(33) 1% on industrial machinery including repair parts and labor, water and energy fuels for manufacturing, etc.; farm machinery and equipment over $250.

(34) Special lower rate for farm vehicles and equipment and manufacturing machinery and equipment. Rate on meals, food, nonalcoholic drinks: Under $1, no tax; $1 or over, 4¢ (3¢ before 6-1-69) plus 1¢ per added 25¢ (33¢ before 6-1-69).

(35) 2%—food for off-premises consumption (1%, before 12-1-69); nonprescription drugs, laundering, dry cleaning, pressing (eff. 12-1-69). 5%—transient accommodations; wine, liquor, beer, food on premises (4% before 12-1-69).

(36) MV excise 4% (3% before 1-1-70).

(37) If state-local tax over $17,000 in 1st or 2d month of any quarter, prepay 90% of that month's tax by 25th of next month to St. Bd. Eq., if notified. Take credit on quarterly return; file by 25 if prepayment.

(38) If tax is over $500 in 1st or 2d month of any quarter, deposit that month's tax with St. Tax Comn. or bank by 20th of next month.

(39) For basis: Actual cost or reasonable market value if property is "susceptible to use tax", if less. If selling to retailer, collect 2% of price as advanced tax.

(40) Internal Revenue Service treats tax as a consumer tax for Fed income tax deductions.

(41) Quarterly by 4-20, 7-20, 10-20, next 1-20 if annual tax not over $600 (MV tax excluded).

(42) Annually by 6-20 instead, for small business.

(43) Starting 9-1-69, tax is general sales-use tax on all tangible personalty, unless exempt. Tax was a selective tax on items specifically enumerated.

Always consult the CROSS REFERENCE TABLE for latest developments

GASOLINE TAX RATES

¶ 285   Where you can deduct and how much. Gasoline taxes are an important deduction in figuring federal and state income tax returns. The total state and federal tax is, of course, deductible if you use the vehicle in a business. But if you use your car for pleasure, it's another matter. On your federal return, the state gasoline taxes are deductible, but the federal tax is not. Delaware is the only state that allows deduction of the federal tax.

    States allowing deduction of state gasoline taxes include Ala., Alaska, Ariz., Ark., Calif., Colo., Del., D.C., Haw., Ida., Iowa, Kan., Ky., Md., Minn., Mo., Mont., Neb., N.J., N.M., N.Y., N.D., Okla., S.C., Utah, Vt., Va., W.Va. and Wis.

    To help figure the deduction, here's a check-list of the per-gallon gas taxes currently imposed:

ALA.	7¢	**MINN.**	7¢
ALASKA	8¢	**MISS.**	8¢
ARIZ.	7¢	(7¢ before 1-2-70)	
ARK.	7½¢	**MO.**	5¢
CALIF.	7¢	**MONT.**	7¢
(8¢ before 9-1-69)		(6½¢ before 7-1-69)	
COLO.	7¢	**NEB.**	8½¢
(6¢ before 6-1-69)		(7½¢ before 1-1-70)	
CONN.	8¢	**NEV.**	6¢
(7¢ before 7-1-69)		**N.H.**	7¢
DEL.	7¢	**N.J.**	7¢
DIST. COL.	7¢	**N.M.**	7¢
FLA.	7¢	**N.Y.**	7¢
GA.	6½¢	**N.C.**	9¢
HAWAII:		(7¢ before 7-1-69)	
HAWAII CO.	11¢	**N.D.**	7¢
HONOLULU CO.	8½¢	(6¢ before 7-1-69)	
KAUAI CO.	9¢	**OHIO**	7¢
MAUI CO.	10¢	**OKLA.**	6.58¢
IDA.	7¢	**ORE.**	7¢
ILL.	7½¢	**PA.**	7¢
(6¢ before 8-1-69)		**R.I.**	8¢
IND.	8¢	**S.C.**	7¢
(6¢ before 4-1-69)		**S.D.**	7¢
IOWA	7¢	(6¢ before 7-1-69)	
KAN.	7¢	**TENN.**	7¢
(5¢ pre 7-1-69)		**TEX.**	5¢
KY.	7¢	**UTAH**	7¢
LA.	8¢	(6¢ before 7-1-69)	
(7¢ before 1-6-69)		**VT.**	8¢
ME.	8¢	**VA.**	7¢
(7¢ before 7-1-69)		**WASH.**	9¢
MD.	7¢	**W. VA.**	7¢
MASS.	6½¢	**WIS.**	7¢
MICH.	7¢	**WYO.**	7¢
		(6¢ before 7-1-69)	

    ⋙**WHAT TO DO→** *If you have all your bills,* total the number of gallons and multiply by the tax rate per gallon. *If you don't have bills,* you can approximate the deduction this way: Divide your total mileage for the year by the average number of miles you get to a gallon (this gives you the approximate number of gallons you used during the year); multiply the result by the tax rate to get your total deduction.

© 1970 by Prentice-Hall, Inc.—State Tax Guide   **¶ 285**

CIGARETTE TAXES—RATES, INCIDENCE, PAYMENT, REPORTS

¶ 286   **The main features** of the state taxes on cigarettes are given in the chart below. If incidence of the tax is on consumer, tax will be deductible on income tax returns in some states (by law). It is not deductible under IRC, nor in states in line with current Fed.

RATE PER PACK OF 20	INCIDENCE	PAYMENT METHOD	MONTHLY REPORT REQUIREMENTS (Who, when and to whom)
ALA. 12¢ (13, 30) ...	Stamps	Consumer(14)	Wholesaler jobber 20th, Dept. Rev.
ALASKA 8¢	.Seller	Reports	Licensee last day, Tax Comr.
ARIZ. 10¢	...Seller	Report	No fixed report dates
ARK. 12¼¢.. (17)	Seller	Stamps(1)	Distributor 10th, Comr. Rev.
CALIF. 10¢	..Consumer(14)	Stamps(2)	Distributor 25th, St. Eq. Bd.
COLO. 5¢(3)	.Wholesale	Stamps	Wholesaler 20th, Dept. Rev.
CONN. 16¢			
D.C. 4¢ (32)	...Consumer	Stamps	Distributor(4) 10 Tax Comr.
DEL. 11¢ (19)	Seller(15)	Stamps	Wholesaler, retailer 15th, Tax Dept.
FLA. 15¢	....Seller	Stamps	Agent 20th Tax Dept
(6)	......Consumer	Stamps	Wholesaler, agent 10th, Dir. Rev.
GA. 8¢	......Distributor	Stamps	Distributor 10th Comr. Rev.
HAW. 40%	...		
(7)	......Seller	Stamps	Wholesaler, retailer last day Dept. of Tax
IDA. 7¢ (26)	.Seller	Stamps	Wholesaler 15th Tax Coll.
ILL. 12¢ (26)	.Seller	Report	Distributor (8) 15th Dept. Rev.
IND. 6¢	......Consumer	Stamps	Distributor 10th (9) ABC
IOWA 10¢	...Seller	Stamps	Permittees 10th Tax Comm.
KAN. 8¢	.....Seller	Stamps	Wholesaler 10th Dir. Rev.
KY. 2½¢.	..... Consumer	Stamps	Wholesaler 20th Dir. Rev.
LA. 8¢.	.......Seller	Stamps	Dealer 15th Coll. Rev.
ME. 12¢ (18).	Consumer	Stamps	Distributor 10th Bur. Rev.
MD. 6¢	......Seller	Stamps	Distributor 20th Comptr.
MASS.12¢(21)	Consumer(14)	Stamps	Distributor 20th Comr. Corps. & Tax.
MICH. 7¢	....Seller	Report	Licensee 20th Rev. Dept.
MINN.13¢(22)	Seller	Report	Distributor 18th (23) Comr. Tax.
MISS. 9¢.	..... Consumer(14)	Stamps	Distributor (10) 15th Tax Comr.
MO. 9¢ (5,16).	Consumer	Stamps	Wholesalers 20th Dept. Rev.
MONT. 8¢	...Consumer	Stamps	Interstate Carriers to Bd. Eq. (no fixed dates)
NEB. 8¢	.....Consumer	Stamps	Retailer, wholesaler 10th Tax Comr.
NEV. 10¢ (19)	Seller	Stamps	Wholesaler 15th (24) Tax Comn.
N.H. 30% (12)	Consumer	Stamps	(Monthly reports not required)
N.J. 14¢	.....Consumer	Stamps	Distributor 20th Dir. Tax.
N.M. 12¢	....Seller	Report	Distributor 20th Bur. Rev.
N.Y. 12¢	....Consumer	Stamps	Agent 15th Tax Comn.
N.Y.C. 4¢	....Consumer	Stamps	Agent 15th City Treas.
N.C. 2¢ (27).	.Consumer	Stamps	Distributor 20th Comr. Rev.
N.D. 11¢ (6)	Seller	Stamps	Distributor quarterly (11) Tax Comn.
OHIO 10¢ (28)	Consumer	Stamps	Wholesaler 10th Tax Comr.

(Notes to chart appear on page 292-B)

ⓒ 1970 by Prentice-Hall, Inc.—State Tax Guide

¶ 286

292-B **Charts — Cigarette Taxes**

RATE PER PACK OF 20	INCIDENCE	PAYMENT METHOD	MONTHLY REPORT REQUIREMENTS (Who, when and to whom)
OKLA. 13¢ ..	Consumer	Stamps	Wholesaler, retailer 10th Tax Comn.
ORE. 4¢	Consumer	Stamps	Distributor 20th Tax Comn.
PA. 13¢	Consumer	Stamps	Dealer 10th Dept. Rev.
R.I. 13¢	Consumer	Stamps	Dealer, distributor 10th Tob. Admr.
S.C. 6¢ (25) .	Seller	Stamps	(Monthly reports not required)
S.D. 12¢ (6) ..	Consumer	Stamps	Distributor, wholesaler 15th Comr. Rev.
TENN.13¢(20)	Consumer	Stamps	Distributor 15th Dept. Fin. & Tax.
TEX. 15½¢ (31)	Consumer	Stamps	Distributor 10th Comptr.
UTAH 8¢ ...	Seller	Stamps	(Monthly reports not required)
VT. 12¢ (18) .	Consumer	Stamps	Distributor 15th Comr. Tax.
VA. 2½¢ (3) .	Seller	Stamps	Wholesaler, storer 10th Dept. Tax.
WASH. 11¢ ..	Seller	Stamps	Wholesaler, retailer 15th Tax Comn.
W.VA. 7¢	Consumer	Stamps	Wholesaler 15th Tax Comn.
WIS. 14¢ (29)	Consumer	Stamps	Mfg., wholesalers 15th Dept. Tax.
WYO. 8¢	Consumer	Stamps	Wholesaler 20th St. Equal. Bd.

NOTES to chart (corresponding to numbers in parentheses in the chart):

(1) Payment with report for stamps purchased on consignment.
(2) Payment with report for tax not paid by stamp or meter.
(3) City taxes are also in effect in some cities.
(4) Machine dealer and operator report on 15th.
(5) City and county taxes are also in effect in some cities and counties.
(6) 8¢ before 7-1-69.
(7) Wholesale price is basis.
(8) Manufacturer reports on 5th.
(9) Report drop shipment on 15th.
(10) Wholesaler and manufacturers also report.
(11) 10th of Jan., Apr., July, and Oct.; monthly reports may be allowed.
(12) Sales price is basis.
(13) Some cities and counties also impose tax.
(14) Not deductible on state return.
(15) Deductible on state return.
(16) 4¢ before 7-15-69.
(17) 8¢ before 4-21-68. 12¾¢ after 6-30-70.
(18) 10¢ before 6-1-69.
(19) 7¢ before 7-1-69.
(20) 8¢ before 6-1-69.
(21) 10¢ before 6-2-69.
(22) 8¢ before 5-30-69.
(23) 20th before 7-1-69.
(24) Metered stamping machine report by 10th. (25th before 7-1-69).
(25) 5¢ before 7-1-69.
(26) 9¢ before 8-1-69.
(27) Eff. 10-1-69.
(28) 7¢ before 8-19-69.
(29) 10¢ before 9-1-69.
(30) 10¢ before 10-1-69.
(31) 11¢ before 10-1-69.
(32) 3¢ before 12-1-69.

¶ 286   Always consult the CROSS REFERENCE TABLE for latest developments

index

Grazing rights, 186

Hatch Act (1887), 169
Hawaii
  assessment of property in, 80
  business taxes in, 89
  income tax in, 44, 47
  property taxes in, 101, 103
  sales taxes in, 62
Health services, 4, 9, 10, 11, 58, 151
  federal grants for, 170, 175
Heller, Walter, 186, 188-89
Holmes, Justice Oliver Wendell, 136
Homestead exemptions, 87-88
Hospital construction program, 172
Houston, Tex., sales tax in, 108

Illinois
  income tax in, 53
  local sales taxes in, 108, 111
Improvements, reduction of taxes on, 99-106
  administration of, 103-4
  distribution of burden in, 103
  inconclusive experience in, 100-102
  motivations for, 99-100
  revenue loss from, 102-3
Income taxes, 32-33, 38, 43-54, 65
  capital gains and, 67-68
  credits on, 50
  development of, 43-46
  disadvantages of, 50
  economic growth and, 196-97
  elasticity of, 39-41, 47
  features of, 47-50
  federal, 13, 21, 37, 50-53
    economic growth and, 151
    farm losses deducted from, 92
    municipal securities exempt from, 135-40
    rate increases in, 119
    rates of, 40-41, 47
  federal relinquishing of tax sources and, 167-68
  federal-state cooperation in, 155-56
  graduation of rates of, 53-54
  instability of yield from, 58
  limitations on, 32
  local, 107-10
  property taxes and, 102
  state, 13, 21, 25, 35, 50-53
    federal collection of, 159-61
    federal credits on, 179-84
  withholding of, 23-24

Indiana
  income tax in, 53
    credits on, 181
  sales tax in, 59-60
Industrial development bonds, 141-45
Inheritance taxes, 26, 32, 33, 38, 41, 65-74
  competition in, 207
  credits on, 180
  estate taxes preferable to, 70-72
  on farm property, 93
  federal aid to states in enforcement of, 68-69
  history and universality of, 67-68
  lack of interest in, 69-70
  revenue potential of, 72-74
Interest rates, 13, 120
  debt limitations and, 132
  factors affecting, 124
  federal, 138
  maturity schedule and, 128
  reductions in, 137
  on revenue bonds, 125
  rise in, 119
  savings in, 123
Internal Revenue Service, 51, 155, 157, 160-61, 163
International Association of Assessing Officers, 166
Interstate commerce, taxes on, 31

Jackson, Andrew, 186
Jamaica, property taxes in, 101
Japan, accessions tax in, 71

Kentucky, local income taxes in, 108

Land taxes
  exemptions from, 101-2
  See also Property taxes
Land use, assessment based on, 93
Land value, 92-94
Licensing requirements as consumer taxation, 35, 55
Liquor taxes, 23, 35, 43, 56, 62
  collection of, 163-64
  federal, 150
Local consumer taxes, 107, 108
Local income taxes, 107-10
Local nonproperty taxes, 107-13
  as Depression innovation, 108
  income taxes as, 109-10
  problems in, 108-9
  sales taxes as, 111-12
  state aid in collection of, 110-13

DISCHARGED   DISCHARGED

DISCHARGED

DISCHARGED

DISCHARGED

DEC 1 0 1977

DISCHARGED